MW01244968

Project Hatfield:
(Russell Williams Investigation)

How a colonel
became a killer

Cal Millar
Ian Robertson

This book is dedicated to victims and those who investigate their cases.

Acknowledgements

The writing of any book, especially one requiring research into realities, is not properly accomplished without the help of myriad sources.

How a colonel became a killer is no exception.

We will be forever grateful to those who helped provide exhaustive details required in our study, plus insightful guidance in considering what facts and accounts to include. We cannot thank them all by name, and some are identified and quoted in the following chapters. A few who deserve special mention are Joe Warmington, a diligent and forceful columnist at the Toronto Sun; Julie Kirsh, the always-helpful head of the Toronto Sun research department and Sun Media's Director of Electronic Information; Bill Glisky, managing editor of the Intelligencer, Belleville's daily newspaper; Chris Mallette, its city editor and reporters Luke Hendry, W. Brice McVicar and Jason Miller.

There were many police officers and some military personnel who provided additional information which helped put details into perspective and writers from various media outlets who gave assistance to track down family members and others who were directly affected by the everlasting pain that Russell Williams inflicted.

(Most of the photographs in this book were officially made public by Canada's Department of National Defence, the Ontario Provincial Police and the Ontario Ministry of the Attorney General, prior to or during court proceedings involving Russell Williams. Photographs in Brighton, Belleville, Kingston, Ottawa and Tweed were taken by Ian Robertson and images of the authors are by Toronto photographer George Onuska.)

ISBN-13: 978-1477590874
ISBN-10: 1477590870

This book is available from www.amazon.com

Introduction

This book deals with an incredibly difficult subject – a well-respected, up-and-coming commander in Canada's military who was unmasked as a cold, calculating and eventually brutal sexual predator. People around the world are fascinated by the exploits of unusual killers and, since he is certainly not typical, there was world-wide media coverage after the arrest, confession and later sentencing of Russell Williams. Once the pilot of dignitaries, including the country's monarch, the former colonel in command of Canada's largest air force base committed scores of clandestine burglaries. His specialty was targeting the homes and intimate possessions of young girls and women, two of them succumbing to the unfulfilled desires that rapidly spiraled out of control into murder. Stories about two victims who survived his degrading and unusual sex assaults, plus the two women he killed, filled local, national and global media reports for weeks after his arrest and the highly-publicized confession that resulted in him ending up in prison for many years to come.

Unlike newspapers, television, magazines and other publications that dealt with the horror of what Williams did, this book is designed to take readers step-by-step through his escalating crimes. It also discloses the sheer – and often much unappreciated – genius of how police officers joined forces and unearthed evidence to not only solve the mystery of the slayings and what led up to them, but how it was used to trap the killer into removing his mask. And they did so relatively quickly, once the pieces of a largely-scattered puzzle began to fall into place. Many observers, especially those with little knowledge or appreciation for how real-life investigations are conducted and who rely too readily on quick CSI moments, castigated the police and military for not having stopped Williams earlier. His life and dark times, however, were not based on a script that either he or his captors could follow.

We have extensively detailed how, where and when he stalked victims in order to build an extensive trophy collection of victim's garments and underwear, plus the unique and painstakingly catalogued combination of images he captured with almost military precision, using both digital and video cameras. Many of the descriptions gleaned from police documents and transcripts of his recordings are not for the faint of heart, especially since some are words coming from the grave. Indeed, they are highly disturbing.

But this is not a novel. This is a study into the rare world of a serial criminal, one who thankfully was caught soon after committing his first slayings, in a pattern which experts were left in no doubt would have led to more killings. Much of what the following chapters contain has not been generally revealed. The book will also introduce you to a number of notorious killers who photographed victims before or after they were killed. Most of them are more deviant than Williams, but you will recognize that the colonel was on a path that could have made him an even more dangerous individual than these homicidal maniacs had he not been captured.

Williams was not someone who left clues to taunt police and gloat that he was still free to rape and kill, but was definitely a calm, calculating criminal who did everything to cover his tracks and prevent investigators from linking him with his various crimes. The purpose of introducing various sexual predators and murderers is not only to acquaint you with the mayhem they wreaked, but by comparison to demonstrate how rare a creature Williams was in this abhorrent environment. He stands out.

Russell Williams is a person without emotion, a man
without a soul – a statement we do not make lightly. He
moves mechanically and focuses on minute details in
everything he does. For more than two-and-a-half years,
he carried out a series of crimes almost without detection.
One of the most amazing things about this case is that
many of the people whose dwellings were entered and
robbed were not even aware that they had been victimized.
Even if some individuals realized their homes had been
entered, only a handful of them reported the burglaries to
police. And that is another fact the public is barely aware
of to this day, if at all.

It is true that Williams began his crime spree by breaking
into houses and rummaging through underwear drawers.
But as he grew bolder and eventually sexually attacked
victims before achieving his desired and ultimate goal to
commit murder, it appears obvious that he was intent on
committing the perfect crime. Eventually he was foiled by
modern forensics, modified police procedures that track
serial sex offenders and killers, skilful interrogation
techniques, dogged police work and a series of
coincidences that brought him to a police roadblock. You
will read that his presence at the roadside stop soon led to
his downfall.

No other killer is known to have videotaped and
photographed victims as they were being murdered – also
keeping precise notes as though he was conducting a high
school experiment. The documentation provided by
Williams and summarized in this book is a treasure trove
for police, criminologists, behavioral scientists and
psychiatrists. It gives a glimpse into an extremely
disturbed mind and raises questions that experts no
doubt will be left to ponder in coming years.

This book is not meant in any way to champion him for
the time he escaped detection. Far from it. Our purpose in

setting out so much graphic detail is to give some insight into the difficulties encountered by law enforcement when dealing with serial criminals in different jurisdictions. The book also deals with the victims, plus the impact on their families and friends and the relatively small communities on which Williams preyed. Nothing can bring back loved ones who fall victim to a depraved killer. But they are the ones who must be remembered – not the animal who took their lives.

Chapter One

His hands piloted the aircraft that carried Queen Elizabeth and Prince Philip on their May 2005 visit to Canada.

They also guided the plane that ferried Canada's Prime Minister Stephen Harper to various destinations across the country.

But those same hands killed two women in separate murderous attacks during a 29-month crime spree, a short drive from Canada's largest military base.

Marie-France Comeau was stationed at the base and knew the man who took her life on November 24, 2009.

The other victim, Jessica Elizabeth Lloyd, was selected randomly in January 2010. "Tell my Mom I love her," she told her killer, before lapsing into unconsciousness.

A woman, who by court order must be identified by the alias Jane Doe, was sexually molested when an intruder entered her home as she slept on September 17, 2009, and Laurie Massicotte was terrorized and molested 13 days later by a man who broke into her residence. They were not raped, but both were forced by the attacker to pose naked while he took a series of disgusting, degrading, humiliating and graphically explicit photographs.

Initially, the cases were investigated separately. A few days after Lloyd vanished, however, the various police agencies involved were advised that the incidents were linked and a single individual was responsible for the crimes. The Ontario Provincial Police and the Belleville Police Service formed a multi-jurisdictional task force and began an investigation, called Project Hatfield, to track down the culprit. Even though the investigators were now aware that the four major incidents were linked, they had no idea the perpetrator was also responsible for more than 80 sexually motivated break-ins over an 873-day span during which hundreds of female undergarments had been stolen.

Detectives also had no way of knowing that their suspect would be the only known person in the world who has documented every aspect of his crimes with photographs, video tapes, sound recordings and computer generated notes. The shocking images found by police during numerous searches include graphic close-up photographs taken with a hand-held digital camera while each woman was being sexually assaulted and video tape depicting moment by moment details as his two victims were murdered. He also preserved the words spoken by his victims. In the case of Jessica Lloyd, she asked the killer to let her mother know that she loved her. There have been cases in which criminals have photographed their prey in the early stages of a crime, especially in sexual assaults and murder cases. But until the arrest of this serial killer, investigators worldwide had never encountered someone who compiled a written and photographic record of each crime they committed and the sounds from victims as they were brutalized.

Forty-six-year-old David Russell Williams was a colonel in the Canadian Armed Forces when he was arrested on February 7, 2010 after confessing to the murders and sexual attacks during a masterful interview conducted by Detective Sergeant Jim Smyth of the Ontario Provincial Police. It was only three days earlier that Williams had become a suspect in the killings. Up until that time, no one could have imagined that the man who commanded some 3,000 men and women serving in 8 Wing and other units at the Canadian Forces Base in Trenton, about 110 miles south of Ottawa – Canada's capital city – could have committed such heinous crimes. He was well respected and considered above reproach, but had rapidly developed a very dark side.

Corporal Marie-France Comeau

What appeared to be an idyllic existence began spiraling into depravity on Sunday, September 9, 2007 when he broke into a home on Cosy Cove Lane, at the north end of

Stoco Lake on the eastern outskirts of Tweed, a village community of 5,600 people. In fact, the home was beside the bungalow where Williams was living and a place where he and his wife had on several occasions been invited to have dinner with the couple who lived there with their children. The family was unaware of anyone having illegally entered their house until Ontario Provincial Police investigators advised them that Williams had broken in three times. During the first break-in, he took 25 photographs inside the bedroom of their 12-year-old daughter. There are eleven pictures showing him standing in front of a mirror wearing only a pair of panties and sexually gratifying himself while lying on the girl's bed. The clock in the camera, which records the time each photograph was taken, indicated that Williams was in the girl's bedroom for at least two hours and 44 minutes. Before leaving, he stole six pieces of underwear. Back home, he loaded the photographs into a private area on his personal computer. He categorized each picture so that he could relive the experience over and over, but his meticulous records also allowed police to uncover every aspect of William's secret life following his arrest.

Police eventually charged Colonel David Russell Williams with two counts of first degree murder, sexual assault and forcible confinement of a 20-year-old woman, plus the sexual assault and forcible confinement of a mother of three children. He also faced 82 charges of breaking and entering a number of homes in Tweed and Ottawa and stealing female undergarments totaling in the hundreds. Williams, once considered a rising star in Canada's military, not only stole the lingerie as trophies from his break-ins, he also took photographs of himself wearing various bras and panties.

Investigators were aware that Williams lived in close proximity to the Tweed home where one victim had been sexually molested and photographed in the middle of the night by an intruder. He was one of several neighbors who were contacted by police in their attempts to find anyone who saw or heard anything around the time the attack occurred. But Trenton's base commander was an individual above reproach and not a person anyone would suspect of being involved in such a depraved and degrading assault.

It was only through a series of coincidences that Williams surfaced as a suspect five months after the two women encountered the intruder. Profilers and forensic experts who had been working on the attacks and the slaying of Marie-France Comeau didn't determine the cases were connected. Similarly, investigators from the Belleville Police Service had no idea that the disappearance of Jessica Lloyd was directly linked to the crimes the Ontario Provincial Police were investigating, even though they occurred within a 100 mile radius.

When the cases were eventually tied together, there was a high degree of urgency because the individual was now known to have killed and at the moment could be holding Jessica captive. The most important piece of evidence was a set of tire tracks found adjacent to her home, which confirmed that the suspect had been driving a sports utility vehicle. It was a key clue and a team of police officers was assigned to set up a roadblock in the vicinity of the missing woman's home on February 4, 2010. They were ordered to stop all vehicles, question everyone they encountered and obtain tire track impressions from any SUVs fitting the profile of the vehicle which had been in the field. The police officers were a bit late arriving at the site on Highway 37 and investigators lost the opportunity to speak with the occupants of numerous cars that had passed Lloyd's house before the roadblock was in place. Williams, however, had been delayed leaving his office and was driving the second vehicle to be stopped at the spot-check. It took only a few minutes for a police officer to ask him some questions while a police technician quickly took a tire impression from a rear wheel. Williams told police during the brief interview that he was the base commander in Trenton and was heading to his home in Tweed. At that point the police manning the roadblock were confident he wasn't a suspect.

Williams would have passed through the location at least half an hour earlier if a series of events hadn't delayed him leaving the office. Just as he was closing the door, the colonel realized he'd left his raincoat behind and returned to get it. When he left for the second time, he met a captain in the hallway and told the young officer that he needed to talk to him. They chatted for almost 40 minutes and it was that delay which brought Williams to the roadblock shortly after it had been set up.

Also, since the constables who stopped Williams were convinced he wasn't the suspect, 10 hours passed before they relayed his name to the command post which had been set up to review information on a real time basis in the hope of finding the abductor and rescuing the missing woman. Rather than dismissing Williams as a suspect, police analysts ordered the tire impression forwarded to forensic experts and notified the detective inspector in charge of the investigation that Trenton's base commander had surfaced as a suspect.

Up until this point, the Ontario Provincial Police had been working closely with Military Police investigators since the murder victim was a Canadian Forces corporal. They had shared every piece of information, but now the OPP began operating in a cone of silence to ensure nothing they discovered over the ensuing days would be leaked to Williams, who had been routinely briefed on the ongoing investigation by his military police officers. Even though his name had come up through the normal course of the investigation, he wasn't considered even a strong suspect

– but the lead detective on the case didn't want to take any chances and made the bold decision to keep the military in the dark.

Jessica Elizabeth Lloyd

Key personnel have admitted privately that they didn't expect Williams would turn out to be the person responsible and when he was asked to come in for an interview three days later, investigators fully expected he would have a plausible explanation and they would be eliminating him as a suspect. Still, they reasoned, he could have vital information or might implicate someone who had permission to drive his vehicle. As a result, arrangements were made to have teams of police available to follow up leads and a judge was also on stand-by to sign any search warrants that might be necessary to safely rescue the abduction victim. Rather than getting fresh tips, the skillful interview with the base commander unearthed a litany of sexually motivated break-ins that eventually escalated to molesting women and then murder.

The totality of the crime saga was actually detailed in a series of interviews with Williams after the initial interrogation that led to his arrest for the murders of Comeau and Lloyd. The first interview took place on February 7, 2010 and Williams was subsequently questioned by Detective Sergeant Smyth on February 11, 16 and 17, also on March 4 and 5, then on May 11. It was during the follow-up questioning that Williams provided codes and passwords that allowed police to locate the images and other documentation of his crimes which were concealed deep in his computer.

He told the investigator he entered his neighbor's house for a second time shortly before midnight on Friday, September 28, 2007. The family was away but their door was open. He again went to one of their daughter's bedrooms and took pictures after stripping naked and putting on underwear removed from drawers and a laundry basket. Twenty pictures were taken between 11:37 p.m. and 12:33 a.m. followed by another set of photographs snapped between 8:02 a.m. and 8:19 a.m. on September 29. Police were never able to ascertain if Williams had stayed in the house overnight or entered that morning when more pictures were taken. Since police were unable to determine if separate entries occurred, they linked everything together for the element of the second break, enter and theft charge that Williams faced when formally arraigned in connection with the two killings.

The third break-in at that home didn't take place until Friday, May 23, 2008, but in the meantime Williams had

DND photo
Colonel Russell Williams

entered several other houses in the Tweed area and another on Cara Crescent in Ottawa. That home was a block from 545 Wilkie Drive, a house Williams and his wife, Mary Elizabeth Harriman, bought in 1995. When he was transferred to Trenton in 2004, she continued living in Ottawa while her husband stayed several days a week at their waterfront cottage in Tweed.

Williams was in the first phase of a pattern that forensic psychiatrists see as stepping stones to more serious crimes such as physical assaults, rape and eventually murder. Until September 9, 2007, Williams gave no hint that his life was about to escalate out of control. He ran the base, attended top level meetings with military and political brass in Ottawa, travelled the world to oversee flight operations which originated from the Canada Forces Base in Trenton and appeared to have a normal family relationship with his wife. They purchased the cottage in 2004 as a get-away home where they could spend time to relax. It was less than three hours away from Ottawa and a convenient 35 mile drive to the Trenton base. He could also easily travel from the lakeside getaway to attend frequent meetings at Canada's National Defence headquarters and other venues in the National Capital Region.

Harriman and Williams were married on Saturday, June 1, 1991 but had no children. Considered a socialite couple with many friends, they attended numerous functions in Ottawa and Williams would often be invited to government and diplomatic soirees when his work took him to foreign countries, including the United States, Europe and the Middle East. He was born in Bromsgrove, Worcestershire, England on March 7, 1963, but as a preschooler was brought to Canada by his parents, Cedric and Christine Williams. It was at the age of six when his father, a scientist at the nuclear research laboratory in Chalk River, sought a divorce from his wife after discovering that she was involved in a torrid affair with another scientist at the facility, 110 miles northwest of Ottawa. His mom, who went by the name Nonie, married the other scientist, Dr. Jerry Sovka, soon after the divorce was finalized. The newlyweds took Nonie's children, Russell, and his younger brother, Harvey, to live in Scarborough, a sprawling city which at the time formed the eastern portion of Toronto's metropolitan area. While growing up, Williams – who adopted his stepdad's last name – attended several schools in a neighborhood known as the Scarborough Bluffs, a rugged shoreline along Lake Ontario directly north of Rochester, New York. He spent his first two years of high school at Birchmount Park Collegiate Institute, but when his mother moved to South Korea after Dr. Sovka was recruited to supervise construction of a Canadian-built nuclear reactor, Williams was enrolled as a boarding student to complete his studies at Toronto's elite Upper Canada College.

Although of no real significance, but what some may consider an eerie coincidence, when Williams graduated from high school, he began taking courses at the same University of Toronto campus where Paul Bernardo was enrolled. Bernardo and his wife, Carla Homolka, a clean-cut couple dubbed the Barbie and Ken Killers, murdered three teenaged girls in a homicidal rampage that bears uncanny similarities to the slayings committed by Williams. There is no evidence that he knew Bernardo or ever had contact with him. However, it is obvious that the future colonel would have been aware of what happened in what can only be described as a house of horrors where Bernardo and his wife lived in the quiet community of St. Catharines, about 10 miles from Niagara Falls and the border with the United States. Williams would also be familiar with Bernardo's earlier role as the Scarborough Rapist, during which 17 women were sexually attacked in Toronto's east end. That crime spree began while Bernardo was enrolled at the university but through bungling, mix-ups and communication failures, it took six years for detectives to identify him as a serial offender and link him with the various rapes and murders. Some of the rapes occurring in the area at that time were not linked to Bernardo and investigations were recently opened to see if Williams could be responsible. Investigators from Toronto's cold case homicide team are also reviewing evidence to see if he's implicated in an unsolved killing.

Ironically, because of the flaws in the Bernardo investigation, the Ontario government appointed a serial predator crime investigations coordinator and developed procedures which are designed to help police quickly find and apprehend individuals who go on murder and rape rampages. Once the unit's computer had linked the four crimes – the murders of Lloyd and Comeau plus the rapes of Massicotte and Jane Doe – the task force led by OPP Detective Inspector Chris Nicholas began making full use of another program known as the Major Case Management Manual, which was adopted after Bernardo's arrest.

Using this computer-guided tool, which directs multi-jurisdictional investigations, it took only one day to identify Williams as a potential suspect. Until that time, police officers involved in the separate investigations had questioned numerous individuals but were not able to zero in on a person of interest for Comeau's murder, the sexual assaults or the missing Belleville woman. They did get what were considered some very strong leads on possible suspects, but all investigations led police down dead end roads and there was nothing concrete to help them solve the case until the link between the crimes was established. The special investigative unit, which was formed to identify serial predators, uses a specialized analytical intelligence computer to comb through tidbits of information from major crimes such as sexual assaults and homicides, to uncover any similarities. It wasn't until after the Williams case that the existence of this mainly-secret unit became publicly known.

In 1987, Williams graduated from the University of Toronto with a degree in Economic and Political Science and immediately joined the Canadian Forces. He became a pilot in 1990 and served two years as a flight instructor in Portage la Prairie, Manitoba before being posted to the 434 Combat Support Squadron in Shearwater, Nova Scotia. The maritime base is responsible for coastal patrols and protecting eastern Canada from enemy submarines, navy vessels and unidentified aircraft, including planes flown by drug smugglers. His skills as a steady, competent, no-nonsense pilot were recognized by his superiors and Williams was recommended for a position with the 412 Transport Squadron in Ottawa. It had him transporting government officials, including Canada's prime minister, foreign dignitaries, and military top brass to destinations across the country and overseas. As a captain, he was ferrying some of the world's most influential and important people and in 2005 was assigned to fly Queen Elizabeth and her husband, Prince Philip, on their Canadian tour from May 17 to 25. The visit took them to Alberta and Saskatchewan for celebrations marking the 100th anniversary of the two provinces joining Canada. Not only did Williams undergo extensive background investigations to ensure that he had the highest possible security clearance, he also underwent psychological evaluations to expose any impediments that would preclude him from having the lives of VIPs in his hands. Nothing was ever found and no one noticed any change in his character during his later 873-day crime spree.

Williams was named manager of multi-engine pilots after being promoted to the rank of major in 1999 and four years later was given approval to attend a two-year course at the Royal Military College in Kingston, Ontario, where he received a Masters in Defence Studies. Upon his promotion to Lieutenant-Colonel, he was put in charge of the 437 Transport Squadron in Trenton, which was playing a vital role supplying Canadian and NATO (North Atlantic Treaty Organization) troops in the Middle East through a base known as Camp Mirage that was set up near Dubai in the United Arab Emirates. Williams was put in charge of Camp Mirage and made frequent trips there between 2004 and 2007.

He wasn't an individual who committed the perfect crimes, just someone who police would never initially think to include in their list of possible suspects. When homes in his neighborhood were broken into, investigators didn't bother to question Williams other than asking him if he'd noticed anything unusual. The same queries were asked of other neighbors, but no one could recall seeing anyone they considered suspicious hanging around the area. Although the break-ins at his neighbor's residence were never reported, police began receiving calls about other entries. In fact, only 17 of the burglaries were reported. It was in October 2007, when the owners of a house on Greenwood Road in Tweed told police they saw a housebreaker run off when they arrived home. The break-in was on October 20, but it was another 10 days before they reported the burglary and investigators were unable to collect adequate forensic evidence. The couple, who were parents of twin 11-year-old girls, didn't initially call police because they thought nothing had been stolen. They only alerted authorities when they heard about another break-in. Those victims were the first people to see Williams, but were only able to describe him as "a tall male" because he bolted from the home as soon as they walked in. When questioned about the occurrence, Williams described it as a close call. The house was on a street running south from Sulphide Road, only a block from his home. He also thought someone from the residence had tried to chase after him on an all-terrain vehicle and he wasn't sure if anyone in the family had caught a glimpse of his face before he managed to escape.

The modus operandi was consistent with his pattern during the first two entries at his neighbor's house. On the evening of Friday, October 19, 2007, Williams broke into the home after finding the door unlocked. He made his way to the bedrooms and rummaged through drawers before collecting 14 items of clothing consisting of panties, bras and swimwear in adult and child sizes. Photographs on his computer were taken between 9:31 p.m. and 9:38 p.m. showing drawers in which the young girls kept their underwear, plus freshly washed items in a dryer. Other pictures were taken in the master bedroom. The following evening, despite the close call, Williams again entered the house through an unlocked door and during a four-minute period from 10:44 p.m., he took photographs of underwear that he found in dresser drawers in the room that the twins shared. At some point later, the clothing stolen from the house – where the couple had lived for 18 years – was painstakingly laid out and separately photographed. Each picture was then labeled and stored among the hundreds of file folders which investigators discovered on Williams' personal computer.

Contained among the collection of images were 41 photographs taken between 5:04 p.m. and 5:38 p.m. on Saturday, September 29, 2007. They show Williams standing and masturbating in the bedroom of his neighbor's house while dressed in the 12-year-old girl's undergarments. Investigators located another 28 photographs, possibly taken at his residence, with him wearing panties and bras which had been stolen from the Greenwood Road home.

Williams looked impressive in his uniform. Square-jawed and standing around six-feet tall, he not only exuded authority, but was the depiction of what a military leader should look like. There was no doubt who was in charge when Colonel Williams made his way around the sprawling Canadian Forces Base in Trenton. He got the same respect from those living in the community around the base and from residents of Tweed as well as the neighbors around the home he previously owned on Wilkie Drive in Ottawa, and a new house he and his wife purchased in December 2009 on Edison Avenue in the city's west end. While working, Williams stayed in Tweed and spent weekends with his wife in Ottawa. She sometimes would join him at their lakeside retreat. Within two months of the couple moving to their new home, however, investigators from the newly-formed multi-jurisdictional investigative task force needed answers to some questions.

Forensic identification officers from the Ontario Provincial Police had found some DNA evidence, but there wasn't enough to conclusively show the same person was responsible for Comeau's murder and the two sexual assaults. Detectives from the Belleville Police Service were in the early stages of searching for Jessica Lloyd, who had been reported missing, and were not directly aware of the homicide and sex attacks. But they learned that the cases were connected after feeding information into a computer system operated by Ontario's Serial Predator Crime Investigations Coordinator. Despite initially not having a DNA link or being able to identify the culprit from among the convicted felons – who had been ordered by the courts to submit saliva and skin tissue samples to Canada's national DNA bank – the Serial Predator Crime Investigations Coordinator's computer analyzed evidence from the abduction and came up with potential links to the unsolved OPP cases.

The investigation into the slaying of Marie-France Comeau began in November 2009 when her body was discovered in the bedroom of her home, 10 miles west of the Trenton base. Police turned up nothing at the murder scene that suggested the slaying could be connected to the earlier sexual attacks months before. However, profiling experts with the Ontario Provincial Police were convinced the person responsible for the sex-related crimes had likely been arrested in the past for misdemeanors such as trespassing or Peeping Tom offences. They also suggested that the suspect may have committed break-ins. Investigators searched criminal record files, hoping to identify the killer, but never found anyone who could be considered a strong suspect. It was a time-consuming and arduous task, but absolutely necessary in leaving no stone unturned in their hunt for the killer.

Corporal Comeau, a flight attendant with the Canadian Armed Forces, was brutally murdered at her home in Brighton, a picturesque town with a motto of where the past meets the future. The 37-year-old woman had served with the military for 12 years and was under the command of Colonel Williams at the Trenton base, a 15 minute drive from her home at 252 Raglan Street. On November 25, after failing to report for duty, her body was found in the master bedroom of the five-room residence. She had been savagely beaten, raped and strangled – but more than 24 hours passed before anyone knew Comeau had been murdered.

Her commanding officer wrote a note expressing his condolences to Ernest Comeau, the murdered woman's father. "I would like to take this opportunity on behalf of the men and women of 8 Wing Trenton to express my sincere condolences on the tragic death of your daughter." The message went on to state: "Marie-France was a professional, caring and compassionate woman who earned the respect of all with whom she came in contact. She set high standards for herself and others and was devoted to the well-being of those around her. Marie-France made a lasting impact in Trenton and will be sorely missed by her many friends. Please let me know whether there is anything I can do to help you during this very difficult time. You and your family are in our thoughts and prayers."

The letter was signed "With our deepest sympathy" by – D. R. Williams, Colonel, Wing Commander.

Ironically, hours before Comeau was murdered, Colonel Williams was arrested, put in handcuffs and incarcerated as part of a "Jail and Bail" fundraiser for the United Way. He was charged with being too young to be a wing commander. With the frivolity of that event, no one could imagine Williams would be involved in the savage sexual attack that ended Marie-France Comeau's life.

The homes in her tidy subdivision, just off Ontario Street, are almost identical. They have two-car garages which protrude from the houses and form alcoves to the main entrance. Comeau's home has a light rust brick front with a similar colored roof that makes it stand out from the houses on either side, which have light facades and bluish shingles. With no back fences, anyone had easy access to the rear of homes which line Raglan Street. There was a wooden patio and sliding door at the rear of her house, but police determined that entry was made after a 30-inch-wide basement window was forced open. The basement was unfinished, with sheets of plastic covering the insulation on the cement walls. The ceiling duct work and wooden joists were fully exposed. The only item of furniture downstairs was a double bed in the northwest corner. In the basement, after her body was discovered, investigators found a bloodstained duffle bag, a flexible plastic band similar to the equipment used by police to bind the hands of prisoners when making mass arrests, cloth binding knotted around a support beam near the bed, blood spattered in several locations on the cement floor and footprints made by someone who had walked through the gore. There was also blood on the banister and landing at the bottom of the stairs leading to the main area of the house, plus blood smeared on the wall.

Pete Fisher, a reporter with Northumberland Today, wrote the first article about Comeau's tragic death. "Northumberland OPP are investigating the death of a woman found in her Brighton home Wednesday afternoon," he informed readers of the weekly newspaper. He identified the victim and mentioned her role with the 437 Transport Squadron. "The military offers their condolences to Corporal Comeau's family and friends," was one of the comments made by Captain Mark Peebles, a public affairs officer at the Trenton base. "Marie will be missed by comrades at 437." The front page article told about the body being discovered at 12:58 p.m. when police, fire and ambulance crews were dispatched after her boyfriend ran from the residence. He was yelling to neighbors that someone was dead inside the house.

Williams received an email message at 12:13 a.m. on November 26 officially advising him of Corporal Comeau's death and that the circumstances were suspicious. He responded at 6:41 a.m., saying he was aware of the incident but wanted to be informed of any developments. Military Police were assigned to assist the Ontario Provincial Police and Colonel Williams was routinely updated on the progress of the investigation.

Comeau's body was on the bed, her head resting to the side of a blood-soaked pillow. She was born on April 19, 1972 and joining the military had fulfilled her dream of following in her father's footsteps. He served 42 years with the Canadian Forces. His daughter enlisted as a reservist in 1995 and later traveled the world as a military flight attendant. Framed photographs in her home were memories of many of the places she had visited.

When her killer broke in, it wasn't the first time he had been inside the residence which she moved into a year earlier. While she was away on a military flight on November 16, 2009, the man who eventually killed her slipped into the house through the same window after parking his car half a mile away in a wooded area. The window is actually five feet wide by two feet deep, but the sliding glass opens only to a width of 30 inches. Being physically fit, the intruder had no difficulty maneuvering through the ground-level opening and dropping five feet to the basement floor. Although Comeau lived alone, she was dating Paul Belanger, also a member of the Canadian military at the Trenton base. Sometimes he would stay at the house when Marie-France was away, to care for her two cats, but wasn't there when the initial break-in occurred. Once inside, the burglar made his way to her ground-floor bedroom. While rummaging through an underwear drawer, the intruder found a couple of sex toys. He donned some of her underwear after stripping naked and also took photographs while holding a purple-colored gratification device. After spending at least one hour and 24 minutes in the home starting just after midnight, he stole seven pieces of underwear. Despite his denials, Marie-France thought Belanger had gone snooping through her personal things while she was away. Because she blamed her new boyfriend, she didn't report the incident to police.

Jessica Lloyd was reported missing on Friday, January 29, 2010. Described as a hard-working and reliable employee, her colleagues at Tri-Board Student Transportation Services in Napanee – a community of 15,500 people, about 25 miles east of Belleville – knew something was wrong when she didn't arrive on time. She had never missed a day without notifying them during the two years she had been with the company. After calls to her home went unanswered, a supervisor telephoned Jessica's mother, Roxanne, around 9 a.m. to ask if she might know where her daughter was.

Jessica lived alone in what had been her parent's house at 1548 Highway 37. In 1990, her father had the home built in a rural area that later was absorbed into the city of Belleville, today a community of 50,000 residents. He was hoping to live out his years with his wife and their two children when they moved from Ottawa after his retirement following a 25-year career with the Canadian Navy. Jessica, who was 14 when her dad died, continued living at the home with her mother and her older brother, Andy, but bought the residence in May 2009 when she got a full-time job.

Roxanne Lloyd lived only a short drive from her daughter's house and arrived at 9:30 a.m., where she found her car in the driveway. The trip to the home on the main highway between Belleville and Tweed had taken her passed the office of her daughter's doctor and she stopped by briefly in the event that Jessica was ill and had either called or gone for a checkup. After unlocking the front door and going inside, she saw Jessica's keys, purse and BlackBerry communication device, but her daughter wasn't there. It was at this moment that the search for Jessica Lloyd began. Mrs. Lloyd called several relatives and friends of her daughter to find out if anyone had heard from her. Those frantic calls brought people to the house. Panic was beginning to set in. No one was sure what to do. The house was a bit of a mess and some family members started to tidy up. They vacuumed and put things back in place while Jessica's mother kept calling anyone she could think of who might know where her daughter had gone. Then came the moment of realization; the Belleville Police Service must be notified.

Russell Williams didn't know Jessica, but his pilot trained eyes saw her through a window as she was working out on a treadmill when he drove by her home on Wednesday, January 27, 2010. He was travelling from the Canadian Forces Base at Trenton to his residence in Tweed. Williams returned to her home the following evening and when Jessica left around 7 p.m. to visit a friend, Dorian O'Brian, he broke in through a kitchen window. The intruder went through the house to confirm that the young woman lived alone, then left. Jessica returned around 10 p.m. and sent a text message to O'Brian at 10:36 p.m., telling him she was safely inside and retiring for the night. Waiting and watching while hiding in a bushy area between two rocks about 500 feet from the rear door, Williams saw her come home. Later, still standing outside, he saw the light go off in her bedroom.

He had earlier driven from his home in Tweed and backed his silver-colored 2001 Nissan Pathfinder down a mud- and snow-covered roadway along a tree-line at the northern end of a farm field. It was a spot he thought wouldn't be seen by passing motorists. Hidden by the darkness of night, he made his way along the perimeter of the field and waited until Jessica was asleep before entering her home through a patio door, which he had left unlocked while in the house hours earlier. Like all previous occurrences, Williams used military tactics ranging from reconnaissance and the element of surprise to camouflage and disguise in order to lessen the likelihood of law enforcement linking him to the crime scene. But for a man intent on committing the perfect crime and getting away with murder, Williams made some critical errors during the abduction of Jessica Lloyd.

Wearing dark pants, a black sweatshirt and what appeared to be a black balaclava, Williams used a flashlight to guide his way through the darkened house while carrying some sort of duffle bag to the woman's bedroom. He found her sleeping face down on the oak frame queen-size bed and was about to render a blow to her head with the heavy flashlight when she woke up. Jessica, dressed in gray track pants and a black tank top, was ordered to remain face down by the masked assailant before he tied her hands behind her with green rope and covered her eyes with duct tape. During a four-minute period starting at 1:19 a.m., Williams took a series of photographs of Jessica in the hallway of her home. In the pictures, her eyes are closed and she's still wearing her sleepwear. The final photograph in this series, taken at 1:23 a.m., shows her with duct tape over her eyes.

Williams took pictures to keep a record of every crime he committed. On Thursday, November 1, 2007, he broke into a home at 38 Cosy Cove Lane through the patio door and took a total of 19 brassieres and panties back to his residence, later photographing and then cataloguing each item in files on his computer. The residents, who had owned the home for a little over a year, were not aware that anyone had been in their house until notified by police after Williams was arrested. He returned to the home during the early morning hours of November 2, took a number of pictures while inside and later loaded them onto his computer. The photographs, taken between 12:32 a.m. and 2:53 a.m., show underwear in a drawer in one bedroom and items of lingerie which he had spread out on the bed and on the floor. There was also a picture of Williams exposing himself in a camisole while kneeling amidst the lingerie on the bed. When back home on Saturday, November 3, 2007, Williams took four pictures of himself wearing items he had stolen from the house as well as a photograph of himself standing completely naked. All these images were filed on his computer.

After an almost five-month hiatus, Williams was back in Tweed on Saturday, March 15, 2008 when he went through an unlocked door at 72 Cosy Cove Lane, where a couple with three young children had lived for 11 years. Photographs taken in the parent's bedroom between 11:09 p.m. and 12:35 a.m. on March 16 show an underwear drawer and six garments spread out on the bed. The family was not aware their home had been entered or that anything was missing, but on March 17, Williams took photographs of himself wearing some of the lingerie he'd stolen from the house the previous day. One photograph shows him rubbing himself with a piece of the woman's underclothing.

On Friday, March 28, Williams broke into a house at 61 McRae Court in Tweed and stole 14 panties and bras after spending less than half an hour inside. He also took photographs in three bedrooms, which show underwear drawers, laundry baskets and some underclothing that he had displayed on the beds. He also recorded images of family photographs that were hanging on the wall, including pictures of the couple's teenage daughters. Even though some lingerie was stolen from the house, the couple had no idea that anyone had broken into the premises and knew nothing about the break-in until police notified them after Williams was arrested. Several hours later, Williams entered a home at 38 Cozy Cove Lane for the second time after finding the patio door open. He stole three pair of panties and took 38 photographs between 2:45 a.m. and 5:15 a.m. while the family was away. During his time inside the house, Williams snapped photographs of himself wearing lingerie that he took from drawers, plus a number of pictures of himself on a twin size bed dressed in bra and panties while masturbating. There are also photographs showing lingerie hanging from an erection while he is standing nude in a bedroom. Williams is masturbating in a number of those pictures. Later that day, he set the self timer on his camera and took photographs of himself at his home while wearing some of the lingerie stolen in the recent break-ins.

It was obvious that Williams had started on a path which would no doubt escalate to more serious criminal activity. But at this point, no one was aware that he was anyone other than the well-respected commander of Canada's largest military base. The colonel also seemed comfortable and content breaking into his neighbors homes while they were away.

On Friday, April 4, 2008, he entered 52 Charles Court through an open door and took 22 pieces of lingerie. It was the first of nine break-ins he would commit at the home. Williams returned the next evening and took 27 bras and panties. All of the items were photographed and later put in secret files hidden in compartments on his computer. Photographs were also taken with underwear laid out on the beds as well as items of underclothing in drawers and storage closets. There is no evidence of any other break-ins through April, but on Friday, May 9, Williams slipped into a home at 1723 Cara Crescent in Ottawa.

This is the first sign of what profilers consider as an escalation of the pattern of behavior in the modus

operandi – method of operation – that a criminal follows
when committing crimes. He had moved from the familiar
surroundings of his quiet rustic neighborhood in Tweed
and became a bit more daring in a municipal area where
homes were more likely to have burglar alarms and a
greater expectation of streets being patrolled by police.

Williams climbed through an open window and made his
way to the bedroom area, where he took photographs in a
room where the couple's daughter slept. He took pictures
of trophies and awards the older teenager had won and
also photographed various pieces of underwear in
drawers, in her laundry hamper and on the floor. When
Williams left, he took 15 items of underwear and between
May 11 and May 27 posed for 78 photographs of himself
modeling the lingerie he stole from the girl's room. A

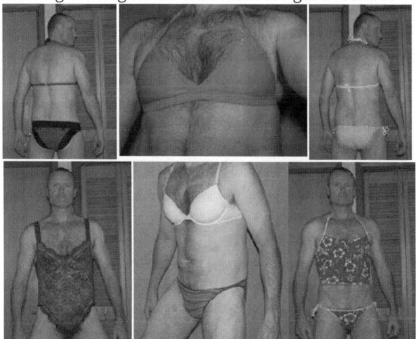

Colonel Williams modeling stolen underwear

number of the pictures show Williams masturbating and
ejaculating. The residents were not immediately aware

that their home had been entered, but called Ottawa Police on June 3 after their daughter discovered some recently-purchased lingerie was missing and the couple noticed a screen had been removed from their living room window.

Possibly because of the time delay or perhaps because of the precautions taken by Williams, police were unable to find any evidence to help identify the individual who broke into the home. The investigative report indicates the screen was off, but there was no other visible damage.

Break-in number twelve occurred back in Tweed on Wednesday, May 21, 2008 after Williams spent 30 minutes picking the front door lock at 18 Cosy Cove Lane while the owners were away. He took a couple of photographs of himself during the few minutes he was inside the home, but didn't steal anything. When the owners returned to the residence where they had lived for five years, they noticed nothing out of the ordinary and were not aware that anyone had broken into their home until told of the entry by police after Williams was arrested. Two days later, he took two pairs of female underwear after entering 66 Cosy Cove Lane while the owners were away for the day with their almost teenaged daughter. It was the third time Williams had broken into their home. While inside the girl's bedroom, he took a series of photographs during a two-minute period starting at 1:31 p.m. They show her bed, the underwear drawer, some of the girl's clothing in a closet and other garments in a laundry hamper. Between 1:50 p.m. and 2 p.m., Williams took 17 pictures of himself while rubbing his genitals with underwear he found in the room. Later in the evening, while at home, he took photographs of the two pieces of clothing he took from the home. All the photographs were stored in folders on his computer.

Driven by uncontrollable urges, Williams was out again during the daytime hours of Saturday, May 31, 2008. Scouting for a home to enter, he saw an open window at 124 Charles Street and climbed through. There was no one home and he wandered about before making his way to a bedroom where he stole some pajamas and lingerie. He also took several photographs. Over the next two days, additional pictures were taken showing Williams at his home wearing the stolen clothing. He also catalogued the items on his computer along with other images of lingerie in drawers inside the house, located only a block from his cottage residence.

Williams had graduated from nighttime break-ins to entries where it took 30 minutes to pick a lock in broad daylight. It still seemed unimaginable at this point, that a respected military officer could eventually escalate his criminal behavior and become involved in forcible confinement, rape and then murder. But in the summer of 2008 and for the next 18 months, he was content to maraud around the neighborhoods where he was comfortable and break into homes while residents were away.

The road to his extreme antisocial behavior took a sharp turn in September 2009 – when Williams broke into a home in Tweed where a 20-year-old woman was sleeping. Her live-in boyfriend was out of town and she was in the house with her two-month-old daughter. It was the first time that he had ever entered a home knowing there was someone inside. By doing this, he graduated from crimes with only a slight chance of being caught to an extremely risky situation which would draw a great deal of police attention. It was as though Williams had a desire to be caught. But it's also possible he was developing a superiority complex and honing his skills with the idea of committing the perfect crime.

Officially listed as counts 73 and 74 on an indictment, the documents charge that on Thursday, September 17, 2009, Williams forcibly confined and sexually assaulted a victim subsequently identified in the court only as Jane Doe. In Canada, the identity of sexual assault victims is protected unless the individual formally asks the judge to allow their name to be made public. Williams didn't know the young woman, who had lived in the home for only a month. She was asleep when an intruder in the darkened bedroom pushed her head into the pillow. She didn't see his face, but during the ordeal had the impression that her attacker was between 30 to 50 years old, someone around six feet tall with an average build. He made a raspy sound while breathing and appeared to be making his voice seem deeper and more intimidating. His face was close to hers and she noticed that he was clean shaven. She thought he was dressed all in black with a tight-fitting sweater, whose sleeve at one point during the attack the young mother thought she had ripped. He wore hiking boots and no glasses, but he did have on a ring which could have been on his wedding finger. She also told investigators her attacker smelled dirty.

It was only 13 days after the attack on Jane Doe that Williams committed his second sexual assault. In the meantime, he continued breaking into homes and stealing underwear. Incredibly, one of those break-ins was at Doe's residence, a day after his depraved attack on her. After climbing through an open window on September 18, Williams stole some of her panties and bras. The following day, he photographed the 15 pieces of stolen clothing and stored the images on his computer. There were other photographs which had been taken during this break-in. Found later on the computer, they show pictures of the woman's bedroom, including photographs of lingerie on her bed, in a drawer and on the floor. He also took pictures of a number of framed photographs hanging on her bedroom wall, which he stored in three separate file folders on his computer.

Williams returned to Jane Doe's home late in the evening of September 19, but her boyfriend was there and he didn't attempt to break in. However on Tuesday, September 22, no one was home and he gained entry through an open window. Williams took photographs of himself standing naked and looking at lingerie from a dresser drawer in her bedroom. He also took photographs of some personal identification, including her driver's license and an insurance benefit card. Before leaving, he gathered up a few dresses as well as some of her panties and bras which he took with him. During the early morning hours of September 24, 2009, Williams spread out various pieces of the young woman's lingerie at his home and took pictures of each item.

He changed his pattern on the evening of September 24 when he broke into a house at 76 Cosy Cove Lane. He had selected his next victim and was doing what could best be described in military terms as reconnaissance, to figure out what would give him total advantage over the young woman and minimize the risk of his capture. This turning point also brings into close focus the cowardice that the colonel had demonstrated since beginning his crime spree. It is now clear he was on a path to commit rape and murder, but needed to build up courage with a series of petty crimes and a trove of trophies which brought him instant gratification and reward. Williams no doubt will be a clinical study in future for psychiatrists, criminologists and criminal profilers. But from the perspective of police officers who had dealt with thousands of cases through the years, he took a deliberate road with a specific objective. A man considered a bright light in the military and someone who would no doubt achieve the pinnacle in the career he had chosen, he was also fostering dark and sinister thoughts which eventually became part of his real world.

The woman picked for his second attack was 45-year-old Laurie Massicotte, who lived three houses away from his residence. Williams had seen her several times and thought she lived alone, but needed to know if she had a boyfriend who would sometimes stay overnight. On Thursday, September 24, he found an open window and went inside. He was there long enough to steal a pair of her panties and look around for any sign of a man's presence. Williams also took pictures in the woman's bedroom. They show undergarments in a dresser drawer, framed photographs on top of the dresser and pictures of her bed. Forty-eight hours later, back inside the home, he stole some of Massicotte's nighties and panties and took

Ian Robertson photo

Laurie Massicotte

several photographs before fleeing. The images loaded into his computer show her bed with lingerie spread out and some underwear in a drawer. He also used the self-timer on his camera to take pictures of himself wearing some of her panties. Each photograph was documented and stored on his computer.

On Wednesday, September 30, 2009, Massicotte was sleeping on the living room couch when Williams punched her repeatedly in the face. She hadn't changed for bed but had fallen sleep while watching television. Fearing for her life, Laurie attempted to pull herself up, but the intruder hit her several more times while telling her to keep quiet. She tried to focus and see his face, but without glasses and the blows leaving her dazed, she saw only a blurry outline of her attacker. Laurie continued struggling for about 20 minutes while Williams continued punching – all the while trying to keep her head turned away so she couldn't see him. "Be quiet," he ordered. "You are making it worse."

The attacker warned her that other men were in her house and taking everything. She was told he was there to keep her under control. Laurie didn't hear anyone else and could only think the attacker was there to rape and kill her. She struggled as hard as she could to get away, but Williams was much stronger and used his elbow to pin her down while warning her not to look at him. Realizing the way she was being held was making it difficult for her to breathe, she begged him to cover her face so she wouldn't be able to see him. At that point, he grabbed a pillowcase and put it over her head. Dazed and bleeding, she stopped resisting, but was now hyperventilating and had the sensation that she was going to suffocate. Her head was also pounding from the beating. She requested a drink of water and aspirin for her headache, also asking if she could just be blindfolded instead of having her head covered.

Williams turned from being an attacker to a comforter, leading her to another room to get some water – but not before binding her hands with what felt like a piece of wire. He assured her she was safe and promised she wouldn't be killed just before telling her that he was leaving the room to go and check on the men who were there to ransack her home. Returning a moment later, he closed the blinds and then began asking probing and personal questions about her life. As he talked, she felt a knife, but her attacker only used the weapon to cut the binding on her wrists. He then secured her hands with the pillow case before commencing a sexual assault that lasted a little over three hours. She begged him to stop, but he fondled her breasts and pulled up her skirt before ordering her to turn around so that he could unfasten her bra. Williams told Laurie he had a camera and would be taking pictures.

From Saturday, May 31, 2008, until Williams confronted his first victim 16 months later, only a handful of the break-ins were reported to police and virtually no evidence was found when police did examine the homes in which burglaries had occurred. The residents of 7 Charles Street, who had lived in Tweed for seven years, didn't know anyone had broken into their home on Friday, June 6 and Saturday, June 7. Williams had picked the lock and stole 35 pieces of lingerie. He attempted to break into a house at 577 Apollo Way in Ottawa on June 14, but the occupants arrived home with their two teenage daughters and he fled. The owners did notice that an attempt had been made to pry open a door leading from the garage, but didn't call police because they didn't realize anyone had broken into their living area.

On Monday, June 16, Williams entered another house on Cara Crescent in Ottawa, where a sex toy and 87 pieces of lingerie were stolen. After returning from an out-of-town trip, the owners, who lived there with their 24-year-old daughter, found the front door unlocked and an unsecured basement window. Police weren't called immediately because nothing appeared to have been taken, but when the daughter came home she realized her personal items were missing. The numerous photographs taken by Williams in the young woman's bedroom indicate he had been in the house for about two hours that morning. The 46 images stored on his computer from this break-in show underwear in drawers, laundry baskets and on the floor, as well as copies of framed pictures of the young woman and her friends that were hanging on her bedroom wall. He also photographed her high school diploma and graduation picture. A series of other photographs appear to have been taken while Williams was at home. They show the woman's undergarments wrapped around his genitalia and a photograph of a stolen vibrator secured to his sex organ with a piece of lingerie, along with a note reading "merci beaucoup" and the daughter's name.

On Saturday, July 12, 2008, Williams went a third time to the home at 7 Charles Court in Tweed and picked the lock to gain entry. Inside, he stole 17 bras and panties and took a number of photographs between 11:09 and 11:14 p.m. that show lingerie and other clothing in drawers and on the floor. The pictures were loaded into his computer along with photographs taken on July 20 and October 6, 2008 of undergarments he had stolen from the house. All images on the computer were laboriously itemized and stored in files which documented the date, time and location of each photograph.

Sixteen days after breaking into the Tweed home, Williams was out for a nighttime stroll in Ottawa on Monday, July 28, when he discovered an open window at a home on Simoneau Way. The owners and their three daughters, aged 9, 11 and 13, were away and didn't know that anyone had entered their house until they were told by police after Williams confessed to the break-in. He had entered the home, not knowing who lived there, but discovered children's undergarments and two-piece bathing suits in one bedroom. Twenty pieces of clothing were taken and Williams listed them as belonging to a "mystery little girl" in the series of photographs of the garments stored on his computer. Among the 42 photographs were several taken in one of the girl's bedrooms between 3:01 a.m. and 4:05 a.m. on July 29. The images included photographs of underwear in drawers and garments that were laid out by Williams on the bed. He also copied framed pictures of the three girls that were displayed throughout the house and set his camera to take photos of himself as he lay naked on a bed while masturbating on the children's undergarments. There were also pictures found on his computer dated August 19 and 26, showing Williams wearing some of the items he had stolen from the home, as well as others of him masturbating and of the children's underwear which were spread out on a bed sheet at his home.

On Friday, August 1, 2008 and the next day, Williams stole a quantity of lingerie and a sundress after climbing through an open window at 90 Cosy Cove Lane. Photographs on his computer show him standing naked in a bedroom at the home. There are also images of clothing in drawers and in the closet. One photograph shows Williams taking a picture of himself through a mirror in the master bedroom while wearing the sundress. The occupants were not home and didn't know about the break-in, only learning what had happened when contacted by police two years later. Williams left the house after the August 2 break-in, then made his way down the street and entered the residence at 72 Cosy Cove Lane through an open door. After taking a number of pictures of underwear drawers and clothing in laundry hampers, he stole several pieces of lingerie. Williams also set up his camera to take automatic pictures while lying naked beside some of the underwear on the couple's bed, plus others while peering into a laundry basket.

Five days later, on Thursday, August 7, 2008, he roamed his Tweed neighborhood again and entered a home at 52 Charles Court through an unlocked door shortly after midnight. It was the third time he had broken into the house and he took photographs of various pieces of underwear strewn around a bedroom. Williams later photographed himself at his home while wearing some

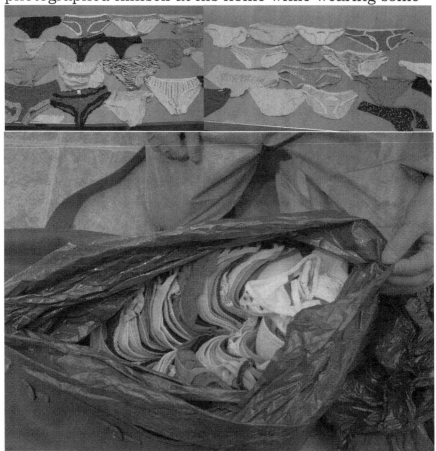
Stolen underwear found in suspect's house

pink panties that were taken during the break-in. To gain entry to 59 Charles Court on Tuesday, August 12, he used a key which the family had hidden outside. He took several pictures but didn't steal anything. A day later, he climbed through an open window at 100 Kanata Lane, but left a short time later. He also didn't steal anything and took no photographs.

On Saturday, August 16, the home at 124 Charles Road was broken into for a second time. After entering through an open window, Williams stole some panties, bras and pajamas, then took pictures in a bedroom. Investigators discovered images on his computer that show family photographs on a bedside table plus several items of underwear in drawers and others that had been set aside to be washed.

The next three break-ins occurred while Williams was at his Ottawa home with his wife. On Thursday, August 21, he entered a residence at 597 Apollo Way through an open door while the occupants and their four children were away. The couple didn't realize that 27 pieces of lingerie had been stolen and were not aware that their house had been broken into until told by police after Williams was arrested. Photographs found on his computer were taken during a 10-minute period from 10:04 p.m. and show a bedroom with a quantity of lingerie. Other photographs include a collage of family pictures that were on display plus itemized images of bras, panties and a slip that Williams had stolen. Two days later, on Saturday, August 23, he entered 1714 Caminiti Crescent while the family was away for the weekend. After returning home, they discovered a screen had been removed from a rear window and called police after realizing that someone had broken in. It appeared the burglar had entered through the rear window and used a side door to leave, but nothing was missing. Williams confirmed he didn't steal anything, but did copy a young woman's graduation picture that he found in a bedroom. He also took photographs of lingerie and copied the young woman's passport photo. On Thursday, August 28, 2008, Williams smashed through a basement window at 1743 Cara Crescent just before midnight and stole four pieces of lingerie. He also took several pictures of clothing on a bed and in a dresser drawer. A neighbor spotted the broken window and called the vacationing family to let them know about the break-in. Ottawa Police were alerted when the occupants returned home, but after checking electronic equipment, jewelry and a liquor cabinet, they didn't believe anything had been taken. After learning that Williams was responsible, images were located on his computer showing pictures that were snapped inside the couple's house, including underwear in a dresser drawer in a bedroom. There was also a photograph of one occupant, which Williams had copied from a passport he found in a drawer, plus several images taken of himself while at his Tweed residence. Two of the photographs, described by police as being close-ups of his midsection, show Williams dressed in maroon panties and a black bra.

All the time while living this existence, in addition to overseeing Canada's largest military base, Colonel Williams was attending top level meetings with high ranking politicians, bureaucrats and other military leaders. He was also flying frequently to bases in Europe and the Middle East, including Canada's secret facility, Camp Mirage, in the United Arab Emirates, to help coordinate Canadian troops deployed with NATO forces to combat Taliban fighters and other terrorists in Afghanistan. He was well on his way to being promoted to the rank of general and possibly destined to one day assume command of Canada's military.

Although going without sleep and spending countless hours on his computer cataloguing the photographs of souvenirs or trophies taken during the continuing crime spree, Williams gave no outward hint that he was leading a Jekyll and Hyde existence with an extremely dark side to his life. In fact, he appeared normal in every way to those who met him through his daily routine. His wife, Mary

Elizabeth Harriman, also told authorities she had no reason to suspect that her husband was prowling the homes of their neighbors in Ottawa and their cottage residence in Tweed to steal lingerie and take pictures. Although Williams is the first person to document his crimes with written notes, digital photographs, sound recording and video tape, a former Toronto homicide detective, Tom Klatt, predicted during an interview for this book that other killers will now start recording their murders. This became graphically evident in May 2012 when parcels containing a severed left foot and hand were mailed to the offices of the ruling Conservative Party of Canada and the Liberal Party headquarters in Ottawa. His other hand and foot were mailed to an elementary school and a private boy's school in the Vancouver area. Police ascertained the body parts were from an individual who had been brutally murdered with an ice pick and then dismembered at an apartment in Montreal. Homicide detectives confirmed the killing and dissection of Jun Lin, a 33-year-old university student from China, had been videotaped and posted on the Internet. There was also evidence of cannibalism.

Police later learned that the suspected killer, 29-year-old Luka Rocco Magnotta, had fled to Europe. He was spotted in Paris after a "red notice" alert was put out through INTERPOL, the international police agency, but managed to escape. Two days later, on June 4, 2012, Magnotta, an aspiring model and porn star actor, surrendered without a struggle when confronted by German authorities at a Berlin café where he was reading Internet news reports of the worldwide manhunt that had been launched for him.

The following news release was issued by the international police agency, based in Lyon, France, after Magnotta was captured:

The arrest in Germany of Luka Rocco Magnotta, a Canadian national suspected of murder and the subject of an INTERPOL Red Notice for internationally-wanted persons, highlights the essential role of international police cooperation and sharing intelligence in fugitive investigations, a senior INTERPOL official has said.

At the request of Canadian authorities, on 31 May INTERPOL issued a Red Notice for 29-year-old Magnotta, wanted for arrest in the killing of a man and posting his body parts to various locations around Canada. German authorities confirmed that Magnotta was taken into custody by police in Berlin today, Monday 4 June.

INTERPOL'S 24/7 Command and Coordination Centre circulated the Red Notice in all four of its official languages, Arabic, English, French and Spanish, to each of its 190 member countries after it was believed Magnotta, who is also known as Eric Clinton Newman or Vladimir Romanov, had fled Canada for France.

Thereafter, INTERPOL Canada and the relevant INTERPOL National Central Bureaus began sharing intelligence on Magnotta's whereabouts. In light of the dangerous nature of the suspected murderer, all information on the case was treated as a priority by INTERPOL's Fugitive Investigation Support unit and its Command and Coordination Centre at its General Secretariat headquarters in Lyon, France.

Throughout the case, INTERPOL's General Secretariat headquarters remained in constant touch with the relevant National Central Bureaus worldwide and specialist fugitive investigation units to ensure a seamless flow of intelligence in following up potential leads provided by both law enforcement and the public.

"Magnotta's arrest demonstrates the benefits of INTERPOL's worldwide network of National Central Bureaus sharing information on dangerous fugitives believed to have fled abroad. Police know that the best way to catch fugitives anywhere in the world is to use INTERPOL's tools and services," said the Head of INTERPOL's Fugitives unit, Stefano Carvelli.

"INTERPOL congratulates all of the authorities and its National Central Bureaus in Canada, France, Germany and elsewhere for their collaborative efforts which led to the rapid arrest of this wanted individual," added Mr Carvelli.

INTERPOL Red Notices serve to communicate to police worldwide that a person is wanted by a member country and request that the suspect be placed under provisional arrest pending extradition.

While police in Canada are concerned with what appears to be a dramatic escalation from the photographing, recording and documenting that Williams did during his killings, law enforcement agencies in Arizona, Florida and California commenced investigations after Magnotta was taken into custody to see if he can be linked to some "corpse mutilation" homicides in those states.

DNDPhoto

Williams with Canada's Defence Minister Peter MacKay

Chapter Two

The pattern of entering unoccupied homes and taking underwear continued for two years, from September 9, 2007, to September 1, 2009. Nine days later, Williams' behavior dramatically changed.

He broke into a Tweed home where a 20-year-old woman was alone with her eight-week-old daughter. Williams had never met the woman, who a short time earlier had moved into the neighborhood with her boyfriend. But he had caught a glimpse of her in the backyard while out in his boat and thought she looked quite cute. The five-foot-two woman, identified in court documents only as Jane Doe, had been visiting her mother for the day on September 16, 2009, while her boyfriend was working out of town for a couple of weeks. She returned home sometime between 9:30 p.m. and 10 p.m. and put her daughter down for the night, before changing into pajama bottoms and a tank top. It was around 11 p.m. when she retired to her bedroom after checking the front door to make sure it was locked. She didn't check other doors or windows because all were secure when she left to go to her mother's home.

Suddenly, someone was holding her head down. She thought it was a nightmare until realizing she had awakened from a deep sleep. Now aware it wasn't a dream, the young woman had one question for her attacker. "Are you going to kill me?" She had no idea who was in the bedroom with her or what was going to happen. Williams assured the victim she wasn't going to be murdered, but wouldn't explain why he was there or what he intended to do. He just continued holding her head against the pillow for what seemed like 30 minutes. His grip was powerful and it was impossible for her to physically resist.

The victim had no idea how long she'd been asleep and Williams told her it was 1 a.m. He wanted to know how long she had lived in the house and she told him a month, but didn't answer when he questioned her about her boyfriend. Totally filled with fear, she had no concept of time and didn't know if her attacker had been restraining her for seconds, minutes or hours. It felt like forever, she later told investigators.

Still holding her head away from him so that she couldn't see his face, Williams maneuvered the terrified woman to the side of the bed. He then repositioned himself, sitting on her lower back and upper legs while putting his hand on her back to keep her pinned down. Jane Doe tried to speak but was struck three times on the head and warned to keep quiet. The attacker also told her to not even think about looking at his face. Despite the warning, she told Williams that from the sound of his voice he didn't seem like the type of person who would do something like this – and he seemed to soften a bit. It was as if he got nicer, she told investigators. After saying he needed to get control of her, Williams grabbed a baby blanket and the baby's receiving blanket, which were near the bed and tried to use them to bind her hands. After failing to fashion a proper knot, he ripped a pillowcase into strips and successfully bound her hands. She was then forced into the living room, where Williams pulled something from a bag that he'd left there after entering the house.

Thinking he might have armed himself with a knife or some other weapon, Jane Doe asked what was going to happen as he pushed her back to the bedroom. "You'll see," said Williams, although he did assure her that he wasn't going to hurt her. Thinking of any type of ploy that might dissuade the attacker, the young woman said she was still fat from having a baby and hoped the words would paint her as someone "unattractive" – and not the kind of person a would-be rapist would target. Williams rebuked her comments, however, saying he thought she was "perfect and sweet" moments before covering her head with a pillowcase.

The new mother began to panic. She was claustrophobic and became overwhelmed with a sense that she was going to die. Williams immediately uncovered her head and fashioned the bedding into a blindfold, which he tightly knotted while standing behind her. After adjusting the makeshift eye cover to make sure she couldn't see, Williams stood in front of his victim. She felt her right breast being exposed as he pulled down one side of her tank top. Then she heard a camera click. Her attacker had taken a photograph. She felt his hand again. This time he lowered the tank top to her waist. Another photograph was taken before he began repeatedly squeezing her breasts. She was then ordered to remove her pajama bottoms and stand naked as he took more pictures. Completely defenseless and unable to resist, she was forced to submit to his request for grotesque poses. This left her feeling shamed, totally humiliated and physically ill. Williams promised he would do nothing more than take pictures and then walked toward her infant daughter's room.

Jane Doe sat on her bed, naked and shaking, again not knowing what was going on. Moments later, she sensed him back in her room and heard dresser drawers opening, but had no idea what he was looking for. The intruder came over and had her stand beside the bed while he fondled her breasts and rubbed his face against hers. He then indicated that he had looked in on her baby and asked her daughter's age.

Williams began moving around the room while telling the young woman to give him time to escape. Ordered to count to 300 before calling the police, she began reciting out loud when she heard him heading to the bedroom door seconds later. She stopped counting when she reached 70.

"Keep going."

The attacker was still there and Jane Doe reached 200 before yelling. This time there was no answer. But she still waited a few more moments before uncovering her masked eyes and phoning friends for help. She also checked to make sure her baby was okay and called police.

The friends, two women and three men, who lived nearby, were at the victim's home within 10 minutes. Two men searched in the vicinity while the others went inside, comforting the young woman during the 15 minutes it took police to arrive in the rural residential enclave. Looking around her bedroom, she noticed the sheets were missing and later discovered that some of her bras and panties had been stolen.

Jane Doe told police she had not heard a car or boat when the attacker fled, but provided details about her assailant, even though she had not seen his face – telling them he had seemed to be like a "Dad" and possibly between 30 and 50 years of age. He also seemed to have an average build, was almost a foot taller than her, didn't wear glasses and was clean shaven. He also wasn't disguised, but seemed to be dressed entirely in black, including a tight black sweater which ripped at one point when she tugged against him. When asked if she recalled anything else, she told police that he was wearing some type of hiking boots and it appeared he was trying to make his voice sound deeper and more authoritative when ordering her around.

She thought he "smelled dirty" and had a ring on one finger, but she didn't know if it was a wedding band.

During the ordeal, Jane Doe thought he took about seven photographs of her with a fancy, possibly digital camera, equipped with a very bright flash.

The first responding officers from the Central Hastings Detachment of the Ontario Provincial Police immediately began checking the area for any sign of the suspect after they realized the victim was being properly cared for. They scanned the roadway, checked adjoining properties and peered across the lake for any sign of someone making a getaway by boat. Nothing seemed out of the ordinary. Roadblocks were set up on nearby Charles Road and people were questioned as they left the neighborhood. No one recalled hearing or seeing anything unusual that night. Police dogs were also brought in to scour the area, but failed to turn up anything of significance to assist the investigation.

Two specialists from the OPP Forensic Identification Services, Jayne Pellerin and Nicole Burley, arrived at 7:35 a.m. and took charge of collecting any evidence that might be useful to identify the attacker. The two constables found that a screen on a side window had been sliced open, but there were no fingerprints or other evidence to identify a suspect. They did notice the sheets and blankets had been stripped from the woman's bed and the cover had been removed from a duvet that was on the floor. In the daughter's bedroom, they located the pillow cases that had been shredded in order to tie and blindfold the young mother. Anything considered evidentiary was photographed, itemized and described in detailed notes before being placed in evidence bags for further analysis at the crime lab. Specific spots in the bedroom and areas on the victim's body were then swabbed in an effort to find DNA samples which can now develop into genetic fingerprints that can pinpoint an individual responsible for a crime with absolute certainty through blood and saliva analysis.

It was later learned that a sample which the identification officers took from the nape of the victim's neck contained enough deoxyribonucleic acid to generate a partial DNA profile. A comparison of samples from convicted criminals failed to turn up a match, but the DNA results were beneficial in ruling out some individuals who had surfaced as potential suspects. The investigation continued for months as police followed every conceivable lead, but eventually they reached a dead end. It was a frustrating and unsatisfactory conclusion to what had been a painstaking hunt for the person who put the young woman through such demeaning trauma. But there was nothing more that could be done on the case, unless someone called police with new information – or the attacker confessed.

It was during the February 7, 2010 interrogation of Williams that he mentioned breaking into the victim's home and molesting the young mother. The statement of facts prepared by police indicates "in the course of a very detailed interview, Mr. Williams acknowledged being the perpetrator of the crimes against Jane Doe." He revealed that he didn't know the victim but had seen her while boating on Stoco Lake and said he thought she was attractive. He explained how, on the morning of Thursday, September 17, 2009, he had cut the screen and crawled through a side window to gain entry to the home. Williams wore a sweatshirt, dark pants and a dark woolen cap, which he pulled down to conceal his face.

Once inside, he admitted making his way to the victim's bedroom and stood over the woman for a few minutes, watching her sleep. He then hit her hard against the side of the head to awaken her, but she immediately began struggling and he used the weight of his body to pin her down. In the interview, Williams talked about removing her clothing and taking photographs before leaving. Not wanting to leave any evidence, he kept one of her tops, all the bedding and a baby blanket that he had touched. In addition, he stole some of her underwear. Williams insisted he told the victim he wasn't going to hurt her or the baby and was only there to take pictures.

Police found nine images of Jane Doe on Williams' computer, along with a two-page typed document detailing his encounter with her. The words he had written mirrored the young woman's terror which she described to investigators. His photographs also depicted the ordeal she was forced to endure. One image taken at 2:47 a.m. shows her blindfolded, sitting awkwardly on the side of the bed with her arms apparently tied behind her back and one breast partially exposed. In the next photograph, she is standing with the bed behind her and her top positioned so that her right breast was fully visible. A third and fourth picture, taken only a couple of minutes later show the victim's camisole-style tank top pulled down. At 2:51 a.m., the top is at her waist but all other clothing has been removed. Her mouth is contorted and she appears to be extremely distraught as five other pictures are taken with her – first standing, then sitting on the bed and finally, at 2:55 a.m. sitting on the floor. In the final picture she is wearing pajama bottoms, but remains blindfolded and her hands are bound behind her back.

Williams also photographed the bedding, a baby blanket and lingerie taken from her home. He catalogued those pictures on his computer before discarding the stolen items at the Tweed dump. Although Williams told Detective Sergeant Smyth that images of all his crimes were stored on two hard drives at his home in Ottawa and on personal computers that he used in Tweed and at the military base, an initial search failed to turn up the pictures. It wasn't until Detective Sergeant Jim Falconer, an expert in the OPP's computer section, delved through a series of complex subfolders and password-protected hidden compartments that hundreds of images were finally uncovered. The photographs confirmed everything that Williams had told them about his involvement in the deaths of the two women, the sexual assaults of Jane Doe and Laurie Massicotte, plus 82 break-ins at private residences in Ottawa and Tweed, where huge quantities of underwear had been stolen.

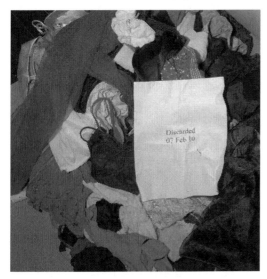

At one point, Williams said he had so many boxes filled with undergarments at his home that he feared his wife would find them and learn of his secret life.

Photo of lingerie Williams took to dump

Chapter Three

Before confronting Jane Doe, Williams gained confidence and courage through an escalating number of home burglaries in the two neighborhoods where he was living. Everyone from criminal profilers to psychiatrists suggest his behavior was a classic case of someone who would eventually become more aggressive and, if not caught, engage in violent sexual encounters before turning to homicide. The critical turning point came on Tuesday, September 1, 2009, when he broke into a house around 10 p.m. on Charles Road in Tweed. The couple who lived there had several children, including a 14-year-old daughter, and Williams admitted when interviewed that he had been yearning for some time to get into the girl's bedroom. He initially tried to enter the house on August 1, but was frightened off when a dog started barking in the basement as he removed a screen from a window. When he returned a month later, he found the rear porch door unlocked. Once inside, he stole five items of lingerie from the girl's bedroom and took a number of photographs before leaving. Williams told Detective Sergeant Smyth that the teenager appeared to be 16 or 17 and he went outside to hide in the darkness and look at her through a bedroom window when she got home. He said he shifted a guitar in her room so that he could get an unobstructed view. While waiting, Williams said he masturbated after stripping naked and was preparing to go back into the house and take pictures of himself on the girl's bed when her father came home. Still naked, he continued standing in the shadows in the backyard watching the house and was there when the girl arrived home about 10 minutes later.

He also detailed the experience in notes hidden among his extensive array of computer files. Her bed was clearly visible from his vantage point on a small ladder in the yard. "I watched her lie down and within 10 minutes turn out the light," he wrote. "Unfortunately I didn't catch her changing. Maybe tomorrow night."

Williams didn't answer when asked by Smyth what he planned to do with the girl if her father had not come home, but denied having any desire to go back into the house at that time.

The photos taken during that break-in were located on Williams' computer and show various images of the bedroom, including pictures of the girl's bed and photographs of underwear in an open dresser drawer. He had also copied family photographs on her dresser. They show the girl's parents and siblings. Police also found a number of pictures of the clothing that Williams had shot after returning to his home, plus other images reflected through a mirror of him looking at himself while wearing the 14-year-old girl's undergarments.

Investigators also found media releases that Ottawa Police had posted on the department's web site, which were related to some of the burglaries perpetrated by Williams in Canada's capital city. Although he did acknowledge developing "a bit of a fetish" for women's underwear in his 20s, detectives were never able to determine the cause or "trigger" that launched his 29-month crime spree. There has been a great deal of speculation, including suggestions in the media that mind-altering pain killers were prescribed to Williams a short time before the first break-in, but no evidence was ever brought forward to confirm that hypothesis. It is almost as though Williams awakened on September 9, 2007 and made a conscious decision to live out some bizarre fantasy.

His thirty-first break-in occurred on Saturday, August 30, 2008 when he entered a residence at 44 Charles Court in

Tweed through an open door. Williams took 17 pieces of underwear, photographed lingerie in drawers and copied pictures of residents that were hanging on interior walls. Police also found a number of images on his computer that show him wearing some of the bras and panties stolen from the home.

Williams was almost caught when an alarm was triggered on Friday, September 5, 2008 while he was climbing through a window of a house at 628 Apollo Way in Ottawa. He hastily retreated when the security company called the house to find out if the alarm had gone off accidentally. Since no one answered, the company notified police and Williams thought an emergency vehicle may have arrived at the house as he fled through the back yard. Nothing was removed from the home and there was no time to snap photographs while inside, but as a souvenir he stored a copy of the news release about the entry, which had been posted on the Ottawa Police website. On Friday, October 3, he broke into the home at 1723 Cara Crescent in Ottawa for the second time and took a quantity of bras, slips and panties. Like the burglary five months earlier, Williams entered the home through an open window and took photographs in the bedroom of the couple's teenage daughter. They show trophies and plaques she had won in various competitions. He also photographed her lingerie in drawers and a laundry basket, and other clothing in the closet. In addition to photographs taken in the home, investigators found images on Williams' computer of some of the teenager's underwear being used for sexual purposes. The family was not aware of this break-in until told by police that he had returned to their home and stolen additional items of lingerie.

Williams stole a couple of bras and more than a dozen panties from a laundry hamper after climbing through an open window at 620 Simoneau Way in Ottawa on

Wednesday, October 8, 2008. He also took a slip, a pair of pants and some tops. The woman who lived there noticed the items were missing as she was getting ready to go to her gym the next day, but didn't call police until October 31 when she heard news reports of a similar break-in in the neighborhood. Williams photographed each item and then catalogued them on his computer. Two days later, he broke into a home on Apollo Way in Ottawa. The owners were out of town, but their two children, including a 14-year-old girl, were being looked after by a relative who was staying at the home. Sometime during the early morning hours of October 9, the relative was awakened by a noise in the basement but didn't see anything when she made her way downstairs to find out what had happened. The next morning she noticed a piece of plastic that had been covering the window was ripped away and the window was ajar. The parents didn't detect anything missing when they returned home and did not call the police, but they nailed the window shut to prevent anyone from getting into the basement area where their daughters slept. Williams told Smyth during his police interview that he immediately left that home without taking anything after seeing two girls, possibly teenagers, asleep in their beds.

William also broke into a home at 622 Stellar Street in Ottawa on Thursday, October 23, but spent less than a minute inside because the burglar alarm sounded. The owners were away, but their daughter, who lives a short distance away, met police around 11:30 p.m. when the alarm went off. A search gave no indication that the premises had been burglarized or that anyone had even been in the house. However, when her parents returned home, they noticed a bucket was covering one of their motion sensors and someone had tampered with a deadbolt on a door. Williams acknowledged being frightened off when the alarm sounded and also told investigators that he stored a copy of the news release about the entry on his computer.

Late Friday on October 24, 2008, he crawled through a basement window of a home at 652 Apollo Way in Ottawa after the owners and their four children left for the weekend. The couple, whose teenage son and three daughters ranged from 12 to 21 years of age, found a rear door unlocked when they returned that Sunday. They then found a trail of mud and leaves on the basement floor and on the stairway leading to the living area. Police who responded to the family's break-in call advised them of several recent underwear thefts in the Fallingbrook area of Ottawa where they lived. An immediate check of the bedrooms revealed a quantity of lingerie and other clothing was missing. Two of the girls found photographs from albums strewn around their bedrooms and when the youngest daughter logged onto her computer the next day she found the French word for thank you – "Merci" – on the screen. Williams told Detective Sergeant Smyth that he had entered the home late Friday evening, returning the following night to collect some additional underwear and left the message on the computer after spotting images of the young girl's friends. He spent at least one hour and 16 minutes inside the house the first night, rummaging through drawers, washing machines and closets before taking 39 pieces of clothing, including bathing suits, underwear, a slip, bras and a dress. He stayed at least one hour and 27 minutes the next night, but stole only three pairs of panties. Williams also took numerous photographs and later stored 76 images from the first break-in on his computer, plus another 86 pictures taken the second time he was in the house.

Images found in files, labeled as "mystery girls" on his computer, indicate he took numerous pictures inside bedrooms where the young girls slept and also copied pictures from albums plus some that were hanging on walls throughout the home. There were also photographs of underwear in drawers, washing machines and laundry baskets as well as pictures showing his gloved hand as he thumbed through and photographed pages of photo albums in one of the bedrooms. Williams also copied university identification belonging to the couple's 19-year-old daughter and pictures of their 12-year-old daughter, plus a letter from the family's doctor, which gave the teenager's name and birth date. Police also found photographs of Williams holding various undergarments and exposing himself while on beds in the different rooms used by the girls. In addition, he had a copy on his computer of a page two article from the community newspaper, the Eastender, about the theft of underwear during residential break-ins.

Shortly after breaking into the Apollo Way home, Williams removed a screen from a window at a Wilkie Drive house where a separated mother was living with her young son and 12-year-old daughter. The woman had gone out for the evening and the children were staying overnight at their father's residence. When she came home, the gate to the back yard was open and some muddy footprints had been left outside the dining room window. When police were called, the woman was asked if any clothing was missing. A check of the bedroom revealed that most of her lingerie and a red silk robe had been stolen. She also discovered that all of her daughter's underwear was gone, but nothing had been touched in her son's room. A steady rainfall had washed away the footprints before police identification officers arrived at the home, but the woman did provide police with a detailed description of the pilfered underwear. Williams admitted going into the house twice throughout the night. After ripping the screen from the window and throwing it into a nearby hedge, he entered the home sometime after 10 p.m. and bundled up 77 items of clothing, consisting of bras, panties, a camisole, bathing suit and a slip. He also took photographs in two bedrooms and other locations in the house. Williams told Detective Sergeant Smyth he left before midnight, but returned about an hour later and collected another 27 pieces of underwear, including a robe which had been hanging on the back of a door.

Williams entered a home at 496 Minnie Avenue in Tweed on Tuesday, November 4, 2008, after finding a window open. He stole 13 garments, including pajama bottoms, a bathing suit, dress, panties, bras and a top. A woman in her 20s, who was staying at the home while her parents were away, didn't realize that anyone had been in the house, but when the couple returned they noticed windows in a bathroom and the basement had been forced open. They also saw a muddy footprint on a tarpaulin that covered their patio furniture, but didn't call police because it appeared nothing had been stolen from the home where they'd lived for 21 years. Williams said he went into the house twice over a short period of time and, in addition to stealing the clothing, had taken a number of photographs which police later located on his computer.

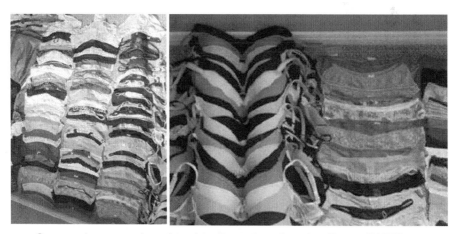

Some photographs of stolen lingerie taken by Russell Williams

There were various images taken in bedrooms, pictures of underwear in drawers and a copy of the daughter's graduation photo. Investigators also found three photographs showing Williams standing inside the house naked from the waist down. On Wednesday, November 12, the base commander stole several bra and panty sets after climbing through an open window of a house at 1735 Cara Crescent in Ottawa. He also photographed the bedroom and some lingerie on the floor. The owners did not know their home had been burglarized until notified by police 15 months later, when Williams was taken into custody. After breaking into another Ottawa home on Canemore Crescent on Thursday, November 20, he took some undergarments and a bathing suit from the bedroom of a 15-year-old girl. She noticed the theft, but her parents didn't call police because they thought the teenager may have been the victim of a prank by some of her step-siblings, who visited regularly. Williams said he gained entry through an open door while the family was away, then took several photographs, including copying pictures of the teenage girl and her younger brother. Images related to the break-in show Williams later wearing and fondling some of her underwear.

On Friday, December 5, 2008, he stole a quantity of clothing, including panties, bras and pajamas from a home on Simoneau Way in Ottawa after breaking in for the second time. Williams slipped through an open window and took numerous photographs of undergarments belonging to two young girls and copied framed pictures of their friends that were hanging on bedroom walls. The following day, he photographed himself dressed in some of the lingerie he'd removed from the home and also posed nude while holding various pieces of lingerie. The images were later found by police on his computer. Five days later, on Wednesday, December 10, Williams broke into a home on Wilkie Drive in Ottawa while the owner and a girlfriend, who sometimes lived at the house, were on vacation. Entry was gained by ripping away a screen and forcing open a kitchen window. A neighbor called the police after discovering the break-in the next day, but it wasn't until the residents returned on Sunday, December 14 that investigators learned some 20 items of clothing and seven sex toys were missing. After

Williams was arrested, they found photographs taken inside the home, which show several items of lingerie in drawers and closets. There were also photographs of the dildos that Williams had positioned on the floor along with several of the woman's undergarments.

After he broke into a family's home on Cara Crescent in Ottawa twice over New Year's, a 15-year-old girl was so frightened she couldn't go to sleep in her own bedroom. The owners were vacationing with their three children when Williams found an open window and went inside late in the evening of December 31. He returned several hours later, in the early morning hours of Thursday, January 1, 2009. During his first illicit visit, he stole 68 garments from the girl's bedroom, then another eight items of clothing when he returned. Also stolen were photos of the teenager, which had been taken for a local modeling agency, and some lipstick impressions she made with her lips on a piece of paper. Williams snapped pictures in two bedrooms and copied a number of photographs including some taken at a wedding. Investigators said a reflection of him is visible in a mirror in some of the photographs that show him wearing a shirt, jeans and winter boots. Other pictures, which police believe were taken during the second break-in, show him naked or wearing some of the girl's clothes. When the 15-year-old realized a stranger had broken in and removed items from her bedroom, she was gripped with fear and had to sleep in a guest room with the family's dog.

Photographs of the clothing taken from the home, consisting of the teenager's intimate apparel, a top and some bathing suits, were catalogued under a file labeled "HNY" on Williams' computer. He told Detective Sergeant Smyth that the initials were an abbreviation for Happy New Year. Ottawa Police forensic investigators also discovered seminal fluid on the top of a dresser in the girl's room. However, there wasn't enough material for crime lab scientists to develop a proper DNA profile which could have been used to connect anyone to the break-in spree once a suspect was taken into custody. Although police weren't able to link Williams to the entry with his genetic fingerprint, they did find the girl's clothing, the lipstick impressions and her modeling photographs in boxes in the basement of his Ottawa home.

On Saturday, January 17, 2009, he failed to pry open a rear patio door at a residence at 561 Apollo Way in Ottawa while the occupants were on their honeymoon. When the couple returned, they noticed someone had tried to break into their residence, but since their home wasn't burglarized, they didn't call police. On the same night, Williams entered 1646 Orford Crescent after finding the front door open and stole seven sets of bras and panties. He randomly took a number of photographs throughout the house of lingerie in closets and drawers which were later stored on his computer. It was Valentines Day before he attempted to get into another house. In the late evening hours of Saturday, February 14, when the owners were out of town with their two infant children, Williams removed a basement window and was attempting to crawl into the home when the alarm sounded. The owners called a neighbor to check the premises as soon as they were alerted by their security company. Williams fled before the neighbor arrived and had no opportunity to steal anything. On Saturday, March 14 and the following day, he failed to break into a home on Apollo Way that he'd entered five months earlier while two girls were sleeping in the basement. The father had nailed the window shut after the previous entry and Williams was unable to get in. On Sunday, April 12, 2009, he did gain entry to 1684 Canemore Crescent in Ottawa and took a quantity of bras and panties. The owner and her 18-year-old daughter were away for the Easter holiday weekend. The woman's three sons remained at home, but were out between 4 p.m. and 10:30 p.m. when the break-in occurred. They noticed the door was ajar and called police after finding a dresser drawer on the floor in their sister's bedroom. Williams also admitted taking pictures during the burglary. They were located during a search of his computer, along with other images that show him wearing various items taken from the young woman's bedroom.

Williams attempted to pick a lock at 7 Charles Court in Tweed on Friday, April 17, 2009, but was unable to get into the home. The next day, he found an open door at a Charles Court home. After entering, he stole two pairs of panties and took photographs of the bed, a sex toy visible in the open drawer of a nightstand and a clothes hamper containing several pieces of lingerie. He also copied several framed photographs of a young woman who lived in the house. It was the fourth time Williams had broken into the home and police later found images on his computer, which show him wearing various pieces of underwear stolen from the residence. Several pictures focused on his midsection and police described them as extremely explicit. On April 19, Williams climbed through a window at 490 Minnie Avenue in Tweed and took six bra and panty sets. The owners were not aware of the break-in until notified by police in March 2010. The couple told investigators they didn't believe anything was missing, but their 21-year-old daughter, who sometimes stayed at the house, remembered having a feeling that some of her underwear had gone missing. A check of two external computer hard drives, which Williams kept hidden at his Ottawa home, contained photographs of him wearing the young woman's underwear, including close-up pictures of his midsection that were also described as explicit. Williams made his way into the Charles Court home for a fifth time on Saturday, May 9, after finding the door unlocked. He took a pair of panties and after stripping naked, began copying photographs in the bedroom of the young woman who lived in the house. The pictures included copies of her university degree, which was hanging on a wall along with her portrait. He took pictures of a sex toy and items in her lingerie drawer, and also set the camera to take photographs of himself while he was in the young woman's bedroom. Investigators later found images on his computer of Williams either totally naked or wearing only a pair of panties while exposing himself.

On Thursday, May 28, 2009, he climbed through an open window to gain entry to a home at 591 Simoneau Way in Ottawa, but fled without taking anything when a vehicle driven by the owner's son pulled into the driveway. The burglar went back into the home on Tuesday, June 2, and stole 28 lingerie items consisting of bras, panties and a camisole. Williams took photographs of underwear removed from drawers in a bedroom, then returned two days later and stole another 21 pieces of lingerie. While in the house the second time, he stripped naked and took photographs of himself on the bed wearing some of the stolen items. Williams also copied photographs from a couple of wedding albums and a picture of a group of teenagers enjoying a day at the beach. Some photographs which Williams took of himself while in the house show him masturbating over a pile of lingerie. On June 5, he forced open a window at 1644 Orford Crescent in Ottawa, but was frightened off when the owners arrived home. Fourteen days later, he successfully entered another Ottawa home on Cara Crescent, where a man and his 24-year-old daughter were living. They were away for the weekend when Williams climbed through a basement window and collected 186 garments, including panties, bras, slips, bathing suits and some dresses. A quantity of expensive jewelry was left untouched. The young woman found her underwear drawer emptied and freshly-washed lingerie in the laundry room was missing. Williams spent more than two and a half hours in the home, where he took more than 200 photographs, including several of himself naked or wearing some female underwear while in the woman's bedroom. He also photographed a wall plaque that bore the woman's name and a personal letter she had received from a local bank branch.

In addition to the photographs stored in a number of folders on his computer, investigators discovered a very lewd letter written to the victim – but there is no indication it was ever mailed to her. The letter, which purports to come from a teenager with the initials JT, apologizes for taking the woman's underwear and stresses that he didn't "mess" with them. "I'm sorry I took these because I am sentimental too," stated the letter, which contained several obvious spelling errors. "Don't worry because I didn't mess with them." It goes on to refer to a fragrance from her panties with a vernacular term and some rough street language. "I should know," the letter continues. "I've been doing this for a while. But I am going to stop because my Mom will (expletive deleted) kill me if I get caught. She is pretty sure I can be something. Besides your place was kinda like the mother lode and I really like that I have a bunch of undies you put on just after you...."

The letter continues: "I started this with a chick I knew from high school ... who lives down the road from you. I thought it would be cool to have some of her undies. It seems right that I finish with a special chick like you. If you decide to call the cops, tell them that I am sorry for the trouble and they won't hear from me again. Now that I know all about you, I think it might be cool to meet you. Maybe younger guys don't turn you on but I think we could be good together. To me teenage chicks are impressed too easy. I guess I would like to be with somebody more experienced."

The letter writer refers to a basement washroom and again offers a halfhearted apology, hoping that he hadn't upset the 24-year-old woman too much. There is a postscript which reads: "Since I sorta feel guilty about wasting the cops time, these are the places I hit, so they can close their books." He ends the letter with a complete list of the Ottawa homes where break-ins had occurred.

Although there wasn't a similar break-in for more than a month in the Ottawa neighborhood, the spate continued in Tweed in the nighttime hours between Friday, July 10 and July 11. And there was an obvious escalation in the offender's pattern. Williams made his way to the home on Charles Court, which he'd broken into five previous times. But instead of entering the house, he found a hiding spot in the backyard. Aware that a young woman lived there, he spent 30 minutes peering at her through the rear windows of the house and determined she was alone. When the woman undressed to take a shower, Williams took off his clothes and, while naked, broke into the house. When interrogated about this incident, he admitted to becoming bolder because he wanted to take more risks. Once inside, he made his way down a hallway, passing the bathroom where the woman was showering and going into her bedroom. He considered taking the underwear she had been wearing, but instead stole another pair so that his intrusion wouldn't be obvious. Williams didn't take any photographs there, but did store images which he took later of her panties and bra. He also kept a journal record detailing his experience. "On naked walk from back forty, after having watched (individual's name) for 30 minutes or so, and confident that she was home alone, I entered her house naked just after she got into the shower. Very tempting to take her panties/bra from bathroom. Decided it would be entirely obvious that someone was in the house while she was in the shower. Took panties from panty drawer instead."

On Tuesday, July 21, Williams tried breaking into 38 Cosy Cove in Tweed while the occupants were away, but couldn't open any of the windows or doors. It would have been the third time he had been in that house. Three nights later, Williams entered a cottage at 700 Sulphide

Road that an older couple owned, but didn't steal anything. He did take some photographs, which police later found on his computer. A neighbor who kept an eye on the property for the owners noticed a screen was damaged, but thought it may have been caused by the wind. Police were not called because there was no indication that anyone had broken into the cottage and nothing was missing. Back in Ottawa on Saturday, July 25, Williams removed a screen from a rear window to gain entry to a house on Mathieu Way while the residents were away on a mini-vacation. He stole 36 items of underwear and bathing suits from the two bedrooms that were used by the couple's three daughters, aged 14, 18 and 21. Williams returned the next night and stole 16 bras, panties, a dress, top, pajamas and another bathing suit after entering through a rear door that he had left open. During both break-ins, he took photographs that included images of himself either naked or wearing various items of clothing while masturbating, plus photos of underwear in drawers, laundry baskets and on their beds. In addition to using his camera to score memorable trophies for his collection, he also stole framed photographs of the daughters at various ages, including the graduation picture of one girl from her elementary school. Williams went back a third consecutive night, but the family had come home and he had no opportunity to break in. Although the owners discovered that the window had been forced open, their daughters didn't indicate anything was missing and the burglary was not reported to police.

This is the last break-in that occurred in the Ottawa neighborhood where Williams was living and the furthest distance from his house. It was just over half-a-mile away and would have been about a 10-minute walk from his home. Police have never determined why the specific homes were targeted when Williams strolled through the residential area, but it's possible he could have driven around and watched from his vehicle as students were arriving home from high school. Officially there were 82 break-ins at 48 homes. Twenty-five entries took place in Ottawa and the remainder in Tweed. Only 17 of the burglaries were reported to police.

Although the burglaries ended in Ottawa, there was an attempted break-in on Saturday, August 1, 2009 at a home on Charles Road that Williams really wanted to get into because a teenage girl lived there. She was 14, but Williams thought she was 16 or 17. A screen was pulled from a window, but when a dog started barking, he replaced the covering before running off. Stripping naked the next evening, before breaking into a home at 72 Cosy Cove in Tweed for the third time, he left without stealing anything or taking any pictures. At the end of the month, Williams went into a house on Charles Street late on August 27, 28 and 29 – in total nine attempts or successful entries without any residents knowing. After getting into the home on Thursday, August 27, 2009, however, Williams was forced to flee after finding a man asleep in a bedroom. But on the subsequent nights, he entered through an open door and took several pieces of lingerie as well as taking pictures of underwear and several sex toys. He also took photographs of his reflection in a bathroom mirror, as he masturbated while wearing some of the woman's underclothing.

On Tuesday, September 1, 2009, nine days before the second anniversary of Williams' crime spree, he finally entered the Charles Road home in Tweed where the older looking 14-year-old girl lived. No one was home and the back door was open, giving him easy access. In the girl's bedroom, Williams took five pieces of lingerie, consisting of panties, bras and a camisole. He left almost immediately, but waited outside to see if he could catch a glimpse of her when she returned home. While hiding in the darkness, he masturbated after stripping naked. Williams was thinking about going back and stretching out on the girl's bed, but her father came home and his plan was foiled. He continued waiting until the teenager arrived home about 10 minutes later and watched until she turned out the light. During an interview with Detective Sergeant Smyth, Williams said the girl wasn't visible while changing from her street clothes to get into bed.

It was seventeen days later, on Thursday, September 17, 2009, that Williams cut the screen of a side window to gain entry to Jane Doe's home, located a short distance from his waterfront residence on a Stoco Lake cove. Before heading to the 20-year-old mother's house, he packed a small bag with some tools, a flashlight and the digital camera used to photograph underwear in scores of residences that he'd entered in Ottawa and Tweed over the previous two years.

Chapter Four

Investigators spent most of September 17 and the next day interviewing Jane Doe and her neighbors, while also striving to locate any physical or forensic evidence they could find to identify her attacker. In the late evening hours of September 18, after police had left the area and the victim had gone to stay at her mother's home, Williams brazenly returned to the house and entered, just before midnight, through an unlocked window. He stole bras and panties, 15 pieces in total, and also took a number of photographs in the woman's residence. Police later found them stored in three different folders on his personal computer.

The photographs in her bedroom, recorded between 12:19 a.m. and 12:27 a.m. on September 19, 2009, were of lingerie on her bed, on the floor and in a dresser drawer. He had also copied several pictures hanging on the wall of her home. Shortly after 10 a.m. while back at his house, Williams individually photographed each piece of lingerie he had stolen from Jane Doe and catalogued them on his computer. That evening he returned to her house, but noticed her boyfriend's car and didn't try to enter. On September 22, however, he again found the home vacant and made his way inside through an open window. Fifteen clothing items, consisting of bras, panties and several dresses, were taken and Williams also took some photographs during the break-in. Among the photographs recorded between 11:03 p.m. and 11:29 p.m. were images of Jane Doe's personal insurance identification card and driver's license; Williams standing naked while peering into the lingerie drawer; and a thong hanging from his erect penis. Just after midnight on Thursday, September 24, he photographed the items of lingerie stolen from her home and stored the images on his computer.

Later, on the evening of September 24, Williams entered
Laurie Massicotte's home at 76 Cosy Cove Lane after
finding a window open. The house was only three doors
from his cottage residence, but he had never met this
neighbor. Once inside, he stole a pair of panties and took
a number of photographs. Images found later on his
computer showed her bedroom, bed, family photographs
atop her dresser and undergarments in her lingerie
drawer. He returned two nights later, stole a pair of
panties plus sleepwear and took several pictures.
Photographs police found from the September 26 break-in
show some lingerie on her bed and the inside of a drawer
containing other pieces of her underwear. The
photographs were taken over a 10-minute period starting
at 10:36 p.m. There are also pictures Williams took later
at his home, which show him wearing a pair of
Massicotte's stolen panties.

As the clock turned to midnight on Wednesday, September
30, 2009, he again crawled through a window of
Massicotte's home. Williams knew she was there alone
and brought along what is traditionally called a "rape kit"
by those in law enforcement – to guarantee he would have
everything on hand to control his victim. The 45-year-old
woman was curled up in a small blanket after falling
asleep on the couch while watching episodes of Law and
Order and Without a Trace on television. She was
awakened by a blow to the head and at the same time felt
herself being pushed forward and held down. She
struggled but was struck repeatedly. The attacker warned
her to keep quiet, saying he was with a group of men who
were ransacking her home. "They are taking everything."

Williams was a strong, muscular man. He held his hand
and then his forearm over her face. She couldn't breathe
and was terrified that she was going to die. Massicotte
struggled to break from his grasp, but gave up after 20
minutes. He was totally overpowering her. There was no

way she could escape. All the time she was struggling, Williams repeatedly warned her to calm down and stop. He told her she was making the situation worse for herself. Massicotte was having trouble breathing and needed to sit up or she would die. Williams was adamant that she wasn't allowed to see his face. She begged him to just cover her eyes while pleading with the man to let her sit up and catch her breath. Her assailant finally relented and used a pillow case as a blindfold, just as he had done while attacking Jane Doe.

Psychiatrists would have no difficulty branding Williams as a psychopath if it wasn't for the behavior exhibited with Massicotte. He helped her get a drink of water after bringing an aspirin from the medicine cabinet to ease a headache she developed from the beating he'd inflicted. Williams spoke with compassion in his voice and seemed genuinely interested in things his victim told him about in her personal life. But he was also firmly in control and after blindfolding Massicotte, he bound her hands with wire earlier tucked into his rape kit.

Once satisfied that she would no longer resist, Williams told Massicotte he was going to check on the gang of burglars who were also supposedly in her home. The woman later told police she heard no one else in her residence, but just being told that others were in the house was deeply frightening. Williams returned moments later and began asking questions about her personal life, while closing curtains and blinds on the room's windows. Shaking with fear, Massicotte still believed her life was coming to an end, but the man gave his word that she wasn't going to die. Williams said he was there only to take her picture.

Massicotte had lived in the single-story house in the rural lakefront community on the outskirts of Tweed for 10 years. She had moved in with her second husband and they had raised her three daughters from her previous marriage. The relationship fell apart, however, and the couple separated. When the three girls finished high school, they went to live with their father in a larger community where there was more to do and better prospects for getting jobs. Massicotte by then had adjusted to living alone and felt safe on Cosy Cove Lane, a street she thought was tucked away in the wilderness – a place that evil would never find.

Now blindfolded with her arms bound behind her back, she was a victim at the mercy of a man who had broken into her home. Williams began touching her breasts and ordered her to face away from him. She begged him not to hurt her. Saying nothing, he raised her shirt and fumbled with the clasp on her bra in an attempt to get it off. He made some comments about her boyfriend while Massicotte continued appealing for him to stop. She also begged him to spare her life as the sexual molestation dragged on.

Using a knife he had brought, Williams cut a pillowcase into strips to blindfold her eyes so that she would never be able to describe his face to a police artist or provide investigators with details of his general appearance. From the moment the attack began, he had used brute force to keep Massicotte's head turned away from him. While pinning her down on the couch, the attacker placed the blanket she was wrapped in over her face. Continually being warned not to look at him, Massicotte knew she wouldn't be left alive if she even tried to catch a glimpse of her assailant. Even though he demonstrated some compassion, she realized that his demands were deadly serious and that she would have to go along with whatever he wanted – in order to survive.

The wire securing her hands was extremely tight and she had the sensation of it slicing through her skin. She had also lost feeling in her hands and started complaining about the pain. Williams cut what turned out to be plastic flexicuffs, and retied her hands behind her back with other strips from the oversized pillowcase. After making sure that she couldn't get her hands free, Williams pushed Massicotte onto the couch. He then began roughly caressing her stomach and forcefully sliding his hand under the elastic of her pajama bottoms and panties while grunting over and over that he was going to photograph her as she was being held captive. She couldn't understand why he wanted her picture, but Williams said he would be giving it to the men who were ransacking her house. At that moment, the attacker stood up and light from a camera flash penetrated the cloth that covered Massicotte's eyes.

It was around 1 a.m. when she had drifted off to sleep. Massicotte remembers hearing the music at the end of Without a Trace, but can't recall how the episode ended. She wanted to go to bed, but decided to rest for a few minutes before retiring for the night. Massicotte doesn't know how long she was sleeping before the blows came raining down on her head. But she knows the ordeal she endured lasted about three and a half hours.

Williams sat on the couch beside Massicotte and repositioned his hand, trying to work his fingers between her legs. She was whimpering and had urinated as fear took total control of her. The attacker grabbed his knife and sliced through her shirt and bra. Her breasts were fully exposed as he admired her beauty and again started insisting that he was going to take more photographs. Massicotte asked the assailant's permission to pull the blanket around her, but her request was refused. Instead, Williams stood up, told her to relax and snapped another photograph.

Overwhelmed with embarrassment and completely humiliated, Massicotte lost her will to resist, fearing that any further efforts to deter the intruder would put her in mortal danger. Lifting her body as he removed clothing, which left her naked from the waist down, she again became defiant when ordered to part her legs so that he could take some close-up pictures of her lower anatomy. Williams struggled for five minutes before promising not to rape her if she would cooperate and let him take the photographs he desired. At that point Massicotte began obeying his orders to pose in different positions while her attacker took a variety of pictures and her living hell continued. She knew he didn't have the knife in his hand while he was snapping pictures, but it was obviously within reach and any second it could be plunged into her body. There were so many things going through her mind, but the most important thing for her was staying alive. She would do anything she could to survive.

When first confronted, she was repeatedly pummeled and then told to be quiet. Her attacker didn't want her resisting. Massicotte clung to the initial impression that the person seemed somewhat kind and believed he was there to control her while other individuals were rummaging through her home and taking whatever they wanted. She didn't hear the sound of anyone else, but not being able to see, had to believe that the intruder wasn't alone. After being told to be quiet, she found herself at times talking to her attacker almost in whispers during the terrifying and torturous ordeal. But when he left three and a half hours later, she was alive.

Every second that Williams was in her home, Massicotte thought he was going to kill her. She was continually threatened. And if she didn't cooperate, there would be lots of pain. Her face was already stinging from the punches. She was living a real-life nightmare. During an interview with a McLean's magazine writer, Massicotte said it felt like she was in a horror movie and didn't know what would be happening in the next scene. Her hands remained tied behind her back. She was helpless. The attacker for most of the time was right beside her or no more than a few feet away, but every so often he would leave the room. He several times said that he was going to see what was happening with the men supposedly in her house. Massicotte thought at one point she might be gang-raped.

Each time Williams returned to the room, he wanted her posing for more photographs. She was told to stand and heard the camera clicking while sensing the illumination of the flash through the blindfold. He again left the living room and Massicotte had the impression that he walked down the hall. Her head instinctively turned to where she heard sound, but she had no idea what he was doing, where he went or if he really was talking to others who had invaded her home. The attacker spoke the moment he stepped back into the room, demanding to take one more photograph. She was told to kneel and put her head down. Massicotte was reluctant and hesitated. It was like she was being ordered into a position to be sacrificed.

"Don't make me get you into position," Williams snarled as Massicotte dropped to her knees and bowed her head, waiting for whatever was going to happen.

There was a click of the camera as her attacker took another photograph.

Her ordeal was almost over. Williams said he was going to help the other men and it was almost 10 minutes before he returned. A blanket was placed over her head and he snapped another picture before telling her he was leaving. "Please don't put the photographs on the Internet," she pleaded as Williams wandered around the room picking up anything that might link him to the attack. As he left

the house, her tormentor told Massicotte it was 4:30 a.m.
Thinking he might still be standing watching, she waited
about 25 minutes before calling for help. Frozen with fear,
she was still sitting blindfolded and bound on the couch
when police arrived.

The Ontario Provincial Police received the 911 call at 5
a.m. and it was 17 minutes before two officers reached the
Cosy Cove Lane home. They found the rear door open and
discovered her on the couch with only a blanket covering
her semi-naked body. Masicotte's eyes were covered, her
arms held behind her with a loosely-tied pillowcase and
flexible plastic strips. The woman's pajama bottoms and
underwear were on the floor. A black top and brown bra
that had been cut through the middle were dangling from
her body. The police also discovered a rear corner window
was open, but didn't see anyone in the surrounding area
after searching the neighborhood with other officers who
had responded to Massicotte's emergency call.

The victim didn't have any serious physical injuries apart
from redness and swelling to her face. Hoping that
forensic and identification investigators could obtain DNA
or other similar evidence to positively identify her attacker,
the police asked Massicotte to remain with her arms
fastened behind her back. It was about five hours before
the binding was removed from her hands and she could
freely move.

Meanwhile, she underwent intensive questioning as police
tried to gather as much information as she could recall
about the man who broke into her home. She hadn't seen
him, but thought he was between 30 or 40 years old. She
had the impression he wasn't a lot taller than her
because, when they were standing, his face seemed close
to hers. There was no indication that he had consumed
alcohol. She also remembered that he wasn't wearing
gloves and thought that he may have been wearing

something with short sleeves because his arms were bare. Massicotte also thought his voice seemed familiar and that her attacker could be someone she knew, but at the time couldn't think of who it might be.

Forensic investigators dusted the living room and other parts of the house for fingerprints, including an aspirin bottle on the coffee table, but didn't turn up anything linked to the intruder. They took numerous photographs so that they could depict the crime scene to a jury once Massicotte's attacker was nabbed, but they found no DNA or any other material to positively identify the person who broke into the house and sexually molested her.

Additional officers were called in to go door to door in an attempt to find someone who saw or heard something that could help the investigation. Although still blindfolded, Massicotte tried to provide police with every detail she could remember, including the fact that she didn't hear the sound of a car or any other type of vehicle when her attacker left. It was soon determined that there had been no gang of men in her house and the place was not ransacked. Her attacker had been alone and his mission was to photograph the victim and commit sexual assault. People living nearby also didn't see or hear anything that assisted the investigation, including Russell Williams, the newly-appointed commander at the Canadian military installation in Trenton, who lived three houses away from the home where the woman was attacked. The police who spoke to him when they came to his front door could never imagine the Colonel as a suspect. Other officers who stopped him at a roadblock almost seven months later, near the home of abduction victim Jessica Lloyd, also didn't think there was the remotest chance that the base commander could be responsible. In that case, they waited 10 hours before alerting OPP analysts that the colonel's SUV matched the description and had similar tires to a vehicle involved in Lloyd's disappearance.

Evidence collected at Massicotte's home was used to
eliminate a number of individuals as suspects, but it also
helped implicate one of her neighbors after she told
investigators the voice she heard sounded a lot like Larry
Jones. He was a 65-year-old man who lived just down the
street and had been in the woman's home with his wife,
Bonnie, a number of times. Police obtained a search
warrant and raided the home where Jones had lived for
more than 40 years. They seized his computer, some video
recordings, a hunting knife, some clothing, boots and a
camera. He was also taken 16 miles to the Ontario
Provincial Police detachment in Madoc, where he was
questioned for more than three hours. Jones was given a
polygraph test and police demanded he volunteer his
fingerprints so they could be compared with evidence
found in Massicotte's home. Until Williams was arrested,
Jones remained a person of interest in the assault on his
neighbor. He lived under a cloud of suspicion and was
shunned by some people who had known him for years.

During the interview with Detective Sergeant Smyth,
Williams said he had never met Massicotte, but knew she
lived alone because he had broken into her home several
times prior to the September 30 attack. On the night he
confronted the woman, Williams said he peaked through a
window to make sure she was alone, then opened a rear
window after removing the screen. When he made his way
to the living room, he saw her on the couch where she had
fallen asleep while watching television. He inched towards
her and then instantly smashed his flashlight against the
side of her head, but the blow didn't knock her
unconscious. Massicotte began to struggle and Williams,
who was wearing a dark sweatshirt and pants while
concealing his face with a cap, used the weight of his body
to pin her down. In an attempt to calm her, he told her he
wasn't there to hurt her, but was part of a gang who were
ransacking the house. It was his job to control her.
Describing the woman as scared, Williams said she was

filled with fear and convinced she was going to be murdered.

He told about blindfolding her and taking pictures, of using his knife to cut her shirt and bra to expose her breasts and then pulling off her pajama bottoms. Williams estimated he was there about two hours and a half and took a couple of pieces of her underwear back to his house, only a few hundred feet away. After the attack, he went to bed and left for work that morning as though nothing had happened. He also explained that he chose Massicotte because she lived alone and had assumed she would be an easy target.

A picture he took of the underwear stolen from her home was later found on external hard drives linked to his computer, along with 29 photographs taken between 2:52 a.m. and 4:44 a.m. According to a statement of facts prepared by police, they "graphically depict" the attack. Williams told police exactly where they would find the hard drives at his home in Ottawa, insisting he didn't want them tearing the place apart. He said damaging the house would break his wife's heart.

The first image in the series of photographs shows Massicotte sitting fully clothed on the couch. She is blindfolded and her arms are behind her back. The next two pictures show the woman sprawled back on the couch with her blouse open and pulled onto her arms, exposing her breasts. Another seven images show her lying naked from the waist down, with her legs apart. Several of those pictures taken between 3:59 a.m. and 4:06 p.m. are close-ups of her pelvic area. The next 10 images show Massicotte standing. Some pictures were taken with the camera positioned at floor level, pointing up at her. Two of the nine remaining images show his victim sitting on the couch covered with a blanket, a third shows the blanket pulled back slightly to expose her breasts and photo 24 shows her from behind while she's kneeling. Two images, identified as photos 25 and 26, were taken of her left side as she knelt on the couch. Her arms are clearly tied behind her. In photograph 27, she is sitting on the couch with part of her face showing – the camera positioned to show part of a man's penis in the foreground. Photograph 28 has Williams exposing an erection while standing in front of Massicotte as she sits on the couch covered with a blanket.

The final photograph is a picture of Russell Williams posing in front of a mirror with a piece of the woman's underwear covering the lower portion of his face and the black toque he was wearing pulled down so that only his eyes are visible. The photo confirms he was wearing the clothing he described during the interview with Detective Sergeant Smyth: a dark sweatshirt and pants. Among the other souvenirs related to the attack, which were stored on Williams' computer, were two photographs taken October 8, 2009 of Massicotte's panties spread out on a flat surface along with a note indicating that they were discarded that day. There were also photographs of pages from the Tweed News, with articles pertaining to the attacks involving Jane Doe and Laurie Massicotte, plus images from an OPP website and various news outlets detailing the attacks on both women. Williams also had photographs posted on the computer that he took of himself while setting fire to some newspaper pages, and as they blazed away in his fireplace.

On October 24, 2009, he broke into a home at 690 Sulphide Road in Tweed through an open door, but left almost immediately when he realized a man and his two sons lived there. Four pictures he took while inside the house, which were later located by police on his computer, show the interior of three bedrooms and a poster of a woman on one of the walls. The home's owner, who had lived there for more than 20 years, had no idea anyone had entered until notified by police after Williams was arrested. On November 5, 2009, he entered a house on Minnie Avenue and took some panties, a slip and a dress. The 21 photographs taken during a 51-minute period show a bedroom where the owner's daughter slept, her underwear drawer, clothes hanging in a closet and some family photographs displayed on a shelf. It was his second time in the home and Williams wrote a note detailing the break-in:

"Unlike last year's entry, after which I'll guess they had no idea that I'd been in the house, I made no effort to conceal this entry. In fact, I left plenty of signs that I was there (screen from back room window was left removed, with window left wide open, and the screen from the lower bathroom, where I actually gained access (like last year) was left removed – again with the window wide open. As well, I closed the back door, but didn't lock it.) On the way home the next night (Friday), at 8:00-ish, I noticed that they had returned home, and that the outside light above the back room door was on (I'd never seen this light on...)."

On the evening of November 7, 2009, Williams took 22 pieces of clothing from a home on River Street West in Tweed after entering through an unlocked door. The items included panties, bras, a skirt and a slip. The owner, who lived at the home with her two daughters, one age 15, was shocked when told about the burglary after Williams admitted entering the house. She had no idea that anyone had been in their home and didn't realize anything was missing. Photographs taken by the intruder prove that he was in three bedrooms and had taken pictures, mostly in the teenager's room. They show underwear on the floor and in a drawer, plus some family pictures in frames on the dressers. There were several trophies, which the girl had won in skating competitions, but Williams photographed only one with her name clearly visible on an engraved plate.

The locations where he had been committing burglaries for the previous two years abruptly shifted on Tuesday, November 17, 2009, when he entered a home to the south in the Belleville area, along the route he regularly took from his residence to the military base in Trenton. Sometime during the early morning hours, when the man and woman who lived in the home were away, Williams crawled through a window of the house on Highway 37 and took three sex toys from the enclosure of a bedside table plus a quantity of lingerie. When the wife, a music teacher at the Trenton base, returned home around 4:30 p.m., she found the door unlocked and the items missing from the bedroom. She initially contacted nearby friends to ask if they were playing some sort of a prank. When no one acknowledged being in her house, she became concerned and decided to spend the night with one of her friends. To avoid embarrassment, police were not called. Later that evening, Williams climbed through the same window and this time left a note for the woman after taking all her bras and panties, an adult movie and more sex toys. His message read: "Go ahead and call the police. I want to show the judge your really big dildoes." During both entries, Williams took photographs in several rooms over an hour-long period. When he returned, he took additional photographs which were all stored on his computer. When police later recovered the images, there were several photographs which Williams may have taken of himself during the break-in as he stood in front of a mirror while wearing one of the woman's panty and bra sets. There were also two photographs of the computer screen in the couple's home, displaying the challenging message that Williams had written.

Police were called immediately after the woman came home sometime between 7:15 a.m. and 7:30 a.m. and found her lingerie missing along with the note left by the intruder. When interviewed after his arrest, Williams wouldn't admit to knowing the music teacher from the base, but said he had seen a younger woman around the home at times when he was driving by. That break-in occurred the same day he entered the home of Corporal Marie-France Comeau to make sure that she lived alone. Although police have nothing to disprove Williams' contention that he didn't know the music teacher, it seems too much of a coincidence that he just saw her while passing her home. He admits checking military records to find Comeau's address, and on the same day he broke into the young corporal's home, Williams suggests he randomly selected another house to enter which happened to be the residence of a civilian who worked at the base. It's quite likely the civilian employee from the base had been targeted for death, but for whatever reason Williams only left taunting notes before focusing his efforts to make Comeau his victim. He hasn't said anything or made statements to confirm that possibility, but a couple of people close to the case are convinced that Williams intended to rape and kill the woman in the house on Highway 37 – but because she was married, he couldn't find a perfect window of opportunity that would guarantee him time alone with her.

Chapter Five

On Monday, November 16, 2009, Williams drove to
Brighton, 46 miles southwest of Tweed, to find the home
of Marie-France Comeau. He had met the 37-year-old
woman on one of his flights and wanted to make sure she
lived alone. Williams never acknowledged to investigators
that he had targeted Comeau for rape and possibly
murder, but confirmed that he checked personnel files to
get her address and details of her work schedule. When he
first made his way to her home at 252 Raglan Street, he
knew she was overseas on military business and was
making what could be best described as a reconnaissance
mission to stake out a would-be prey.

Home where Marie-France Comeau was murdered

If Comeau had a boyfriend or there were others living in
the home, there would be no opportunity for him to slip
into her residence and feed an abhorrent sexual appetite
that would have a fatal consequence for his victim.

The colonel was at a point of no return. Although continuing to function in a normal manner at work, he had spiraled completely out of control in a dark world fueled by evil, uncontrollable forces which had festered unchecked somewhere deep in his mind. Williams was now a man who needed to kill in order to quench his lust.

It was in the evening hours of Monday, November 16 that he parked his car in a wooded area to the east of Comeau's home. After walking almost half a mile, he forced a basement window at the northeast corner of the house. Finding no evidence inside that anyone was living with Comeau, he made his way to her bedroom and began snapping photographs, including images of lingerie in a dresser drawer and a laundry basket. The time stamp on his camera indicates he was in the house at least one hour and 24 minutes. More than 50 pictures were taken there, some of her bedroom and others of sex toys that he discovered. In several photographs, Williams is exposing himself while wearing some of the corporal's underwear and putting what police described as a "purple" sex toy inside the lingerie and against the lower part of his anatomy. He also photographed her military uniform, her name tag and an insurance benefits card which displayed both her name and picture. A number of undergarments were taken from Comeau's house, which Williams later photographed at his home and catalogued on his computer.

Comeau knew immediately when she returned that someone had gone through her things and confronted Paul Belanger, a military colleague she was dating. She accused him of kinky and weird behavior, which Belanger vehemently denied. Comeau, however, wasn't really convinced and just let the matter drop. She had no thought that anyone had broken into her home and never considered calling police.

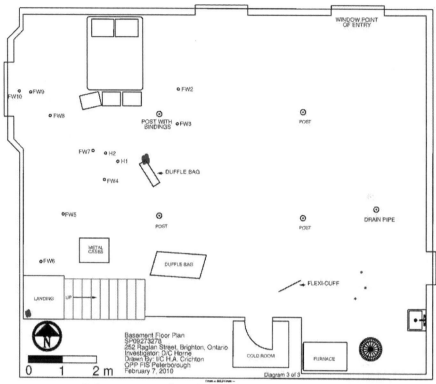

Crime scene drawing of Comeau's basement

One week after the initial break-in, Williams returned to Comeau's home. He spent the evening of Monday, November 23 in his office at the Trenton base. When he left, sometime between 10:30 p.m. and 11 p.m. he turned off his BlackBerry, the telephone and messaging device that linked him to the military command in the event of an emergency. When he passed through the gates, it appeared the base commander was on his way home. But instead of driving northeast towards Tweed, he headed west to Brighton, a community of 11,000 people on the shore of Lake Ontario, 15 miles from his office. Parking his vehicle in the same spot where it was left on his previous visit, Williams again walked through overgrown scrubland to reach Comeau's house. This time he was carrying the rape kit which he'd earlier taken to Massicotte's home. There were a few lights in windows of homes in the neighborhood, but most of the houses were in total darkness and none of the residents were anywhere in sight. Wearing a dark sweatshirt and Docker pants, Williams was virtually camouflaged while working his way towards the young woman's residence. He saw only her car in the driveway and while standing outside her bedroom window, heard Comeau talking to someone on the telephone. It was obvious she was alone and that this would be his opportunity.

Forcing open the same two-foot by five-foot window that he had used the first time to gain entry, Williams eased himself through and dropped to the cement floor of the unfinished basement. Before slipping in, he covered his mouth and nose with a small scarf and pulled a cap over his forehead to conceal his face. He told investigators that Comeau would recognize him not only as the base commander, but because she had served as a flight attendant on one of the aircraft he had piloted on a mission to the Middle East. Hoping to wait until his victim was asleep, Williams hid beside the furnace for 30 to 40 minutes. He didn't make a sound, but Comeau's cat sensed his presence and sat staring at the stranger after going downstairs to a litter box. When the feline ignored her calls to come upstairs for the night, Comeau made her way to the basement. She saw the cat staring at something near the furnace located in an alcove at the southeast end of room. Curious to see what had its attention, she focused her eyes while walking towards the darkened corner – and saw someone attempting to conceal themselves.

"You bastard," she screamed, as Williams lunged at her and landed several blows to her head with a red-colored flashlight he was carrying. Covered only with a shawl, Comeau struggled to fight off the intruder while trying to back away, but was overpowered by Williams when she tripped over the rape kit that he had left on the basement

Police photo of basement were Comeau was beaten unconscious

floor. The only items in the room were a full-size bed located in the northwest corner, three blue storage containers at the foot of the bed, a covered litter box, some cardboard boxes and a metal container.

She had no idea who her attacker was. The masking over his face covered everything but his eyes. Blood spattering from a laceration on her scalp showed the attack began near the furnace and the pair moved in a north-westerly direction before Comeau fell backward after stumbling over the duffle bag that Williams had brought with him to carry out the attack. She was pinned down at that point while being shackled with plastic zip ties. There was a large amount of blood on the floor plus swishing patterns painted with her gore-soaked hair. This indicated to investigators that she had been thrashing around, trying to fight off the attacker as he struggled to restrain her. Once subdued, Williams tied her hands with a rope. The binding was fastened so tightly, it left abrasions on her wrists. Forensic investigators also found bloody footprints leading to one of four metal jack-posts that supported major crossbeams in the home. It appears that Comeau was dragged across the basement floor and tethered to the post by some items Williams found in a pile of laundry. He also wrapped her body with a piece of rope which he had brought with him.

Two photographs were taken of Comeau at 12:21 a.m. on November 24, 2009. They show her secured against the post with rope pulled around her thighs and between her legs. She is naked, but her shawl was draped over her left side. There is also duct tape covering her mouth and a portion of her face.

To prevent anyone from looking in and witnessing the attack, Williams began to sweep the house in search of windows in the basement and living area after making sure his quarry was tightly secured. He also went outside and replaced the screen on the basement window so that there would be no immediate sign of a break-in, should a police officer or anyone else come along and check the property. When he initially moved away from the bound victim, bloody footprints show that Williams went to the window on the east side of the basement and looked at her neighbor's home before going upstairs. Forensic investigators were able to follow bloody footprints and map out the route Williams took while moving through the house, plus the locations where Comeau was dragged during the murderous attack.

On the main level, he found the victim's house key and inserted the blade into the front door lock before snapping off the top portion to prevent anyone else with a key from gaining immediate access to the home. He then tossed the set of keys, which contained the broken one, on the island counter in the kitchen before continuing to scout the house to make sure no one would be able to peer in and witness the events that would unfold over the next couple

Police aerial photograph of Comeau's house shortly after her murder

of hours. Comeau's bedroom blinds were closed, but Williams draped a sheet over the entire window to eliminate any possibility that someone could peek through a tiny opening. Knives from the kitchen were stuck into the top of the window frame to hold the dark pink sheet in place. Williams did everything possible, not only to prevent anyone from seeing what was going on, but he also had a plan to collect anything that might become contaminated with his DNA to ensure investigators couldn't directly link him to the intrusion and attack. It was as though he had picked an opportunity to commit the perfect crime.

Before returning to the basement, Williams also removed night lights from electrical outlets in the living room at the front of the house as well as in a nearby sitting room furnished with a couch and television. Footprints left by his bloody boots show he made his way down the stairs and went directly to Comeau, who was still trussed up against the metal support post. The clothing and rope securing her to the post was untied and she was pushed

Blood on basement floor and landing leading to main floor

towards the basement stairs at the south side of the home. At the base of the steps, it appears the woman again began struggling and either tripped on a single step leading from the basement or was pushed forward. Unable to break the fall because her hands were behind her back, Comeau fell heavily against the wall and was knocked unconscious. Investigators found an indentation where she hit the drywall when pitched forward. There was also blood on the basement floor, the banister and a light switch, in addition to a large amount on the wall and the carpet where she fell. Williams began dragging the victim up the stairs, but stopped and took four pictures. The photographs at 12:51 a.m. show the unconscious and naked victim lying on her back with her arms tied behind her. One picture is a close-up of her pubic area. Another shows her upper torso, along with severe injuries to her head. When observing the photographs, police also noted that the duct tape had been removed from her face and mouth.

After taking the digital images, Williams resumed dragging Comeau up the basement stairs and carried her through the foyer to her bedroom at the back of the house. She was placed on the queen-sized bed and a burgundy-colored towel was wrapped around the top part of her

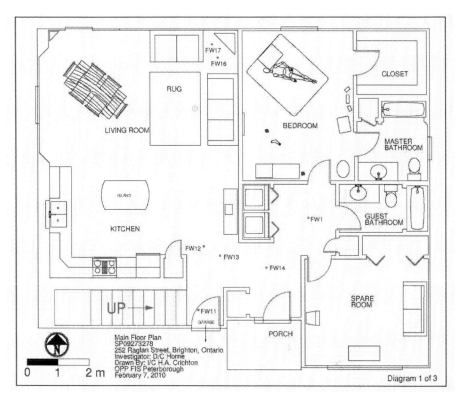

*Police drawing showing main floor of Comeau's home
and bedroom where she was murdered*

head to stem the blood. Duct tape was stretched around the towel and other strips were placed across her eyes and mouth. Another strip positioned down the front of her face left only a small opening at her nose, which allowed her to breath. She was then sexually assaulted for the next one-and-a-half to two-hours. Williams also videotaped his attack on Comeau.

A synopsis of the video tape from the Ontario Provincial Police Child Sexual Exploitation Section first shows Comeau naked on the bed in a fetal position, facing the camera with her wrapped head resting on a pillow. Her hands are bound behind her back with what police described as a green industrial-style rope, with the excess portion coiled into a figure eight. The camera pans from the bed with its burgundy sheet and pillowcase set to the matching comforter, which Williams had draped over the bedroom window. There is the sound of someone moving around the room and the screen goes blank before it becomes obvious the camera has been put in a stationary position so that it can record what is going on in the room. It is focused on the bed and clearly shows the victim still in the same position.

A naked man with a black balaclava pulled over his head moves into the picture and then climbs onto the bed. In a kneeling position, he roughly pulls the victim's left knee and positions his body to commence the rape. Comeau appears unresponsive, her head flopping to the side, unaware that she is about to be sexually attacked. Fresh blood is visible when Williams reaches over to reposition her head when it flopped from the pillow as he pulls her onto her back. "No," the victim mumbles as the camera records him moving his body over hers.

The digital camera was on the bed and Williams reaches out with his right hand during the rape to pick it up and take graphic, close-up images of the assault. Comeau isn't moving and appears to be semi-conscious. Fifteen photographs were taken between 1:17 a.m. and 1:39 a.m. showing the victim on the bed prior to being raped. Three more photographs, taken during a three-minute period starting at 1:43 a.m., show Comeau on the bed and Williams standing nearby wearing only the face-masking balaclava. He is looking directly at the camera in two photos, but in the third his attention is focused on the victim while he's molesting her. The eight graphic images depicting the rape were taken between 1:47 a.m. and 2:01 a.m. as the video camera continued to record both the video and sound of his attack on Comeau.

After sexually assaulting the 37-year-old woman, Williams gets off the bed and ambles over to check the still-running video camera. It is recording images of Comeau collapsed backwards, but struggling to get up. With her hands secured behind her, she flounders awkwardly while rolling back and forth in an attempt to sit up. She is groaning, but the tape over her mouth is muffling her words. Finally swinging her legs to the side of the bed, she manages to get herself to a half-sitting position, but is too weak to remain upright and slumps against the headboard. A moment later she falls to her side and curls into a fetal position. Feebly attempting to pick at the rope with her fingers, Comeau is struggling to talk, but investigators were unable to make out what she was saying even after attempts were made to enhance the audio recorded on the video camera.

Williams again begins recording video images of Comeau on the bed. He zooms in while she is on her right side, still in a fetal position, and then puts the camera down before walking back into the picture. Once on the bed, he positions himself behind her and again starts raping the defenceless victim. He changes positions several times, but Comeau remains virtually motionless and seems to be almost unconscious throughout the ordeal. It also looks as though Williams is using considerable strength to flop her dead-weight body into positions which allowed him to continue the sexual assault.

The 21-page, real-time description prepared by the investigators is a sickening account of the ordeal the corporal experienced at the hands of her commanding officer. It details each of his movements while sexually attacking her as well as the various things he does while intimately examining the victim and mauling her. On the video, he is seen bending to closely inspect intimate areas of her body. At times, Williams seems to be contemplating what to do next.

After the second violation, he again walks over to adjust the video camera. As he goes out of frame, Comeau is motionless, her head on the pillow and hands bound behind her. A moment later, Williams makes his way back to the bed and forces the woman into a face down position while kneeling over her. Comeau tries to speak but her words survive only as muffled groans. Williams orders her to "get up on your knees" and begins raping her a third time. Comeau finally makes herself understood to Williams, but he leans forward and in a low voice whispers "no" before reaching back and picking up the digital camera to take close-up still photographs of the assault. Eleven pictures are taken between 2:06 a.m. and 2:19 a.m.

While face down, Comeau managed to rub away some of the duct tape which allowed her to access a little more air and make her words more clearly understood. She also found strength to struggle a bit against her attacker's weight and the video shows her head turning towards him.

"Get out. Get out," she cries. "I want you to leave. I want you to leave."

Williams ignores her pleas. He says nothing and appears totally emotionless while pointing his digital camera to take photographs of her face as she pleads with him to stop.

"Get out," she says again while struggling to breath.

Williams calmly puts the camera down and continues the assault. Comeau seems to lapse into a semi-conscious state. She struggles at times, but is more like a rag-doll while being manoeuvred into different positions during the attack. She is repeatedly raped and at times Williams takes various pictures with his digital camera in addition to images being recorded on the video camera. He also used his flash to take some of the close-up photographs, including images of his actual sexual intercourse with the victim.

Comeau would attempt to shift herself into more comfortable positions whenever Williams let up on his attack, but with her hands and arms secured behind her, she was totally defenceless and unable to prevent him from posing her body any way he wanted. After raping her in a number of different positions, Williams finally flopped Comeau onto her back and stretched out over her. At this point during the sexual assault, Williams looks back toward the video camera, pulls off the balaclava that was masking his face and puts it on the pillow beside her. He initially covered her face with his left hand, but moved it down over her body while kissing her right cheek. Williams then glances back at the video camera. There is a smug look on his face and he gives a half smile while continuing to rape the victim.

At this point in the attack, he turns his head several times to stare at the camera and then instinctively puts his left hand over her eyes. He is wearing his wedding ring. Moving forward, her tormenter presses his face against her right cheek before repositioning himself so that he can watch his sexual gyrations. The video also shows him roughly fondling her body.

With her arms wrenched behind her and from being shifted into various grotesque positions, Comeau is in obvious pain and is often heard groaning. She tries at times to speak, but the duct tape prevents her words from being distinctly heard. The pain stops momentarily when she's forced onto her stomach, but instantly resumes when Williams continues his assault. It is as though she is being subjected to some type of military torture as the attacker tugs at her arms and elbows.

"Get up," Williams orders. "Get up," as she's pulled back onto her knees.

While kneeling unsteadily and with her head bent downward, the attacker wriggles himself between her legs so that Comeau is now straddling him. She groans and struggles to speak. You can see her lips moving beneath the tape covering her mouth as she tries to plead with him to stop. "Please," she says as he continues his attack. She groans again and then you hear the words: "Oh, my hands." Her words are now more recognizable as she begs him to untie her. Comeau wants him to unfasten the flexible cuffs on her wrists, insisting she won't try to escape. Williams says nothing, but snaps more photographs while she is on top of him. Seemingly drained of energy, she slumps forward.

"Don't fall over," Williams warns. "Don't fall over."

Williams extricates himself from his position under the victim and shoves her to a sitting position on the edge of the bed. As he reaches to adjust the video camera, Comeau slumps over and then collapses sideways. She struggles for a few moments to sit back up, but Williams reappears and briefly kneads her breasts before rolling her onto her back. He lowers his head to again closely examine her pelvic region and kisses her between the legs before repositioning himself and biting one of her breasts. The bed is creaking as he mercilessly renews the rape. The defenceless woman tries to speak, but "please" is her only audible word.

Noticing the duct tape might be coming away from her eyes, Williams stops briefly to press the covering back into place with his right hand before renewing the attack. A short time later, he pulls away and tells her to "stay there" while he gets off the bed. Comeau is groaning and starts rolling towards the edge, but her attacker leaps back to stop her from falling to the floor. He stands watching for a few moments to make sure the victim isn't going to move, then walks out of the camera's view. Williams can be heard rummaging in the room while the video shows his victim motionless on her side, with her head at the end of the bed and her left leg dangling over the edge. Reappearing on the camera, he's seen clenching a tube of lubricant jelly between his fingers. It appears as though he doesn't want to touch anything and investigators believe Williams was trying to make sure there would be no fingerprints at the crime scene.

He continues raping Comeau after applying the lubricant, but stops briefly on occasion to take photographs with the digital camera. Eventually Williams looks directly at the video camera while cupping his hands to capture his seminal fluid. He begins backing slowly from the bed and is seen with his hands entirely covering his genitals to prevent semen from dripping anywhere in the room. Williams then walks out of view and towards the en-suite bathroom as the camera continues to focus on his victim. She is breathing deeply and lifting her hips, trying to ease the pain of having her arms bound behind her. Comeau attempts several times to sit up, but doesn't have the strength and curls once again into a fetal position near the edge of the bed.

Returning to the bedroom, her attacker is holding a tissue and appears to wipe several areas before again walking from the room. There is the sound of a toilet flushing and seconds later, the video fades to black while the camera continues recording sounds from the bedroom. Another section of the video shows the naked man in front of the dresser, appearing to search through the drawers. At 2:23 a.m., Williams begins taking a series of 12 photographs of Comeau during a thirteen-minute period. The first shows the victim curled on the bed, but after the video camera is again switched on, she is seen sitting on the edge. Her feet

Comeau's bedroom with bloodstained pillow and drape on window

are on the floor and her head is drooping to the side. Reflected in a mirror, clothing from the drawers can be seen strewn on the floor and then Williams starts to take pictures with his digital camera. Still naked, he is again wearing the balaclava.

"Put your head up," he instructs, while leaning towards Comeau to snap additional photographs.

Her head doesn't move, but seconds after the photo is taken, she slips from the bed, landing heavily on her knees.

"Stand up, stand up," demands Williams, who repeats his order a third time.

Comeau is defeated. She is slumped over with her head hanging down, whimpering.

Williams leans close to her and angrily demands that she stand up. But when the woman doesn't move, he puts down the camera and grabs her by the shoulders, yanking her onto the bed in a sitting position. She is gasping. Her breathing seems labored and uncontrolled. Comeau groans while being grabbed around the waist and sadistically thrown onto her stomach. Unemotionally, the attacker looks at her convulsing on the bed, then walks out of view after glancing briefly towards the camera. Williams moves it slightly before walking back to the whimpering victim. Leaning forward, he again starts raping her, but leaves a short time later for the washroom. The video records the sound of a flushing toilet and running water. Looking at his hand when he comes back in view, he wipes it across his leg, then walks over and shuts off the camera.

When interviewed, Williams said he didn't wear a condom, but avoided climaxing with his victim to prevent police from obtaining any evidence that would link him to the crime. Despite his precautions, forensic investigators were able to collect material from under her fingernails and through a vaginal swab. While the resulting DNA profile did not pinpoint Williams or reveal the identity of the attacker, it would not have excluded him in a pool of possible suspects.

At one point when Williams went to check the front of the house to make sure no one had heard the commotion, Comeau fled into the adjoining bathroom in an attempt to barricade herself. The attacker returned, forced his way in and struggled briefly with the victim before dragging her back to the bed. She was punched several times in the head while being subdued. Forensic investigators were able to trace the movements and struggle through blood-spattering and scarlet stains on the washroom sink and bathtub. Analysis of a swab from one of the bloodstains produced a DNA match with Williams, but at that stage of the investigation his name had not come up as a possible suspect, the sample was something that could only be used to tie the perpetrator to the crime scene once an arrest was made.

When the video camera comes back on, Williams is seen tossing some lingerie taken from a dresser over the victim, who is almost completely covered with strewn items. He puts down his digital camera and begins moving around the bedroom while video-recording the undergarments that blanket Comeau. He removes some of the clothing to expose intimate areas and after taking close-up views, returns the camera to its stationary position, which gives a full view of the victim. Williams is next seen collecting the lingerie and stuffing it into a yellow and black duffle bag which he had placed on the floor near the bed. He zips up the bag and it looks as though he is preparing to leave, but the attack isn't over. He grabs the victim by her ankles and begins another rape. Stopping long enough to take hold of the video camera, he starts recording close-up images of the attack, sometimes holding the camera only inches away.

Comeau is struggling and at times her fingers are clearly picking at the rope that binds her arms behind her. When Williams leaves the bed to put the video camera back on its perch, she begins floundering from side to side and is moaning: "No, no, no."

Williams kneels beside her and makes "ssshhusshhing" sounds, telling her to keep quiet. Comeau tries to cry out, but her scream is muffled by the duct tape. He moves her sideways and goes to again adjust the video camera before returning, this time reclining on the bed beside her. After lifting himself to a partial sitting position, he takes off the balaclava and looks at the victim. Williams extends his arm across her and starts rubbing her lower back while leaning close and whispering something into her ear. He moves his hand and brushes his fingers against her face before climbing from the bed and again goes over to readjust the video camera.

Returning seconds later, Williams kneels over her and uses the weight of his upper body to pin her to the bed. He has his arm under her neck and his face pressed against hers. She tries to talk but can only mumble, possibly in response to his continued whispers.

"No, no...please," says Comeau, her words clearly understandable.

He remains, however, pinning her with his body for more than a minute before Comeau begins to struggle. "I don't want to die," she says. "I don't want to die."

Williams forcefully urges her to keep quiet. "Shh, shush," he whispers, while not letting her move. Although not confirmed by anything Williams says in his statements or heard on the video, it is possible that he whispered into her ear that she wasn't going to live.

Comeau is sobbing and moaning: "No, no."

Ignoring her appeal, the attacker glances several times at the camera to assure himself that the images are still being recorded.

"No, no...I don't wanna," she screams, her voice now appearing more muffled, possibly because the weight of Williams on top of her is making it more difficult for Comeau to breathe properly. She is shaking, sobbing and whimpering: "Leave me alone."

Williams sits upright, braces himself with his right arm, then moves his left hand and puts it over her mouth and nose. Her one nostril, the only way she can get air, is now being blocked. He is trying to suffocate her.

Comeau appears lifeless, but she was feigning unconsciousness to make him think she was dead. She takes in some air when Williams moves his left hand to pick up a nearby pillow and covers her face. He puts his full weight on his left arm while repositioning his right arm just above her head to help steady himself over the victim while killing her.

Letting out a muffled scream, she lashes out with her legs. "No," she murmurs while wriggling from beneath him. Kicking out with her legs, she screams: "Noooo," as loud as she could. "I don't wannnt to ddddiiiiiiie."

Williams fell off the bed and pulled down the bedding that was covering the window when Comeau twisted herself around and continued kicking out. He somehow manages to keep the pillow over her face, but she momentarily gets free and yells – "No" – while struggling for her life. He almost immediately moves behind her and keeps trying to smother her while she hysterically screams: "I don't want to diiiiie. I don't want to diiiiiiie. I don't want to die."

Throwing his body across hers, Williams again uses his weight to keep her pinned while struggling to squeeze the pillow against her face. Some of the rope has become unfastened and is bundled between her legs, but her hands remain tied. The tape is also still covering her mouth, but has pulled away a bit and she is now in a life or death struggle. Trying to employ some of the techniques learned in hand-to-hand combat training, Comeau is kicking wildly while working to extricate herself. Rolling to the side of the bed, she forces her attacker to stand in an effort to prevent himself from falling to the floor, but he is able to keep the pillow over her face. She continues to yell – "I don't want to die. I don't want to die. I don't want to die" – but the tape has been pressed more tightly over her mouth and her words are quite muffled.

The synopsis of the video tape prepared by police gives a full description of the events as they unfold and the words being spoken.

"He orders "shut up, shh" and she continually struggles to get her hands free," the typed report states. "He tells her to shut up forcefully. He tells her "stop moving and be quiet, I'll let you breath. Stop, shut up and I will let you breath. Shut up. He tells her shut up. She answers "okay," the report continues. He tells her "there you go, uh, uh, there you go." She says: "I don't want to die" and he says "shh, shh."

Williams stands up, but continues holding the pillow against Comeau's face. He looks directly at her and then glances at the camera. He looks perplexed and seems to be pondering what to do, but his next action is decisive. Reaching into the yellow and black bag on the floor, he retrieves a roll of silver-colored duct tape. Using both forearms to keep the pillow over his victim's face, Williams begins peeling a strip from the roll. Comeau hears the sound and instantly starts tossing about on the bed while screaming out "no, no, no" as the attacker struggles to control her.

"Be quiet," he tells her. "Be quiet and I'll let you breathe."

Comeau yells out "no" repeatedly while thrashing around, eventually plummeting from the bed to the floor.

Enraged with anger, Williams hisses at Comeau to stop making noise. "Be quiet and I'll let you breathe," he repeats, with frustration clearly evident in his voice. "Be quiet or I'll suffocate you...do you understand. Do you understand?"

Comeau isn't visible on the floor, but Williams is leaning over her. "Okay," he says. "You have to be quiet." She is yanked from the floor and put on the bed in a sitting position and Williams repeats the word "quiet" over and over again before she seemingly gives up her efforts to resist. Pressing one hand against the top of her head and holding the pillow in the other, the attacker appears somewhat bewildered before ordering the victim to stand up. When she feels him grabbing the length of rope attached to her hands, she says defiantly with a strong French accent – "I won't do nothing." Clutching the rope and the pillow in one hand, Williams pushes her towards the video camera.

"Okay, okay," she says, her voice very muffled because of the duct tape. "I will walk. I'll walk."

Williams continually urges her to "keep quiet," fearing that somehow his now almost inaudible voice will be heard by someone outside the house. He throws the pillow back onto the bed but is still holding the rope while leading her out of camera range. She says "yes" when he asks if she wants some water and then is pulled back – like a dog on a leash – and steered backwards. Comeau moans when she trips and falls awkwardly against the bed. "Stay there," Williams orders while walking away, but still maintains control as he uncoils the rope so that he can pull her back if she tries to escape.

He moves to the other side of the bed and replaces the bedding that had been ripped away from the window during the violent struggle with his victim. Comeau somehow manages to pull herself from the floor and is moving around, trying to find a comfortable position on the bed. "Stay there," Williams insists in a slightly raised voice while making his way toward hers. She is half sitting on the bed with her right foot on the floor and her left leg bent on the bed. He grabs his balaclava, which has fallen to the floor, and pulls it back over his head. In the video it's now obvious that the masking cloth is not a balaclava.

In fact, it is a black ear-warming band which was used to cover his mouth and nose, along with a hood which he pulled over his forehead, leaving only his eyes visible. He pulls the ear-warmers to his neck, and his face remains uncovered.

When Williams moves back around the bed, he brushes against the sheet that he positioned over the window and it again falls to the floor. The sound startles the victim and she begins to cower, backing further up on the bed. As the attacker wanders about the bedroom collecting his clothing, Comeau asks what's going to happen to her.

"You're going to kill me, aren't you?"

At first he ignores what she's saying and starts to get dressed. He pulls his dark sweatshirt over his head. There is a pause while he positions the garment over his upper torso. Then, looking at Comeau, he calmly says "No."

"Ya," responds Comeau, her voice conveying the feeling that she doesn't believe him. "When are you going to do that...when are you going to leave?" Williams moves around the room putting on items of clothing as he finds them. His victim turns her head. Although she can't see him, she follows the sound and seems to be watching as he pulls on his black underwear, his socks and a pair of jeans. Williams goes to the window and attempts to reinstall the sheet so that no one can look in and see what is happening, but it won't stay up. Moving around the room again, he locates the hooded sweatshirt that he was wearing and puts it on before hunting around and finding his running shoes. Finally dressed, he peels several strips from the duct rape roll and uses them to hold the bedding over the window. He also jams a couple of knives into the space between the wall and the window frame to make sure the sheet is securely in place. During this time, Williams has been glancing repeatedly at Comeau, who is sitting very still, with her head hanging down. The camera records him moving around the room picking up several items from the floor and carrying them to another area of the house.

Returning to the room, Williams walks over to Comeau. "Get up," he orders. "Get up," while pulling her to a standing position. She instantly backs away and spins around into the wall next to the bed.

"I don't want to die," she murmurs. "I don't want to die."

Williams grabs her as she blindly tries to walk past him. "Who said you were going to die," he teases, while leading her out of sight of the camera.

"You are going to kill me, I know," she says. "Go away. Go away."

Williams stands in front of the camera as he pulls the black cap to his eyebrows and the band around his neck over his mouth and nose. He resembles a hooded executioner as he reaches out and grabs Comeau with his right arm.

"Please, go. No, go," she said. Her voice is muffled but she's clearly terrified. "Please go. Go! Just go away. Just go." He tries to quiet her down, but she pleads with him and says "no" repeatedly. Williams maintains a grip on the rope leash while telling her he is going to leave and she won't be killed.

"Go, go, please go," she pleads. "I don't deserve this. Please go. I don't deserve to die." She is quiet for a moment. "Please, go. Please. I've been good all my life." She begs him to just leave and spare her. 'Please go, please. I won't tell anybody you ever came here."

Still holding the rope, Williams is staring at his victim, who was out of view of the camera while pleading for her life. Realizing she is not being videotaped, he moves over and focuses the camera on Comeau, who is now leaning against her dresser while trying to huddle protectively in the corner. Though standing about six feet away, his reflection is visible in a mirror. He is still holding the rope, but is fiddling with something in his hand.

"Please give me a chance," she says, but quickly adds – "I don't think so" – while contemplating what's going to happen to her. "I want to live so badly."

Williams asked if she expects to live.

"Yes," she responds. "Give me a chance. I'll be so good, please. I want to live so badly."

As she is begging, Williams walks over and presses a piece of duct tape over her nostrils and pinches them closed.

"Please. I don't deserve this," she gasps. "I have been good all my life...I will be much better after that."

She slumps forward with her head resting against the mirror that shows Williams' reflection. "Please go. Please go away."

Sliding to her knees, Comeau continues begging for her life: "Have a heart, please. I've been really good. I want to live."

It is 3:30 a.m. Her body convulses and then goes limp. There are no more words and her head simply droops to the side as she suffocates.

Displaying no emotion, Williams picks up the video camera and begins recording images in the laundry room, showing the washing machine, the dryer, some cleaning products and a pile of laundry. He also videotapes clothing in the washing machine before returning to the bedroom

and shutting off the camera. At 3:36 a.m., Williams takes a photograph of Marie-France Comeau with his digital camera. She is sitting lifeless on the floor near the dresser. Her back is against the wall and her hands are tied behind her. Her head is hanging forward with a towel and duct tape covering her face. Another photograph taken at 4:23 a.m. shows Comeau on her stomach in front of the dresser. Naked, with her arms secured behind her back, she is obviously dead.

When the video camera is reactivated, Comeau's naked body is now on the bed. She is face up, with her ankles crossed. Her hair is trailing behind her head, indicating she has been dragged onto the bed. The towel that masked her face is no longer there and the duct tape that prevented her from breathing has been removed from her nose and mouth. She is on the bare mattress. All the bedding has been removed. Williams walks into view on the video and stares at his victim before going over and turning off the camera.

Reactivated one more time, the final images show a burgundy comforter that has been thrown haphazardly onto the bed to cover Comeau's body.

The investigation determined that after Comeau was killed, Williams gathered the bed sheets and washed them with bleach in an attempt to eliminate any trace evidence that would link him to the slaying. Some video and a number of still photographs were taken of the bedding as it was being washed. He also removed the duct tape from her face and later destroyed it so that police wouldn't find his fingerprints or be able to collect any of his DNA on the strips of adhesive that snuffed out the 37-year-old woman's life. Before leaving her home through the back patio door, Williams took nine bras and panties from the dresser as trophies of his first murder. It was around the time he would normally have headed to work, but that morning, instead of going to the Canadian Forces Base at Trenton, he drove 178 miles to the Ottawa area. Once there, he attended an 8:45 a.m. meeting in Gatineau, Quebec with top government and military officials to finalize operational plans for the C17 "Globemaster" transport aircraft which had just been purchased from the Boeing Corporation in Seattle. After co-chairing the meeting, Williams praised all those in attendance, saying the purchase of the aircraft was an historic and outstanding accomplishment and the work done at the meeting demonstrated the value of the four giant cargo carriers to the Canadian military. At some point after leaving the meeting, his mind flashing back to the killing, Williams discarded the boots which had left bloody footprints throughout Comeau's home. And he also burned the rope which had been used to secure his victim's arms behind her back.

Chapter Six

While Williams was outside Comeau's home on the evening of November 23 and listening to her talking on the telephone, the conversation was with her new boyfriend, Paul Belanger. Before saying goodnight at 11:30 p.m., the pair made arrangements to have dinner the following evening. When he telephoned the next day to set a time to pick her up, there was no answer. He left messages on her answering machine, but she never called back. By Wednesday, after repeatedly trying to get in touch, Belanger became frantic and drove to her home. The car was in the driveway, but she did not come to the door when he knocked. Something was obviously wrong.

Unable to open the locked front door, he made his way to the back of the house and discovered that the patio door leading into the living room was unlocked. Stepping inside, he shouted for Comeau. There was no response. Glancing around and not seeing anything that appeared out of the ordinary, Belanger went through the foyer to her bedroom. He immediately saw her lying lifeless on the bed. She was wrapped in a burgundy comforter with a printed tapestry design. The lower corner of her uncased pillow was soaked with blood.

Belanger called 911 at 12:59 p.m. before staggering from Comeau's house.

He was standing outside the Raglan Street home and crying uncontrollably when Constables Chris Dingman and Dustin Shaw of the Ontario Provincial Police arrived four minutes later. Investigators initially thought that Belanger, also a corporal at Trenton's military base, might be responsible for the slaying, but he was later cleared of any involvement.

While a team of forensic investigators combed the single-story home for possible evidence, uniformed OPP officers went door to door through the neighborhood looking for anyone who might have seen or heard anything unusual. Military police were notified that one of the base personnel had been murdered and several email messages were sent through the chain of command to advise senior officers – including Lieutenant Colonel Russell Williams – that Marie-France Comeau had died as a result of a homicide at her residence. Williams was promoted to the rank of colonel a short time before his arrest.

Wearing sterile coveralls to prevent hairs or fibers from falling from their clothing and contaminating the homicide scene, a police forensic team took scores of photographs and collected trace evidence, including blood samples from various rooms throughout Comeau's home. They photographed her body the way it was found on the bed and later at the morgue in the Ontario Forensic Pathology Services facility in Toronto, where Dr. Michael Pollanen conducted a post mortem examination. It was discovered during the autopsy that the victim had been bound and gagged. Although suffocation was confirmed as the cause of death, petechial hemorrhage in her eyes and marks on her neck indicated an attempt had been made to strangle Comeau. Injuries to her head were caused by what Dr. Pollanen described as repeated blunt impacts, and an injury to her back occurred when a metal pin poked into her body while she was tied to the basement jack-post. The head blows caused bruising and lacerations around her left eyebrow, ear and scalp. But it was the sticky residue found by the pathologist around Comeau's mouth and nose that finally revealed the cause of death. Forensic chemists at the crime lab determined it came from duct tape and Dr. Pollanen concluded the obstruction over her mouth and nostrils had prevented the victim from breathing.

Scientists at the crime lab also confirmed that some blood at the murder scene came from Comeau and other swabs picked up traces from a man, which indicated the victim had violently struggled with her attacker. One blood sample discovered in the bathroom adjacent to Comeau's bedroom produced a DNA profile with a random match probability of one in 48 billion people. It was like finding the killer's fingerprint, but police at this stage in the investigation had no idea who was responsible for the corporal's death.

A media release was issued by the OPP's Northumberland detachment several hours after Comeau's body was discovered, but it was a day later when the victim's name was officially made public. A local web-based newspaper carried a story that reported police were investigating the suspicious death of a woman found in her Brighton home. "The victim is identified as Marie-France Comeau, a flight attendant stationed at the Canadian Forces Base in Trenton," the article stated. "Captain Mark Peebles, the Public Affairs officer on the base offered condolences to her family and friends. He told media representatives that Comeau had served in the military for 12 years, but had only been at 437 Squadron for six months."

Although the homicide unnerved residents of the relatively crime-free community, Canada's national media did not immediately pay much attention. Comeau's murder received only a mention in the Globe and Mail, Toronto Star, National Post and Toronto Sun. The slaying was also given coverage by some French-language newspapers in the neighboring province of Quebec, where her father lived. But the murder was "big news" in the daily newspapers of nearby communities, including the Belleville Intelligencer and the Kingston Whig-Standard, along with numerous weekly publications.

The Northumberland News gave details of Comeau's boyfriend discovering her body. Reporters also interviewed neighbors and friends to provide readers with background and any other information they could discover about the victim. The Ontario Provincial Police assigned a detective inspector, backed up by a team of investigators and specialized personnel, who worked around the clock to track down every lead in an effort to find the person who killed the young woman. Two months after the slaying, police continued to appeal for public assistance and told the media that they anticipated a lengthy investigation would be required before the perpetrator could be brought to justice.

At this point, Williams' name had not surfaced in the investigation and they could not have even surmised that

Comeau's killer had been helping his wife move into her dream home, built to their specifications in the Westboro area of Ottawa. It is 10 miles from the Orleans neighborhood where the series of break-ins had occurred. Their former house on Wilkie Drive, where the couple had lived for 14 years, was sold in the summer of 2009, but it wasn't until December that they were finally able to move into the newly-constructed box-shaped home at 473 Edison Avenue. There has never been an explanation about why Williams disrupted his crime spree between the two murders, but it is thought that he likely spent considerable time helping unpack and arrange things at the new dwelling while also hiding the lingerie and photographic evidence related to the various break-ins.

Although Williams took a hiatus, the investigation into the slaying of Comeau continued and in late January 2010, an OPP inspector publicly announced that a lengthy investigation would still be required before the corporal's murder could be solved. The same day that police were appealing for help in the Brighton killing, Williams renewed his crime spree and broke into the home of Jessica Lloyd, north of Belleville. Her abduction generated much more media attention, but it wasn't until the February 10 arrest of Colonel Russell Williams, a shining light in Canada's military who had flown dignitaries – including Queen Elizabeth – that the story began attracting the attention of media outlets around the world. And as more information came out, people realized the highly-respected military officer had been leading a twisted Jekyll and Hyde existence.

Chapter Seven

Russell Williams didn't know Jessica Elizabeth Lloyd. He drove past her home regularly on the way from his office at the Canadian Forces Base in Trenton to his residence in Tweed. But it wasn't until January 27, 2010 that he claimed to have noticed her on a treadmill at the house on Highway 37. It was while driving that Williams spotted her through a basement window at the ranch-style house on the northern outskirts of Belleville. The 27-year-old woman, a hard-working and dedicated person, had just started to exercise to get in shape for an upcoming vacation to Cuba. When Williams locked eyes on her, he instinctively knew she would be his next victim.

About twenty-four hours later, on Thursday, January 28, 2010, Williams entered Lloyd's home through a patio door leading to the kitchen. He wanted to make sure she lived alone and spent a bit of time looking around, but didn't steal anything. When Williams broke in, Jessica was visiting Dorian O'Brian, a long-time friend. She got home shortly after 10 p.m., but saw nothing to indicate that someone had been in her house. At 10:36 p.m., Lloyd sent a text message to her friend, telling him she had arrived home safely and was going to bed.

She got up early each morning to make sure she wasn't late for her job at the Tri-Board Student Transportation Services in Napanee, a half-hour's drive east of Belleville. Lloyd had never missed a day at the company. She had worked there for two years as a transportation planner, preparing schedules for school buses. She was a reliable employee, but on Friday, January 29, she didn't show up for work. When calls to her home went unanswered, worried colleagues telephoned her mother, Roxanne, to find out if something was wrong. Her mom also couldn't contact her and drove quickly to her daughter's rural house to find out why she wasn't answering her phone. She found Jessica's car in the driveway, but there was no sign of her daughter. Not knowing what had happened, she contacted the Belleville Police Service and told the officer who answered the telephone that Jessica had vanished.

The isolated home of Jessica Lloyd in a rural area of Belleville

No one was aware at the time that Williams had entered the home through a patio door shortly after midnight and confronted the sleeping victim in her bedroom. He had driven to the house from Tweed after shutting off his BlackBerry, the hotline link that kept him in touch with the military operation's centre and key personnel in the event of a major incident or disaster that would require the involvement of Canadian Forces personnel. Inside the bedroom, Williams was just about to club the victim with his heavy metal flashlight when she awakened. Although his face was masked, he ordered her to turn away from him and get onto her stomach.

Several hours earlier, the intruder had parked his silver 2001 Nissan Pathfinder beside a row of trees in a farm field at the northern edge of the young woman's property. The SUV was a considerable distance from the well-travelled highway, but was clearly visible to passing motorists and obviously Williams made a mistake by parking the vehicle in that position. Using shadows from the trees and shrubs as cover, Williams made his way around the perimeter of the property to a spot where he could conceal himself in the brush and watch the house while waiting for his victim to return. It was an extremely dark winter evening and there was virtually no chance that anyone could see him hiding in the location he had chosen for his lair, about 100 feet from the house.

Looking south at tree-line in foreground where Williams parked

One of three passersby who reported seeing the four-wheel drive SUV along the tree-line was a Belleville police officer who was patrolling the rural area north of the city. The vehicle caught her interest and she pulled into the slightly-elevated driveway at the isolated bungalow on the east side of the roadway between Sills Road and Harmony Road to determine if the owners were aware that someone had parked on their farm about 500 feet from their home. If not, she was hoping to get permission to go onto the property and check out the SUV, but there was no one at home.

The officer, who was never publicly named, made a cursory check to make sure the home was secure. Before driving away, she wrote a description of the vehicle in her notebook, indicating its color, possible make and the style of the vehicle. But without having a reported crime to start an investigation or authorization to go onto the property, the officer couldn't get close enough to see the license plate.

Belleville Police Chief Cory McMullan later commended the officer, saying she went above and beyond her duty in an effort to find out why the vehicle was in the field. The description of the SUV and its location also assisted investigators in obtaining tire tracks and footprints which led to the spot where Williams had waited until his victim got home. Although not known at the time, the tire tracks and description of the vehicle were the critical pieces of evidence that allowed investigators to break the case one week later.

After getting Lloyd face-down on the bed, her hands were secured with a rope that Williams had brought with him in his rape kit. He later placed duct tape over her eyes and began taking photographs, just like he had done after breaking into Comeau's house. The first three images, taken between 1:19 a.m. and 1:23 a.m., show the victim standing with her eyes closed in the hallway of her home while wearing a black tank top and grey track pants. In a fourth picture taken seconds later, she has duct tape covering her eyes and her hands are bound with green rope behind her back.

Lloyd's sexual assault was also videotaped. The initial images show the victim face-up on the bed. Her breathing is heavy and erratic, and it's obvious that she's frozen with terror.

Bedroom where Jessica Lloyd was repeatedly raped

The bedroom was illuminated with the beam from the flashlight that Williams was carrying, plus four table lamps positioned on nightstands on either side of the bed. Three of the lamps were brought from other rooms after the victim was subdued. The lighting left an eerie, high-contrast image on the video which showed Lloyd with her arms tied behind her back and rope securing her to the headboard. Investigators from the OPP's Child Sexual Exploitation Section, who viewed the video to prepare a synopsis for prosecutors, described the victim as a woman with dark brown hair and a medium build. She was wearing a black shirt and light-colored track pants, and had strips of silver-colored duct tape covering her eyes.

Jessica is alone on the bed, but there are sounds of someone moving around the room. A moment later, the arm of a man comes into view and he places a digital camera at the bottom of the bed. Photographs found later show the woman's attacker had taken several pictures between 1:30 a.m. and 1:41 a.m. of lingerie in the drawers of her dresser and some undergarments scattered about the room. After taking the photographs, Williams walks over to the bed and sets down his digital camera, which had a large lens. His arm extends into view for a second time while he puts a black flashlight on the bed. The video was running for fourteen seconds before Williams comes into full view and walks along the left side of his victim's bed. He leans over to adjust the rope around her leg and then unties the portion that is securing her to the headboard.

His jacket and pants are black. He also has a black balaclava covering most of his face. There are holes for his eyes, but the mask has only been pulled down over his nose. His mouth and chin are visible. Nothing is said, but Williams reaches over and pulls away a section of shirt that is covering his victim's stomach. He briefly glances at Jessica, then steps back before walking out of the video camera's view. He is back a moment later with some sort of multi-purpose tool and unfolds the knife blade to cut away the garment from the upper part of her body. The remaining pieces of her shirt are sliced off before the comforter and sheets are stripped from the bed. The video shows Lloyd being fully compliant as she moves her body several times and arches her back to help her attacker remove the clothing that had been covering her breasts.

Williams again starts taking pictures of the topless woman with his digital camera, while the video records everything in real time as the chilling drama unfolds in the bedroom. The attacker brushes his fingers against the duct tape to make sure it's tight against her eyes, then orders Jessica to open her mouth. She instantly obeys his command and investigators said it was obvious that she was doing everything in her power to cooperate and not upset her attacker. Two photographs taken at 1:43 a.m. show the victim on her back and three more were snapped a minute later as her track pants were being removed. The video shows her on the bed, clad only in panties. Then a flash of light indicates that another picture was made with the digital camera. Prior to other photos being taken, her underwear is pulled off and placed on her thigh. The undergarment is then thrown on the floor before Williams begins moving around while taking photographs of her naked body.

She complies when told to spread her legs and remains in this position while her attacker removes the still-running video camera from the tripod and begins recording close-up images from around her knees to her pelvic area. Jessica is ordered to bend her knees while Williams continues to shoot video of her. Moving up her body, the camera is now focused on the victim's face. "Open your mouth," she's told, followed by an immediate order from Williams to close it. He makes his way to the end of the bed, restores the camera to the tripod before taking more photographs with the digital camera and then walks away. Investigators who reviewed the video described the attacker's movements as slow and methodical. Police later found three images on his computer which were taken between 1:48 a.m. and 1:50 a.m. Showing Lloyd naked on her back with her legs apart, they were dated the day she vanished.

"You want to survive this, don't you," says Williams in a calm voice while standing somewhere off to the side, outside the view of the camera. Nodding and saying yes, Lloyd is told she's doing good. "Okay, okay," she replies with a nervous strain in her voice. Still not visible on the camera, Williams asks if she has a vacuum cleaner.

"Yes," she responds and explains that it is in the closet in the spare bedroom. There are sounds of someone unzipping a duffle bag and rummaging through it while Lloyd is heard on the video recording explaining that there's no light in that room. "You may have to turn on the hallway (light) which is right by the door," she tells the intruder.

He doesn't leave the room, but moves back to the bedside and is seen in the video taking close-up pictures of various parts of her body. Williams has removed his balaclava and isn't wearing any clothes. He asks a number of personal questions and then orders her to spread her legs wider apart while continuing to take pictures. Not realizing what was happening, the victim's body jolts involuntarily when Williams put his hand on her lower pelvic region. "Oh, geez, I'm sorry," Jessica said apologetically, while trying to remain as still as possible while his fingers begin probing her. A ring is clearly visible on his right finger and the video shows that he is closely watching her face for any reaction to his touching. She remains motionless.

Obviously aroused, Williams reaches for his camera and starts taking pictures while touching the same intimate part of her body with his left hand. Moments later, she is ordered to turn over and he climbs onto the bed to push her from her back to her stomach. As she rolls from her back to her right side, the video reveals that her dark brown hair is tied in a bun at the back of her head and the green rope binding her arms behind her back is tied in a large elaborate knot. After being turned over, Lloyd is face down on the right side of the bed. She is ordered to "get up on your knees," then is immediately told to keep her face buried in the pillow. Williams gives a series of instructions which have her moving her buttocks higher into the air and sometimes looking back at the video camera. He also takes some digital images while she's in this position. At one point she asks if he wants her on her right side and he replies "nope" before telling her just to do the same things, but to turn her head to the left. Throughout the ordeal, she was totally submissive and acquiesced to her attacker's every demand. In the statement of facts written by police in preparation of court proceedings, investigators stated: "When directed to position herself a certain way, she would ask in a terrified voice if she was in the right position. She would ask for permission to adjust to a different position that was not as awkward or uncomfortable," the document states. "Throughout the entire sexual assault, she was compliant and cooperative with all of Russell Williams' demands. He tells her such things as 'get your ass around to the right and put your head around to the left' and she asks him for further direction to make sure she complies with his wishes."

The video shows the victim has a scrolling tattoo on her lower back. Williams is directing her so that the design will be visible in the still photographs he is taking. "That's it, stay there," he says while holding his hand against her buttocks to maintain the position she's in while he snaps another picture. At times he will move one of the lamps that illuminated the room and on occasion will brush his hand across her skin to remove a piece of lint or thread so that it won't appear in the images he's recording. Investigators described him as being "very methodical" and he was obviously intent on videoing every moment and photographing each phase of the sexual attack on Jessica Lloyd.

Williams is seen on the video taking the bedside lamp and positioning it at the end of the bed to illuminate his victim. He then removes the camera from its stand and begins panning up and down her right side before focusing on her backside. There are some close-up images in that area, then he zooms in on the rope, which appears to be of high quality and likely designed for repelling. Investigators observe that it is knotted several times. Continuing to move the camera over her body, Williams records images of her breasts before fetching his digital camera to take other photographs. In several frames, he holds the camera out so that he can include pictures of himself with the victim.

After each image is taken, he instructs Lloyd to change her position slightly so that each photograph will be different. The video camera has been running for 14 minutes and 55 seconds when Williams sets the digital camera at the side of the bed and activates the time delay so that he can better position himself in the picture. When the camera snaps the image, he is kneeling on the floor with his face close to the victim's pelvic region. A moment later, Williams engages in oral sex, then intercourse while intermittently taking photographs throughout the rape. He also picked up the video camera, which had been left running near the bed and takes close-up images of the sexual attack at various intervals.

"Spread your legs," her attacker demands, while squirming around to get what he thought would be the best images of the torture she was enduring. Stopping briefly, Williams replaces the video camera on its tripod and takes additional footage of Lloyd on the bed. "Okay, roll on your back." She immediately complies and he renews the rape, stopping every so often to sit up and take digital pictures. He stares almost absently at the tape covering her eyes, but every so often glances back to make sure the video camera is still running. The vital but vile and disturbing police synopsis drones on for 12 pages, describing every lurid and disgusting aspect of the attack depicted in the images that Williams had recorded. The graphic documentation, complete with sound, was a goldmine for the investigators, but it also showed the brutality of the attacker and the depths of depravity that the young woman was forced to endure after Williams broke into her home.

Police, however, saw something else in the video. It was the bravery that Jessica displayed while hogtied and helpless. She was unable to physically resist, but did call upon her emotional strength to cooperate with the attacker in the hope that he would believe she liked him and allow her to live. "Do you want my knees up?" she asks at one point. Jessica also quietly says "yes" when Williams tells her to keep her legs in the air when he halts his rape long enough to take several digital images of her naked on the bed. Another series of photographs between 2 a.m. and 2:03 a.m. shows the victim on her knees with her back to the camera.

Lloyd is ordered onto her back again and from 2:04 a.m. to 2:11 a.m., photographs are taken while she is being sexually attacked as the video camera continues to run. One minute later, she is told to get onto her knees. Investigators note that her hands are bound so tightly by the rope that blood circulation has virtually been cut off and the skin is turning purple.

Williams is constantly giving directions while taking pictures. "Keep your feet up...okay to your right...hold that," he says at various times while moving to get what he thinks is the best angle for his photographs. When he orders her to sit up, she asks if he wants her on her "bum," but Williams scowls and says "on your knees, straight up" while grabbing her shoulder and yanking her up. Lloyd holds her position like a statue. She's on her knees in the middle of the bed, holding her back rigid while Williams moves around the bed recording images of her in that position. In the video, Jessica is sitting so high that her head has gone out of the frame and is no longer visible. Although trying to stay still, she is swaying slightly. At 2:15 a.m., she obeys his command to "sit straight down" and other photographs are taken as she is positioned with her legs folded beneath her.

After finishing that series of photographs, Williams moves from out of video range and is heard rummaging through the rape kit that he carried into the house. He is back in view a moment later and climbs onto the bed beside his victim. Kneeling beside her, Williams fastens a long black zip-tie around Jessica's neck. There is a zipping sound as a second plastic garroting device is tugged securely into place. The attacker then tauntingly asks: "What do you think is happening now?"

Her mouth trembling and fighting back tears, Jessica says she has no idea. Her voice is quivering. She is obviously terrified and Williams climbs from the bed to get his camera and take pictures of the young woman, who is now trembling with the realization that her life might be coming to an end. She struggles to keep sitting up and remain still, but her face is contorted as Williams takes digital images, then records her terror with his video camera. After snapping a few more photographs, her tormentor says, "okay, now is the test," while pulling on the plastic cord. Only inches from her face, Williams says, "you feel that...if I feel something I don't like...I pull on that and you die. Got it!" Jessica nods and then says "okay" as her voice cracks. She then says "yes" to make sure he knows that she understands what he has just told her. She is still bravely trying not to cry as he steps back and takes some close-up photographs of the fear in her face.

"Do you want to die?" Williams asks, almost mockingly, while gripping the tie with the fingers of his right hand.

Moving her head from side to side while muttering "No," she is too scared to speak another word to the man holding her captive.

Still clinging onto the tie, he tells her to open her mouth, then tells her to sit up while taking more photographs with his digital camera. Standing up on the bed, Williams renews his rape of Jessica as she kneels in front of him. Photographs are constantly taken during the attack. He also picks up the video camera to get close-ups of her face and other parts of her body before concluding the assault. She is ordered to keep her mouth open while he takes additional photographs.

"Okay, close your mouth," Williams says while backing away, the digital camera focused tightly on her face as he stands momentarily at the side of the bed before moving out of video range. "Turn a little to your left," he insists, while light from a camera flash illuminates Jessica several times as she maintains her upright position on the bed. Ten photographs between 2:21 a.m. and 2:27 a.m. portray close-up views of the sexual attack and of the victim alone on her bed.

Getting back onto the bed, Williams again positions himself in front of the woman and resumes the rape while threatening to tighten the zip-tie noose if she refuses to fulfill his demands. In some photographs, Williams' hand is clearly visible holding the end of the zip-tie and the video shows the victim breathing erratically and obviously filled with fear, knowing her life could end at any moment. He orders her onto her back. Instead, Jessica stretches face down on the bed. Immediately apologizing, she then rolls over. Williams says nothing, but stands at the side of the bed while taking pictures. At one point he pushes her knee out of the way to get two close-up images of her pelvic area.

Jessica is told to stand beside the bed. After obeying, she asks if her position is acceptable and Williams replies "to your right." He then grabs a bundle of rope trailing from her bound arms and uncoils it while walking out of view.

The camera flash goes off several times as he takes more photographs of the young woman, who is no longer visible on the video. When Williams reappears, he places some light-colored lingerie on the bed. Realizing the video is no longer recording images of his victim, he moves the tripod slightly to show Jessica standing against the wall near the bedroom closet. Her eyes are still taped over, her arms are secured behind her back and she is naked. The attacker moves meticulously around the room while picking up several items from the floor, including a black extension cord and some family photographs that were knocked off a side table. After tidying the room, Williams takes several more photographs before walking over to the victim and moving his hands over her breasts and stomach. Going over to the bed, he selects a pink lingerie set and then bends in front of Jessica, telling her to lift her right leg and then her left while fitting her with a pair of panties. Like a designer with one of his creations, he sweeps his hand across the silky material to wipe away wrinkles, but before stepping back, Williams kisses each of her breasts. He next casually drapes a pink teddy over part of her upper body and again starts taking digital photographs.

Moving towards her, Williams grabs the garment and bends down, ordering her to lift one leg at a time while he tugs the teddy over her hips and adjusts the see-through top over her breasts. He also turns her towards the video camera while he takes more digital photographs. Some pictures are made as he crouches down in front of her, while other shots focus on her face. Lloyd, who has been standing motionless, is ordered to climb back onto the bed and kneel with her face down. She almost falls while trying to feel her way to the bed and apologizes to her attacker, who places a hand on her back to steer his captive across the bedroom floor. As she climbs onto the bed, Williams repositions the video camera to record the next phase of his attack. He zooms in to show the rope securing Jessica's arms, then shines a flashlight onto the large knot holding her hands together.

"Roll over on your back," Williams commands.

Jessica positions herself on the bed with her feet towards the bottom end. Williams tells her to get her knees up and spread her legs, then moves casually around the bed taking photographs. "Put your feet closer together and spread your knees," she is told. At this point, the video camera is moved from its stationary position and close-up images are taken between her legs, before her panties are pulled down to her ankles and she is again forced to endure repeated sexual acts. On several occasions during the assault, Williams stops to take photographs. Three images between 2:44 a.m. and 2:45 a.m. show oral copulation and twelve images taken over a seven-minute span starting at 2:47 a.m. are of Jessica being raped. During the attack, Williams is seen several times looking over at the camera to make sure it is recording every intimate detail.

Williams takes several digital photographs of Jessica after this attack. She has obeyed his order to keep her legs in the air. The video image shows the panties drooping from her left ankle along the lower part of her calf. She is shaking with fear and continues to breathe erratically. "Is it okay if I put my legs down?" she asks. "I'm shaking." Williams is heard answering "yep" before the video screen goes blank.

Between 3:06 a.m. and 3:08 a.m., six photographs are taken. One shows a blurry reflection of Williams in the bedroom mirror. In the other images he is clearly raping the victim. The teddy that was covering her breasts is now around her waist. Three more photos taken at 3:10 a.m. show close-ups of Williams engaged in his sexual assault and seven photographs between 3:11 a.m. and 3:21 a.m.

are of Jessica on the bed, including several with her legs spread apart. It is evident that she has just been raped.

The seventeen photographs taken from 2:34 a.m. to 2:41 a.m. with Jessica wearing panties and the teddy were not the only pictures of her posing in lingerie. Williams forced his victim to model multiple items of lingerie while he took pictures.

Before the video was shut off, she can be seen sprawled on the bed and there are rustling sounds in the background. Williams also comes back into view to take a number of

Jessica Lloyd is held captive in the Tweed home of Russell Williams

photos of Jessica on the bed. He is now dressed and has the balaclava on his head, but it is not pulled down over his face. The intruder had been in Lloyd's home for about three hours and he was now about to abduct her. Before bundling the victim into his SUV, which was parked beside the tree-line, Williams puts back the lamps he took into the bedroom to provide extra lighting. He then re-packed the rape kit which he brought to the house. Although he is not seen in the final sequence of the video at her home, there are sounds of items being packed and a bag being zipped up.

Williams was also able to convince Jessica to leave the house willingly after repeatedly promising that she would be released safely if she obeyed his demands. Investigators found the woman's footprints near the spot where he had parked his vehicle and they learned that the victim sat blindfolded in the front passenger seat while being driven to Tweed. They arrived at her abductor's home at 62 Cosy Cove Lane sometime between 4:30 a.m. and 5 a.m. Once inside, Williams told police he took her to the bathroom so that he could wash away any physical evidence that could be recovered from her body.

When the video camera is turned back on, the victim is standing naked in the bath, bracing herself against the back wall, with the shower spraying over her. Her head is bent forward, but it is clear that her eyes are still covered with duct tape and her arms are bound with the same previously-applied rope. After roving around the tiny bathroom and taking video images, Williams positions the camera on the vanity, then pushes her forward while getting into the tub behind her. He asks if the "water's all right" and she tells him "it's a bit hot on my arms." Williams adjusts the tap and Jessica nods her head to indicate the temperature is now fine. Fondling her breasts before picking up a bar of soap, he begins lathering every area of her body, including between her legs. After rinsing the soap away, Williams gets a towel and dries his victim. "Is there any possible way I could get some clothes?" she asks. "I'm freezing." Williams says nothing and the video screen again goes blank as the camera is shut off.

Three digital photographs were taken of Jessica in the shower between 5:56 a.m. and 5:57 a.m. Also clearly visible is the zip-tie which Williams placed around her neck when he first confronted the woman. During the interview with police, he acknowledged having allowed Lloyd to sleep for a few hours when they arrived at his home, but said she had some sort of seizure as a result of the stress.

There is nothing to indicate how much time has passed, but it's already daylight when the video is turned on again. Jessica is face down on a bed, but it appears to be a different room. She is naked and still secured with rope, which is bundled beside her. The walls are painted a light color and there are white sheets and white pillow cases. There is also a beige comforter trimmed at the bottom with a design of white leaves. The room is strewn with clothing. She speaks, but her words are muffled by the pillow and Williams asks her to repeat herself.

"I don't feel good," she says. Williams asks what she needs. "I have to go somewhere," she replies, and then – obviously aware that she's at his home – asks how far he lives from the hospital.

"Fifteen minutes," he tells her. In truth, however, it would take at least twice as long to reach any of the nearest hospital in Belleville, Trenton or Napanee. When she asks how he's going to take her, Williams walks over to the bed and puts his arm on her, telling her to move over.

"I don't want to move," she says. "I don't want to get up." She is clearly in distress and needing medical attention. Williams pulls down the sheet that had been covering most of her body and rubs her shoulders and lower back.

"Hey, come on," he says, his words almost a whisper, as he moves the pillow away from her face. "Take some deep breaths. Take some deep breaths."

"Get someone who can help me," she pleads. "If you can't take me to the hospital, take me home."

Williams leans over her and strokes her hair with his hand. "Put your head to the side," he says. Leaning even closer, he tells her not to make it worse for herself. "Talk to me, Jessica," he whispers. "Talk to me."

The police officers, who viewed the video and prepared the written synopsis, described the victim as appearing either intoxicated or ill. She was slurring her words. "You have to take me to the hospital," she tells Williams. "You have to take me or I'm going to die."

The synopsis reads: "He is smoothing her hair with his hand while leaning over her and whispering "hey, hey, hey Jessica. Dry your eyes. Dry your eyes. Come on, come on. Roll over." She appears to be vomiting and retching. "You have to take me somewhere," she says. "Please, you have to." Williams lifts her up onto her side and her breasts are exposed. She rolls onto her back and appears to be convulsing. Her eyes are still duct taped. He leans over her and rubs her face, telling her quietly and calmly: "Come on, come on. Don't bite your tongue. Relax, relax. Try and relax. Focus. Stay with me, Jessica." He is leaning over her with his right hand at the side of her mouth, saying: "Okay, okay." He places both hands on her face. She convulses again and struggles to speak. "You have got to take me somewhere. I'm going to die if you don't."

Williams whispers "okay" as the young woman turns and buries her face in the bed. She also starts coughing. The sheets have been pulled back a bit further and the rope that is binding her arms is now also wrapped around her thighs. "Do you need to throw up?" the assailant says, while trying to assist her from the bed, but she says no. She is gagging but still forcing herself to speak. "You have to tttttttake mee sossssomwhere."

The synopsis continues: "He holds her face towards him and whispers "What can I do to help you? What can I do to help you in the meantime? She says "Don't let me bite my tongue. Don't let me bite my tongue." And he continues to hold her face. He tells her to "keep your mouth closed. Keep your mouth closed, okay." And remains directly in front of her face, holding her mouth. She nods vehemently. "Okay," she says. "Okay, okay, hold on" before adding: "We have to go because I only have twenty minutes from the time it starts." He whispers "hold on" as she falls back onto the bed. He helps her to get up from the bed and whispers "okay, okay try and swallow," while she asks him again to take her to the hospital. She is at the end of the bed crouched in the fetal position, appearing extremely distressed and shaking. He calmly goes back to the camera and turns it so that she is clearly back in view while suppressing gags and convulsions. Even while she is in extreme distress, he deliberately turns the camera to capture her.

"She leans over and says "I know I can't put anything in my mouth because I will swallow my tongue" and he puts his hand on her back to steady her. He tells her "stand up, you can stand up." She leans forward and retches while he retrieves a white wastebasket from the side of the bed for her to vomit into. He is completely naked during this section. He is whispering "here's the bucket" and she cries "you have to take me somewhere. She is crying and says "can you put something on me first?" She is crying. "We have to go, we have to go. I don't want to die." She is crying and saying: "I should have told you this last night. I never even thought. I'm sorry." He holds her up and is whispering "shh shss." She is extremely upset and crying and trying to speak... "You have to take me even if you can't take me to a hospital, you have to take me somewhere." She is convulsing and he puts his hand over her mouth.

"We have to go. We have to go. We can't stay here and waste time," she begs him. He tries to hold her up and says "you're doing well. You are doing well, come on." He tells her "come on, stand up" and looks towards the camera while brushing hair out of her eyes. He appears to continually be conscious of the position of the camera even as she is in obvious distress. "Come on, don't bite your tongue. Don't bite yourself," he whispers. She gags and anxiously says "we need to go." He says "I know, come on. I know." She is crying and gagging, saying "we have to go. I only have twenty minutes from when I start having one. We have to go. How long have I been out already? He looks towards the bed and states "you have only been two minutes." She begs him "can you drop me off?" She falls to the floor. Growling and retching, she says: "Please, I'm begging you. Can you?" He looks at the camera and puts his hand towards her mouth. Williams is crouching behind her, holding her chin and leaning over her." Since some of the words in the synopsis are repetitive, it appears the investigators had difficulty detailing the sickening events they were watching.

"You don't understand," Jessica tells Williams. "I'm not making it up." She's crying, but her attacker is unmoved. He whispers her name several times before she again appeals to him. "If you don't take me, I'm going to die."

Williams tells her to stand up and says he's going to get her dressed. Unable to see, she's stumbling around, trying to feel her way in the unfamiliar room. She pleads with him to take the tape from her eyes. "I won't look," she says. "I won't look." Williams tells her to be quiet and indicates he needs to get her dressed. "You are doing very

well," he says. "I will get your jeans." She begs him to
untie her. "I won't do anything," she says. "I promise."
Williams is trying to hold her up, but she slips sideways
and bends over. "I think I bit my tongue," she tells him.
Grabbing her jeans, Williams struggles to get her dressed.
Jessica is disoriented and is waving her arms. "I'm not
going to do anything," she says as her words slur together.
She also starts to cry again. "I'm so sorry," she says. "I
should have told you. Do you promise to take me to the
hospital?" Her voice sounds desperate.

Williams unfastens the rope and pulls the jeans up her
legs, then circles behind her to thread the belt through the
loops. She is bent over and convulsing. "Hang in there,
baby," Williams says. "Hang in there." He finds her
sweater on the floor and begins to remove the rope that is
securing her arms. "I promise, I won't try to do anything,"
Jessica tells him. She also sticks out her tongue and asks
how much of her tongue has been bitten off. He says "not
much" while urging her to hang on. "I don't want to die,
please," she says as he pulls her sweater over her head.
Williams is still naked.

"If I die will you make sure my Mom knows that I love
her?"

Jessica is crying while being led from the room as the
camera is turned off.

Williams did not drive her to a hospital and since the video
wasn't running, there is no record of what happened when
it became evident that she wasn't going to be taken to
anywhere she could get help. Investigators did find some
pictures taken during that time, as Jessica sat in a
crouched position for a short while before collapsing to the
floor. She was asleep for about an hour. Four photographs
were taken between 11:40 a.m. and 1:18 p.m. The first
views show her crouching and the other pictures are of

her sleeping. Dressed, her arms are untied, but the duct tape is still covering her eyes. Williams also took video of her while she was sleeping on the floor.

A few hours earlier, Jessica's mother, Roxanne, was contacted by a supervisor at Tri-Board Student Transportation after her daughter failed to show up at work. It was just after 9 a.m. and this was the first time that Jessica had ever missed work in the two years she had been with the company. Employees said calls to the house went unanswered and no one had heard from her. Her mother started driving to Jessica's house around 9:30 a.m., but stopped at her doctor's office to see if she was there or if the staff had heard from her. Roxanne Lloyd was concerned she might have taken an epileptic seizure and hoped she had received medical help. Her daughter's car was in the driveway, but Jessica was not at home. After seeing her purse, keys and BlackBerry, her mother immediately began calling friends and other family members, hoping that someone would know where Jessica might be.

Sensing how distraught Roxanne was, several people came to the house to do whatever they could, but still there was no trace of Jessica. A couple of relatives busied themselves by cleaning up the kitchen, living room and dining room, but left the bedroom untouched. As they talked, everyone realized that something sinister may have occurred. Just after noon, a call was made to the Belleville Police to report Jessica missing.

The first officer arrived at 12:18 p.m. and requested investigative assistance after learning from Roxanne's mother and others in the house that it was completely out of character for Jessica to be away without letting anyone know. Constable Dan Hounslow and Detective Constable Jeff Holt, a member of the forensic identification unit, began a meticulous search inside the house and in the surrounding property. There was no immediate indication of a crime, but Detective Constable Holt located boot prints leading to and from the rear of the home. He also noticed another set of prints, possibly made by a woman's boot, leading away from the house to the back fence and then to a spot along the tree-line, where a vehicle had

Tire track, impression and tire tread from the Toyota that Russell Williams drove

been parked. It was almost 500 feet from the house and the exact location where the other officer had spotted the vehicle the night before. Photographs were taken, measurements recorded and mold impressions of the footprints and tire tracks were cast. Three other people driving in the vicinity had noticed the vehicle in the field between 9:30 p.m. and 3:20 a.m., which helped investigators develop a timeline to establish when the victim may have been abducted from her home.

Because most witnesses got only a fleeting glimpse of the vehicle while driving by, the descriptions varied from a silver grey Tahoe or Escalade SUV, a light-colored or white pick-up truck, to a dark Explorer sports utility vehicle. A missing person's alert was issued to all police agencies across Ontario, with special attention to Ontario Provincial Police detachments and other municipal departments in close proximity to Belleville. A media release was also prepared. It advised that a 27-year-old woman was missing from her home and a full-scale grid search of the area was organized, which included the assistance of a search and rescue helicopter from Trenton's military base.

No one could ever imagine that Jessica had been taken to Tweed and was now being used as a sex toy by the commander of the base where military personnel were coming out to assist other volunteers to help hunt for her. Around the time her mother was frantically calling anyone she could think of, Williams' camera recorded Jessica asleep on the floor of his lakeside bungalow. He took a video that shows her curled up in a brown, red, orange and white afghan, with her head resting on a blue pillow. She is wearing the same beige sweater that Williams dressed her in when she was begging to be taken to the hospital. His victim has pulled herself into a fetal position next to a black and white striped couch. There is a box of tissue beside her on the tile floor and Williams is directly above her recording video images. As he moves around, the camera still running, a burgundy blanket comes into view, plus the legs of an ironing board. One of her legs appears and it is obvious that she is wearing jeans, while her feet are bare.

"Okay, Jessica. It's time," says Williams in a flat, unemotional voice, as Jessica awakens and lifts her head slowly from the pillow. Still unable to see because of the duct tape over her eyes, she asks if it is okay for her to move before getting into a sitting position. While pressing a tissue against her nose, which she had been clutching in her hand, she holds the blanket tightly around her. Jessica also moves her hand to feel the duct tape covering her eyes. "All set," Williams asks and she nods her head before the video screen goes blank.

The victim is next seen sitting on the toilet in the bathroom, with her jeans bunched at her ankles and her hands folded in her lap. Her head is bent slightly forward, with her hair tied in a loose ponytail. Jessica has a white, beige and red Roots sweatshirt pulled around her and her toenails are painted red. Williams records her as she's fumbling around to find toilet paper and as she feels her way to the sink to wash her hands after pulling up her jeans. "Right in front of you," he says as she's moving her hands through the air while feeling for the taps. After washing her hands, Jessica dries them with a blue towel and then tightens the belt that is holding up her jeans.

Investigators viewing the video noted that the bathroom had light-striped wallpaper, a blue towel on a rack between the toilet and sink, brown tiles on the floor and a small white mat. There is also a waste basket, some brown cupboards, a variety of toiletries on the sink counter and a spray-type cleaning solution.

The captive has already been told by Williams that he wants to take more photographs and have sex with her, and she's prepared to comply with his demands to gain her freedom. The video camera, which had been shut off after the scene in the bathroom, is turned on again and Jessica is now standing in the bedroom. There are numerous items of clothing scattered about, including a pile of lingerie on the bed. Walking over, Williams begins to undress her. He lifts her sweater and pulls it over her head as she lifts her arms to help him remove the garment. She again starts to cry. After getting an assurance that she's okay, Williams takes off her belt and then her jeans, leaving her naked, while he strips off his clothes. "Can you see?" he asks, but even as she shakes her head, he runs his fingers across her eyes to ensure the duct tape is firmly in place. He then fondles her breasts and rubs her stomach before walking over and picking up the digital camera from the bed. Circling slowly, he takes seven photographs between 1:34 p.m. and 1:36 p.m., including some where he crouches in front of her after telling her to spread her legs. The tone of his voice is "flat" and demanding.

From a kneeling stance in front of his victim, Williams crawls over to the bed and selects the flimsy pink see-through lingerie outfit that he had Jessica model during the picture-taking session at her house. He discards it for a moment and then picks it up again before ordering his victim to put it on. Mimicking the slow and deliberate moves of a professional studio photographer, Williams contorts his body while capturing images of Jessica from different angles. She stands motionless and only moves on his instruction. He leans forward at one point to adjust the strap on her top and then lies flat on his back while pointing the camera upward to take several pictures. Between 1:38 p.m. and 3:03 p.m., he takes 154 photographs of his victim posing in undergarments that he took from her home. Visible in many of the images are deep bruises on her arms caused by the rope when she was tied up. The zip-ties are still clearly around her neck – a constant reminder that her life could be choked to an end at any second. Several photographs are also taken while she is again being raped or forced to perform other sexual acts.

The video camera is continually trained on the victim and even if Williams is not in view, a brilliant white light flashes across the scene each time a photograph is taken with his digital camera. Walking behind her, he tells her to take down her underwear. "Top, too?" she asks before stripping naked. "That's a nice tattoo," says Williams, referring to a scrolling design running from her lower back and onto her buttocks. She said it was done four years earlier. He moves one hand over the design while pointing her towards the mirror and touching one of her breasts with his other hand. He also kisses the back of her head and then her cheek while standing behind her and roaming both hands over her breasts. All the time, he is looking at their reflection in the mirror.

Williams fetches another pink see-through top and a bra for her to put on, but since her eyes are covered, she struggles with them and needs help fastening them in place before more photographs can be taken. Getting a pair of panties, he orders her to put them on and becomes aroused while she dresses. He positions himself on the floor with her standing over him while continuing the picture-taking session. Jessica is ordered to turn around while Williams remains on the floor and when he stands up, she is told to take off the see-through cover-up so that he can take pictures of her wearing only her panties and a bra. A few moments later, he begins a sex assault after demanding she kneel before him.

Williams touches the zip-tie around her neck, giving a signal that her life remains in danger. Digital photographs and video recordings are made during the sexual attack and Jessica is forced to change into other lingerie outfits. The insatiable rapist is seen handing her a burgundy bra and matching panties. He watches as she puts them on. After taking photographs from different angles, Williams again demands that she perform a sexual act on him. Jessica is told to stand up and removes the lingerie she's wearing while being kissed on the mouth. She is given another skimpy outfit and Williams watches her putting it on before starting to take pictures. He kisses her several times on the lips and she is fondled repeatedly during the picture-taking session.

Standing with his hands on his hips, Williams admires the outfit she is wearing and tells her that it "suits" her while picking up his camera to take additional photographs. As he kneels in front of her, she makes a half turn to her left with her arms hanging down to the side. He moves towards her and makes an adjustment to her underwear, then lies prone on the floor, pointing the camera lens upward while focusing between her legs. When this series of images is completed, Williams orders her to again kneel in front of him and takes other photographs while she's engaged in a sex act on him as the video camera records everything going on in the room. When finished, Williams kisses her lips. He also whispers something and Jessica begins to remove her bra and panties as he picks up a lemon-green bra and panty set. He watches as she puts them on and then calmly walks over with a pair of scissors and snips off a portion of the zip-tie tail that had been visible in the various photographs he had taken. Presumably Williams didn't want the end showing in the photographs. He had earlier tried tucking the loose piece into the band at the back of her neck, but the tail remained noticeable. Walking her over to the mirror, he again gets on the floor to take pictures with his digital camera. "Spread your legs," she is told.

Stretched out on the floor in front of her, Williams again has the camera focused upward, between her legs. The video shows him sitting up and kissing her stomach before directing her with a touch on the inside of her thigh to turn slightly and move her legs further apart. He shifts himself behind her and continues taking other digital photographs before standing up, then adjusts and smoothes out both straps on her bra. Still standing behind her, he sweeps his hands over her shoulders, down her arms and then over her stomach. Jessica's hands instinctively move in front of her to the spot just touched, but she is ordered to keep her arms at her side so that he can take pictures of her while she's posed in that position. Williams again moves behind her and pulls her arms back while turning her face to the video camera. He also leans forward and kisses her. It is a prolonged kiss on her cheek. She is made to twist a bit more to the left and he again kisses her. He turns her to face him and this time kisses her on the lips, long and lingering while sliding his hands in a tenderly fashion down her arms. It looks strangely like the actions of two lovers, but Jessica is blindfolded and held captive while being repeatedly raped and sexually violated. She is only compliant because she is convinced that, by giving in to his demands, she will eventually gain her freedom.

Picking up the digital camera, Williams takes two photographs before Jessica again starts to remove her bra and panties. As she stands naked, he walks out of view on the video, but returns seconds later without the digital camera. He puts his arms around Jessica and pulls her close to him. Reacting instinctively, she lifts her hands to his shoulders and they stand in an embrace for several moments. Williams has his head nestling against her neck. Stepping back, he goes to the bed and selects a fuchsia bra and panty and demands she put them on. As Jessica struggles to stifle her sobs, Williams again starts kissing her on the lips and rubbing her stomach, an indication everything is going to be okay, but at the same time he reaches for the camera to continue the picture-taking session. "Spread them more," he says while on the floor and pointing his camera upward.

After taking numerous photographs while she stands, Williams tells her to kneel on the floor. "Open your mouth," he orders, while gripping the zip-tie. She obeys and he takes a picture of her in this position before forcing Jessica to engage in another sex act. He continues holding the plastic loop around her neck with his right hand while clicking pictures with the camera held in his other hand. Moments later, she is told to "stand up" and the attacker kisses her directly on the lips before leaning backwards. He stares intently at her face while taking additional photographs. She is told to undress and is standing naked, with her hands at her sides, when Williams reaches forward and touches her hips and pulls her pelvis against his body. He gives her a prolonged kiss before dropping to his knees and begins performing a sex act as she stands with her hands resting on his shoulders. He switches to a sitting position and Jessica seems to almost fall, but puts her left hand on his head to keep her balance during the assault. When finished, Williams gets to his feet and pulls her against him while kissing her.

After positioning her beside the mirror, the attacker selects a see-through baby-doll pink top and matching panties for Jessica to wear for his next set of photographs. As she stands, Williams moves around, snapping images with his digital camera before again lying down and pointing the camera upward as she straddles him. Obeying his next instruction, she unfastens her top and moves the garment away from her breasts. After several more photographs are taken, the victim is again ordered to kneel and she is forced to endure another sexual assault. The video camera continues to roll while Williams takes close-up images of the attack before reaching out and slowly pulling her up with her right hand.

While he walks around the room picking up various pieces of lingerie strewn on the floor, Jessica disrobes and is standing naked when her assailant puts several outfits on the bed. He then selects a light blue, see-through top and panty set and tells her to put them on. She is having trouble getting the top around her and Williams adjusts the garment so that she can feel the opening for her arm. She apologizes for not being able to dress herself. "I'm sorry," she says. "I don't know how to do this up. Do I have it on wrong?" Her captor again assists and then holds the matching underwear in front of her. Reaching out, but not immediately being able to feel the panties with her flailing arms, Jessica again apologizes while pulling them into place.

She is directed towards the mirror and told to stand with her hands stretched out touching the wall, while Williams commences another picture-taking session. He tells her to "move your knees a little bit," which leaves her standing with her legs parted before he sits on the floor in front of her for another series of images. "A little more," he says, while directly photographing her vagina. Moving behind her, Jessica is told to lift the tail of her top and expose her buttocks. He crouches down and tells her to "spread your legs" as he takes additional close-up images. When she is finally given permission to let go of the garment, Williams slips his arm around her waist and turns her towards him while nestling into her neck during a 30-second hug. It appears as though he is engaged in a tender embrace, but then heartlessly steps back and, without emotion, says: "Okay, you can take that off."

When Jessica has trouble unfastening the top, Williams tells her to forget trying to undo the clasps. "You'll just have to pull that down," he says. "Not up." When she is still unable to get it off, he calmly walks over and releases the clasp. As she stands with the top draping from her shoulders and breasts fully exposed, he kisses her lips several times while the garment falls to the floor. He then takes more photographs as she stands with her hands at her side, clad only in panties.

After snapping several pictures, Williams puts the camera down and tells Jessica to completely undress. When she is again standing naked, Williams meanders around the room picking up clothes which have been left scattered on the floor and puts them on the bed. He then touches her arm with his hand and pulls her towards the bed, where she's ordered to sit. As the relentless attacker sits beside her, she asks for a drink of water. "Stay right there," he says, before heading to the kitchen and returning moments later with a bottle of water and his BlackBerry communication device. "Thank you," says Jessica, after taking several sips. Williams is busy typing a reply to a text message and does not appear to hear what his captives said. Standing naked beside the bed, he continues to scroll through a series of military alerts that have been flashed to him over the past few hours. While scanning the text messages, he touches his penis almost unwittingly before bringing his fingers to the miniaturized keyboard in order to answer some of the people trying to make contact with him – just as he did during the killing of Comeau.

Jessica obediently sits after taking several sips of water from the water bottle, but appears extremely frightened and has no idea what is going on during the time Williams has been on his BlackBerry. With no hint of empathy, her attacker then took more photographs of her sitting on the edge of the bed before going over to a lingerie pile beside her and picking out several items he wants her to model. "I'm done with this water," she says, while holding the bottle out to him. "Thank you," she adds, as Williams takes the container after dropping several items of lingerie on the floor near her. From the pile, he selects a blue pair of panties and places them on the bed beside her. Taking Jessica by the hand, he says "okay, come on" and walks her backwards to the mirror. She stands there shivering with her hands in front of her, modestly trying to cover her pelvic region. He asks if she's all right and she tells him: "I'm just a bit cold."

Williams takes the blue briefs from the bed and tells her to put them on. He also notices the design and asks if she's a Leaf's fan, referring to the Toronto Maple Leafs, a National Hockey League team. Jessica giggles. "I take it these are my Leaf's underwear then," she says, while still chuckling nervously. "I just don't admit to being a fan." He tells her that he likes the team and wonders if the players have any idea what underwear some of their fans wear. Walking behind her and smoothing wrinkles from the panties, he tells her the team would be proud of her. Grabbing his camera, Williams stretches out in front of her and again starts taking photographs. "Move back a little more," he instructs. He also touches her ankle and pushes against the inside of her upper thigh to turn her around so that he can photograph her from behind. He says "turn around," then wants her to turn her head towards him, insisting "a little more" as she is urged to spread her legs further apart. Getting up from the floor, he orders her to take off the underwear. Picking up the panties, he tosses them into the corner when she steps out of them. Jessica is now obviously crying and holds one hand near her mouth as Williams walks over and appears to wipe tears from her cheeks. He kisses her after saying something in a whisper that was not picked up by the microphone on the video camera. She seems relieved, possibly after being told she would soon be free, and she passionately responds to his kisses. Her ordeal, however, is far from over.

Williams selects a lace burgundy-colored thong and helps her put it on before taking another series of photographs similar to the ones he had just taken of her in the blue panties. During this session, Jessica starts having trouble breathing and puts her hand to her chest while taking several deep breaths. She appears to be completely overwhelmed by what is happening, but still apologizes for the way she is feeling. Williams pauses for a moment and then gets back onto the floor to take pictures as she stands topless with her legs apart, holding both hands against her upper thighs. After taking close-up images between her legs, Williams rolls himself to a sitting position and kisses her buttocks before standing. He brushes hair from her shoulders and takes several pictures before handing her a white bra to don. He gets her to face the camera by touching her left side and then looks back at the video camera to makes sure it is still recording everything that's going on. Getting back on the floor, Williams takes a series of pictures from various angles, then slides towards Jessica and sits facing her as she stands in front of him. He licks the front of her thong and then partially removes the lingerie while initiating oral sex and taking numerous photographs during the attack. Williams also becomes vigorous and the video shows the victim reaching out and steadying herself against the wall before the sexual assault ends.

The video camera is shut off and when it is reactivated, Jessica is stretched naked on the bed. The zip-tie is visible around her neck and her legs are slightly apart. Williams walks into camera view and then kneels on the bed. A moment later, he leans forward and renews the oral assault on his victim. "Move to your right," she is told, as Williams makes sure graphic video images are being recorded. After several minutes, he sets the self-timer on his digital camera so that he can take pictures while kissing, then raping his victim for almost 15 minutes.

After reviewing the video, and from time stamps on the photographs, investigators realize that Jessica has endured another 90 minutes of torturous terror from her attacker. He has been deliberate and calm while snapping images of the victim throughout the vicious sexual trauma. Photographs 875 and 876, taken between 3:07 p.m. and 3:08 p.m., show Jessica sprawled nude on the bed with Williams performing oral sex. Photos 877, 878, 879 and 880, taken over a five-minute period beginning at 3:08 p.m., reveal Jessica on the bed with her legs spread and include close-ups or her pelvic area. Her eyes remain covered with duct tape and the zip-tie is visible on her neck. The next 10 images, taken between 3:22 p.m. and 3:27 p.m., are of the victim while she is being raped. In the coinciding video, she is clearly wincing and whimpering. The series of photographs includes close-up images of penetration and Williams rubbing himself on his victim's breasts and face. Images 891 and 892, taken between 4:02 p.m. and 4:04 a.m., are of Jessica on her back covered with a white sheet, then with a comforter pulled over her. At 5:45 p.m., photograph 893 shows the

victim sitting on the bed with a plate of fruit on her lap.
She is wearing blue jeans and a Roots hoodie. Her eyes
are still covered, but she is been told she will be going
home.

One hour and 45 minutes later, at 7:30 p.m., Williams
takes two photographs of Jessica stretched out on his bed.
She is fully clothed. The duct tape has been removed, but
her eyes are tightly closed. Between 7:39 p.m. and 7:41
p.m., four other images were taken of her on the bed. She
is shown on her stomach, wearing jeans and the hoodie,
but there is tape again over her eyes and green rope can
be seen binding her arms behind her back. Photograph
number 900, taken at 7:50 p.m., shows her sitting up and
smiling broadly. Two more photos were taken at 8:07
p.m., with Jessica sitting on the edge of the bed with her
feet on the floor. In addition to the clothing, she is now
wearing a pair of shoes. Her eyes are covered, her arms
are bound and she now has a strip of duct tape over her
mouth. But she can breathe freely through her nose.

Jessica is told she will be going home and starts walking
towards the door.

At that instant, Williams moves behind her and raises his
hand above his head. She is clubbed violently with a
flashlight and drops in a stupor to the floor. The attacker
took three photos as Jessica lay bleeding and then, before
she regained consciousness, he grabbed a piece of rope
and methodically pulled it tight around her neck until she
stopped wriggling. Williams had just committed his second
murder.

Three photographs taken between 8:18 p.m. and 8:19
p.m. show Jessica Lloyd face down on the floor. The
flashlight is beside her on the floor and there is an
expanding pool of blood around her head. Although she
received a severe laceration to the back of her head, an

Police tape outside Tweed home where Jessica Lloyd was slain

autopsy determined that the official cause of her death was strangulation.

Williams dragged Jessica's body to his garage and mopped the blood from his living room floor before driving to his office in Trenton sometime between 9 p.m. and 10 p.m. Once there, he reviewed paperwork and grabbed some sleep before piloting an early morning flight which ferried several Canadian soldiers to California. The colonel arrived back in Trenton at 6:30 p.m. on January 30, 2010 and drove to Ottawa, where he spent Sunday and Monday with his wife.

On Tuesday, Williams returned to the cottage residence in Tweed and bundled Jessica's body into his SUV before driving to an isolated spot on Cary Road, about nine miles from his home, where the victim's remains were dumped. After returning home, he spent considerable time wiping the floors and vacuuming various rooms to remove any evidence that would link him to her killing. He also thoroughly cleaned his suburban utility vehicle.

MISSING

JESSICA LLOYD

Height: 5'5"   Weight: 125 lbs
Eyes: Green   Hair: Dark Brown

• PLEASE CALL •
BELLEVILLE POLICE (613-966-0882) or (613-962-3456)
OR ANDY LLOYD (613-?)
IF YOU HAVE SEEN HER!!! *Please help us find her!*

Missing poster produced after Jessica Lloyd vanished

Chapter Eight

The enormity of the case became apparent almost immediately after the Belleville Police Service received the call that Jessica Lloyd had vanished. Initially a missing person occurrence, the investigation soon shifted to a possible abduction, with a strong likelihood that the 27-year-old victim was in extreme danger.

It is rare for police to encounter a kidnapping and there is a potential for officers to become quickly overwhelmed with the complexity of the type of investigation required to locate a victim. That was not the case with personnel at the 125-member Belleville department. From the outset, its officers began a systematic probe which uncovered and preserved critical evidence to track down the individual who had forced Jessica from her home. The first police officers at the home began gleaning as much information as possible from her mother, relatives and friends. Jessica's brother, Andrew, told police about spotting two sets of footprints while checking outside before officers arrived. That was a critical clue and focused investigators on the possibility of abduction rather than making an assumption that the young woman may have gone off on her own to enjoy the company of someone she had just met.

It is interesting to note that although the Belleville Police Service is a relatively small department, its forensic team has an international reputation for the collection and identification of footwear, tire and barefoot impressions. This expertise was a vital element in identifying and tracking down a vehicle, and eventually a suspect in the disappearance of Lloyd. Sergeant Grant Boulay, a 25-year veteran who has hosted courses on behalf of the force's forensic section on track and foot impressions for investigators from international destinations, contacted experts he knew to garner as much information as possible from the footprints and tire tracks found in the field next to the victim's home.

In situations in which an adult goes missing, it's not unusual for law enforcement officials to adopt a wait-and-see attitude. Police realize that people have the freedom to come and go as they choose, and agencies don't want to squander resources on an occurrence that may turn out to be unfounded. In today's society, it is not out of the realm of possibility for a young person to take an unannounced trip or make the decision to spend a few days at a friend's home. This was obviously a quandary that Belleville Police had to deal with when Jessica's mom called to report her daughter missing. But the footprints and tire tracks around her home provided strong hints that the woman was in danger. Family and friends also described her as a conscientious person, not someone who would abandon her responsibilities at work. She had never in the past gone anywhere without letting someone know and it was totally out of character for her to simply vanish. Her house had been tidied up in the hours between the time relatives and friends first learned that she had not shown up for work and until police were called. As a result of their well-intentioned efforts, investigators were unable to immediately assess if there had been a struggle or any type of violence to pinpoint a crime scene.

After weighing various factors, the first responding police officers made the decision to treat the disappearance as serious. They notified the duty sergeant and wheels were put in motion which brought additional police, a forensic team and detectives to Jessica's residence. Preliminary investigation revealed that the young woman had arrived home the previous evening and a short time later had advised a friend via a text message that she was going to bed. Her keys, purse and BlackBerry were inside the house; her car was parked in the driveway and despite attempts by Williams to "clean up and sanitize" the crime scene, there was enough disarray in the bedroom to convince police that something out of the ordinary had occurred.

Step by step, crime scene investigators moved through the house looking for hair, fibres, fingerprints and any other material, including DNA evidence, which could be linked to a suspect once an arrest was made. They also examined combs and brushes for the victim's hair, checked toothbrushes and various personal items and collected saliva or other fluids that might be needed to positively identify a victim should badly-decomposed or skeletal remains be found months or years later.

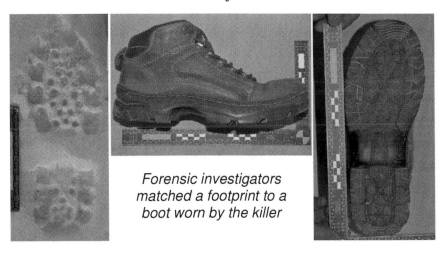

Forensic investigators matched a footprint to a boot worn by the killer

Nothing was left to chance once the decision was made to pull out all the stops and handle the case as a major crime investigation. The police officers who examined the perimeter of the home followed the two sets of footprints in the mud and snow from the back deck to the fence line at the rear of the property. Constables Hounslow and Holt also tracked the footprint impressions along the perimeter to where Williams had left his vehicle during the three hours he was sexually attacking Jessica in her home. Over successive days, investigators conducted interviews with friends and family members, hoping to gather any information that might help locate Lloyd. They also had relatives check clothing and footwear at the house to establish what she might be wearing. A pair of boots she had bought to use during inclement weather was missing and Sergeant Boulay concluded that the smaller footprints behind the home could have been left by the victim. The experts who Boulay contacted for assistance, Jamie White, a collision investigator with Transport Canada, and Thomas Rogerson, a civilian member of the Royal Canadian Mounted Police with expert knowledge of vehicle impressions, suggested police should look for a 1996 to 2002 Toyota Forerunner, a 1999 to 2004 Jeep Cherokee or a 1998 to 1999 Nissan Pathfinder. Rogerson determined a track from the left front wheel was made by a Toyo Open Country tire and additional research by Boulay narrowed the brand to Toyo Open Country HT tires.

The investigative process being carried out by Belleville detectives was very coordinated and followed a mandated Major Case Management System from the Ontario government, which all police services had to follow. The process was put in place for major investigations after a judicial inquiry made recommendations in the wake of mistakes which had prevented police from identifying Paul Bernardo as a sexual predator. Bernardo killed three teenaged girls and raped several other victims during a six-year period until finally being arrested in 1992. The suspect's name had surfaced several times during individual probes of the various cases, but a lack of cooperation and communication between investigators prevented vital information from being shared. Bernardo, who was enrolled at the University of Toronto Scarborough Campus at the same time Williams took classes there, was declared a dangerous offender in 1995 after being convicted of three homicides and a series of rapes. Toronto Police initially linked several sexual attacks in the early 1980s and issued a composite drawing of a person which closely resembled Bernardo. However, he wasn't officially identified as the rapist until arrested along with his wife, Karla Homolka, for the April 1992 killing of 15-year-old Kristen French; the June 1991 slaying of 14-year-old Leslie Mahaffy and the murder of Karla's 15-year-old sister, Tammy, on December 23, 1990.

Homolka, who made a deal for a 12-year sentence in return for evidence against her husband, said she inflicted a lethal overdose on her younger sister while trying to knock her out in order to give Bernardo a gift of "virginity" for Christmas. The couple first met in 1987 while attending university together and were married in the summer of 1991. After their arrests, Paul Bernardo and Karla Homolka were branded by the tabloid media as the "Ken and Barbie Killers" because of their clean-cut, preppy appearance.

There are similarities in the abduction and sexual torture of the two high school students by Bernardo and the terror that Williams' victims endured. But, as mentioned previously, investigators said there is no indication that the pair ever met in university or had any other contact through the years.

Mahaffy was bundled into Bernardo's car after being confronted in the early morning hours of June 15, 1991 on a residential street near her family's home in Burlington, a quiet upscale community on the shore of Lake Ontario, about 45 miles west of Toronto. She was blindfolded and driven to Bernardo's house in St. Catharines, about 10 miles from Niagara Falls, and offered as a sexual playmate to his wife. A month earlier, Homolka helped her husband rape a 15-year-old girl she brought home after getting her drunk during a girl's night out. Bernardo also videotaped his wife as she performed oral sex on the unconscious victim. Mahaffy was given a fatal drug overdose because her blindfold slipped off during the attack and the couple feared she would identify them. After the killing, the victim was cut into pieces and her various body parts were encased in cement before being dumped into a small lake off Highway 406, about 10 miles west of Niagara Falls.

Ten months later, Kristen French was heading home from her Grade 10 class at Holy Cross Catholic High School on April 16, 1992 when Homolka asked if she could help find a street on a map she was holding. As the teenager began intently scanning the map, she was grabbed by Bernardo and pulled into the couple's car. She was threatened with a knife and warned to keep her head down while being driven to their home, less than four miles away. Kristen was held captive in the house on Bayview Avenue in the Port Dalhousie area of St. Catharines for three days and was videotaped while being tortured and raped by Bernardo and his wife. Her ordeal ended when she was strangled with a rope that was looped around her neck. But the murder was not filmed. Her parents knew immediately that something was wrong when Kristen failed to come home from school and police realized they were facing a potential foul play situation when her shoe was found in the parking lot Grace Lutheran Church – the spot where she had been spirited away. Her body was found on April 30, 1992 in a ditch off a sideroad in a remote part of Burlington, the community where Mahaffy was abducted. Both Niagara Regional Police and Halton Regional Police assembled a task force to probe the slayings, but it was not until Homolka contacted a lawyer and gave details of the killings that Bernardo was arrested on murder charges and implicated as the Scarborough Rapist in attacks on 17 women between May, 1987 and June, 1990.

An inquiry was ordered by the government to determine why police had not realized the same person was responsible for the rapes and killings and how Bernardo was not identified after detectives obtained a DNA sample from him while probing the series of sexual assaults. Justice Archie Campbell, of the Supreme Court of Ontario, conducted the public inquiry and recommended that the Case Management program for handling major investigations be revamped. The veteran judge also called for the province's Major Case Management Manual to provide the guidance which police used years later to link the slayings of Marie-France Comeau and Jessica Lloyd, the attacks on Jane Doe and Laurie Massicotte – and put the pieces of the puzzle together to snare Russell Williams.

As detectives completed various phases of the investigation into Lloyd's disappearance, the Belleville Police entered information from the crime scene and details of other evidence into the major case management software system to see if there were similarities with other cases. There was no match to any kidnapping or missing person cases, but the two recent sexual assaults and Comeau's killing produced several common links with the Lloyd case. Details were flashed to Ontario's Serial Predator Crime Investigations Coordinator, who set up an immediate meeting with the OPP investigators who were probing the sexual assaults in Tweed and Comeau's murder in Brighton, and the team of Belleville detectives who were hunting for Lloyd.

On February 4, 2010, a multi-jurisdictional investigation was established and a series of initiatives were proposed to collect as much information as possible from people in the vicinity. Arrangements were made to interview the occupants of 285 homes over the next three days, including everyone living on Highway 37 between Belleville and Tweed, plus all residents within just over a half-mile radius of Lloyd's residence. Police asked people if they had seen or heard anything unusual; if there had been any burglaries or any attempted break-ins at their homes which had not been reported to police and if they had noticed anyone they considered suspicious in the past few weeks. They were also asked if they knew the missing woman and were aware of anyone who wanted to harm her. Police also cleared four known sex offenders who were living in the area.

During the initial brainstorming meeting with investigators from the OPP and Belleville Police Service, it was determined that a key priority should be locating the vehicle that had been parked beside Lloyd's home. They tracked down the drivers of 178 of the 450 vehicles in the Belleville area, but none had a matching tire tread. The team also made what turned out to be a key decision to set up a roadblock near the victim's home on Highway 37, to question drivers and get tire impressions of any vehicles fitting the description from the three witnesses and government experts who had examined the tire marks found near the missing woman's house.

One week after Lloyd disappeared and police were thinking that the person responsible might be an individual who routinely passed the house. The roadblock was to be set up the around 6 p.m., but it was just before 7 p.m. when they were in position and flagged down the first car. Officers were given a list of questions to ask each stopped motorist. If any vehicle fit the profile of the one they were looking for, the driver was to be pulled over and questioned more extensively while tire impressions were taken for later comparison. Williams arrived at the checkpoint in his 2001 Nissan Pathfinder at 6:57 p.m. He was driving the second vehicle that police stopped and because the SUV fit the description, the colonel was asked to pull over so that they could examine his tires.

Williams told them he was Trenton's base commander and regularly travelled that route to his home in Tweed. He admitted driving the highway on January 28, but told police he had not seen anything unusual. He also denied knowing the missing woman.

Investigators later learned it was a fluke that Williams had been stopped, since he should have passed the house more than half-an-hour earlier. Instead, he was delayed for 40 minutes while talking to a captain who he had met in a base hallway moments after leaving his office to go home.

There was also a 10-hour delay in getting information to the command post that had been set up to direct the multi-jurisdiction probe. But as soon as investigators learned Williams had surfaced as a suspect, wheels were immediately set in motion to make sure nothing was overlooked. At this point, detectives assumed that Lloyd was alive and they were hoping to bring her safely home. Undercover surveillance teams were dispatched to keep the base commander's home under observation and follow him while detectives began preparing search warrants that would be needed to collect any evidence should Williams turn out to be Lloyd's kidnapper.

When members of the Major Case Management team learned that Trenton's base commander had been stopped at the roadblock while driving a vehicle matching the profile, there was initial skepticism regarding Williams' involvement. But as other information was developed, the possibility of him being the suspect grew stronger. He lived only a short drive from the home of Jane Doe, the 20-year-old woman who was sexually attacked by an intruder on September 17, 2009, and his residence was in close proximity to the house where Massicotte was attacked less than two weeks later. There was also a potential link with the unsolved murder of Marie-France

Comeau since she worked at the base. In addition, the route Williams often traveled from Trenton to Tweed took him directly past the bungalow where Jessica Lloyd lived.

At this stage, all evidence was circumstantial and police had nothing solid to implicate Williams in the disappearance of the Lloyd woman or the other cases. However, at that point the investigators were confident the same individual was responsible for all the crimes and Williams emerged as a single suspect on their radar screen. Surveillance teams moved in surreptitiously to follow Williams wherever he traveled. Police also undertook the arduous task of drafting search warrants and, on February 7, 2010, Mr. Justice Robert Grayson of the Ontario Court of Justice granted investigators the authority to search the homes and vehicle Williams owned. That same day, undercover officers from the Ontario Provincial Police surveillance unit watched him thoroughly clean his SUV at a car wash in Ottawa. When he left, a couple of the undercover officers seized the material that Williams had vacuumed from the floor, seats and rear compartment of his vehicle.

It was also on February 7, shortly before 2 p.m. when Detective Sergeant Smyth telephoned Williams at his Ottawa residence and casually invited him to the main Ottawa Police Service building. He was told that a follow-up interview was needed to confirm information he'd given when questioned by uniformed officers who stopped his vehicle at the roadside checkpoint near the home of Jessica Lloyd three days earlier. Williams agreed to meet Smyth an hour after his call.

It would be his last hour of freedom.

Chapter Nine

Colonel Russell Williams was casually dressed in a yellow
and black winter jacket, a short-sleeved blue polo shirt
with white horizontal stripes and blue jeans when he
walked into the Ottawa Police headquarters building on
February 7, 2009 for an interview with detectives
investigating four sex-related crimes near his Tweed home.
Obviously nervous, he was trying to act cocky and
maintain the authority he exuded as a military base
commander. After shaking hands with several Ontario
Provincial Police investigators in the lobby, Williams was
led to room 216 on the second floor. It is equipped to
record audio and video statements from witnesses in
addition to those who are under suspicion. The colonel
knew that police wanted to clear him from their list of
suspects in the rape and murder of a female corporal from
the base he commanded in Trenton and the
disappearance of a 27-year-old woman who had recently
vanished from her home in the Belleville area. Three
nights earlier, the base commander was stopped by police
near the missing woman's home and was not surprised
that investigators might subsequently want to talk with
him. Before Lloyd's murder, police had already come to his
door, wondering if he saw or heard anything on the night
a 45-year-old woman was sexually assaulted during an
ordeal that lasted more than three hours at a house only
three doors from where he was living.

Detective Sergeant Jim Smyth, wearing a dark gray suit
and bluish-gray tie, was the only investigator who walked
into the room with Williams. After introducing himself, the
pair engaged in small talk banter as they settled into the
interview room. The seasoned detective casually reached
over and shifted a pair of gloves that Williams had placed
on the table before draping his winter jacket over the chair

where he was now sitting. "I'm just going to move your glove … that's a little microphone," the investigator said, almost apologetically. "Just to make sure it's nice and clear. As you can see, everything in this room is video-taped and audio taped." He then asked if Williams had ever been interviewed by the police in a room like this.

Williams looks around and grins as he glances up at one of four cameras set to monitor everything that goes on in  the room. He then settles in the chair and directs his eyes towards Detective Sergeant Smyth. "I have never been interviewed by police," he said. There is a smile on his face, but a bit of indignation in his voice – a demonstration that he is addressing a person who in the military would be several ranks beneath him. To display even more authority, Williams tells Smyth that he had been interviewed by agents from Canada's National Intelligence Service to get his top secret clearance. Smyth dismisses the colonel's attempt to gain superiority with a simple "oh yeah," then starts addressing him by his first name. "Russell, I appreciate you coming in. An investigation like this, I mean … I'm sure you can appreciate it's been big news. Especially down Belleville way…and, you know, obviously our approach in cases like this is that we don't give up on somebody being alive until we get evidence that they're not. Because of that we're treating Jessica's case as an emergent situation."

Williams answers "absolutely yeah" before Smyth continues: "We're fast forwarding things that we might normally take our time with. And that's why we're here on a Sunday afternoon," he says, allowing Williams to give only one or two word answers of acknowledgement before continuing. "We're going to do a pretty thorough interview today. The reason for that is because the last thing we want is to be calling people back again and again and again." He explains they will go over a number of things and suggests they may be pertinent to Williams while at the same time offering coffee. "I'm a big coffee guy. I don't know if you're a coffee guy or not." Williams wants black coffee, but the Styrofoam cups brought into the room are saturated with sugar. He is chewing gum and apologizes for not being able to take a sip at that moment.

Continuing the interview, Smyth tells Williams he has a simple rule when talking to people. "I treat people, everybody, with respect," he said. "I'll ask that you do the same for me. So what we're going to do is, we're going to start off by going through what your rights are. Okay?" Williams says he's never been cautioned by police before in his life, but Smyth tells him it's just like on television. He explains Williams' rights are guaranteed under Canada's Charter of Rights and Freedoms and that he is not under arrest. "Any time you feel you want to leave here, you feel free to do so," said Smyth. "The door's not locked. Theresa (Detective Constable Theresa Kelm) will walk you down to the lobby any time you want." He also tells Williams to let him know immediately if he wants to speak to a lawyer at any point during the interview. "You just let me know."

He explains that investigators are looking into the disappearance of Jessica Lloyd, but tells Williams it is just one of four cases in the past few months that police are probing. "There have been four occurrences, like I said ... that we're looking into. Two of those occurrences occurred in September of 2009, and very briefly they were up in the Tweed area." Again Williams was interjecting one or two-word responses when Smyth paused. "They involve somebody entering two different women's houses in the evening hours and committing sexual acts," the detective sergeant said. He then mentioned the name of Marie-

France Comeau, indicating that her body had been discovered in her home in Brighton. "One of my people," Williams responded, before Smyth continued. "We believe that there is a sexual component to that crime as well," he said. "Then most recently we have Jessica Lloyd's disappearance. So essentially, when you look at those kind of crimes, we're looking at a number of different potential criminal charges. We're looking at issues all the way from the most serious one, which is first degree murder ... kidnapping and sexual assault ... break and enter with intent to commit sexual assault ... forcible confinement. Clearly, when we find out who's responsible for one or all of those crimes, they could be charged with one or all of those offences...whether it's you or whether it's anybody else, all right."

Smyth was still giving the caution or reading the rights to Williams, but at the same time telling him that they think he was responsible for the abduction of a woman, two sexual attacks and the homicide of a corporal under his command. "That's why it's important that we make sure the people understand what they have and what they don't have to do when they're talking to us. As I said before, any point today you feel the need ... you want to speak to a lawyer, you let me know. We can take you to a room where you can do that in private." After a bit of banter about what arrangements can be made to get a lawyer for him, Smyth tells Williams there are several other things he wants to make clear. "You don't have to speak to me today," he says again, repeating his caution that everything in the room is being recorded.

Williams starts to explain that he is aware of the sexual assaults on the women after being cautioned by Smyth not to tell him anything that a police officer had mentioned to him about the incidents. "Understand these first two attacks that happened are not that far from my place in Tweed," he said. "Well, the second one. We didn't even know the first one had happened, but I understand that was reasonably close as well, but the second one was very close. So certainly at the time the OPP went door to door."

Smyth told Williams he was aware that police had canvassed the area, hoping to find witnesses, but he was now more interested in finding out what he knew about all the cases. "Russell, in a nutshell, that's what we wanted to talk to you about. Those four cases are a concern to us … essentially there's a connection between you and all four of those cases, would you agree … geographically."

Williams acknowledged that he drives past the homes, going back and forth to work or to Ottawa for various meetings. "I would say there's a connection, yes," he said, well aware that he had been stopped at a roadblock three days earlier. "I'll be frank with you," replies Smyth. "Things kind of evolved when the officers talked to you on Thursday night. We kind of went from there." The detective-sergeant said Williams was in uniform when stopped by the police and that connected him to the base where Comeau served. There is also the fact that he lived three doors away from where one of the women was sexually attacked. Williams is then asked to account for his movements when the sexual attacks took place, but he denies recalling anything unusual about his routine while at the base or at home on the specific dates.

"Now I'm going to walk you through November, but I'm going to take you to a date that's probably pretty fresh in your mind, the day that Marie-France Comeau…do you remember how you found out?" Smyth asked.

"I do, yeah. I was sent an email," Williams explained. "As soon as the operations staff in the base learned, they told me. So I got an email. I can't remember if it was late at night or in the morning, but certainly I saw it. I want to say first thing in the morning because I had just come back from Ottawa. I was in Ottawa for…I can't remember what day of the week we're talking about. But I mean obviously when one of your people gets killed…it gets your attention."

Although only Detective Sergeant Smyth was in room 216 with Williams, other investigators, including Detective Sergeant Ed Chafe, Identification Sergeant Frank Cloake, Detective Sergeant Steve Colburn, Detective Inspector David Quigley and Detective Inspector Paul McCrickard, were gathered in a nearby room watching and listening to the interview on a television screen. They were also poring over investigative files from the various occurrences and suggesting questions that Detective Sergeant Smyth should be asking to obtain confessions to the crimes.

Williams said he first met Comeau shortly after being transferred to the base on a day trip spent transporting troops from Edmonton to Trenton on the first leg of their deployment to Afghanistan. He thought it was sometime the previous August or September and she was among the crew on the aircraft. He could not recall exactly when the Military Police informed him that Corporal Comeau's body had been found, but thought he was at home in Tweed when the email message came in.

Smyth continued with his questions, asking about William's background and anything that would "send alarm bells" to the investigative team looking into the four cases. His interrogation was skillful. He built up the pressure and gave Williams no room to maneuver. Weaving his way through a web of evidence, the detective sergeant put the colonel in the vicinity of each crime, but backed off slightly each time an accusation was made, to give Williams the opportunity to confess or call a lawyer. His questions initially were quite general and developed a timeline covering Williams' movements at the time of the various incidents. Smyth slowly introduced pieces of evidence that linked the suspect to the crimes before revealing that teams of investigators were searching his home, the cottage in Tweed and his Canadian Forces Base office in Trenton.

"What would you be willing to give me today to help me move past you in this investigation?" Smyth asks, before suggesting they wanted to take his fingerprints, a blood sample and impressions of the boots he was wearing. Williams says "okay" while his interviewer rambles on about having specially-trained experts outside the room ready to take a saliva swab, fingerprints or anything that Williams will agree to help clear him as a potential suspect.

"Can I assume you're going to be discreet?" Williams asks. "You know this would have a very significant impact on the base if they thought you thought I did this."

Smyth appears sympathetic and assures Williams that they arranged to interview him on a Sunday so not too many people would find out he was being questioned. Before introducing him to the investigators waiting to collect forensic evidence, Smyth did mention to Williams that the military had been assisting them, especially with Comeau's murder. Back inside the room, he suggests to Williams that the break may have given him some time to think. "I know we've been throwing a lot of things at you here, but now you've had some time to think about things," he said. "Is there anything that you're concerned about that Buccal swab matching in any of those four residences?"

Arms folded in front of him and shaking his head from side to side, Williams answers with an almost inaudible "no" before Smyth indicates that DNA is a significant part of their investigation.

Williams is asked about the possibility of an extramarital affair with any of the four women – something he wouldn't want his wife to know. If he did have contact with any of these women in a situation like that, Smyth tells him it would give police an explanation, if his DNA is found to match any of the forensic samples collected at the various crime scenes. "Absolutely not," he said, while turning his head away from Smyth and shifting his body to the left.

"Essentially DNA has become more and more precise," Smyth tells Williams. "When you and I walked in this room earlier today, we could've sat down and talked for 30 seconds. CSI officers could've come in three or four days from now ... did some swabs here and would've found your DNA and my DNA and probably a lot of other people's. And that's what I am getting at ... if you were ever in Laurie's residence, it's quite possible, quite innocent your DNA could be in that residence. Has there ever been a time you've been in there?"

Williams insists he was never in her house and also tells Smyth that he had not visited Comeau's home. At this point, the interview has been going on for just over two and a half hours. "Okay, right," says Smyth. "So you're quite positive there'd be no reason why your DNA would be in any of those locations." Smyth then pressed Williams about the disappearance of Jessica Lloyd, to make sure he didn't know her and had never associated with her in any way. Shaking his head, Williams sat with his arms folded in front of him as the interrogator shuffled through pages of notes in a binder on his lap. The colonel is then asked about the tires on the 2001 Toyota Pathfinder that he drives – just before Williams is told that investigators have tracked the activity on his security swipe card to determine when he was at the Trenton base around the time that Corporal Comeau was murdered.

"I can't remember honestly that that's the day that I had the meeting in Ottawa but if I wasn't at the Base, it was because I was here," William's told Smyth. "I drove to Ottawa in the morning of the day of my meeting. So if it was the Tuesday, then I would have left Tweed. It was a very foggy morning." He said it was mid-afternoon when the meeting ended and he had dinner with his wife at a restaurant near their Ottawa home before he returned to the cottage residence. "I, you know, kissed my wife goodbye and headed back to Tweed to go to work the next day."

Tire tracks from Russell Williams' Toyota found near Lloyd's home

The questioning switched back to the tires on his Toyota. He is asked if he had ever driven his SUV off the roadway near the location where police had set up the roadblock three nights earlier, outside Jessica Lloyd's home. "I want you to rack your brain here," Smyth said. "This is important. So is there anything you can remember doing that, you know, would cause you to drive off the road at that section of roadway?"

Williams shakes his head. "No."

Smyth stares directly at Williams. "Would it surprise you to know that when the CSI officers were looking around her property that they identified a set of tire tracks to the north of her property," he said. "It looks as if a vehicle left the road and drove along the north tree line of Jessica Lloyd's property. Tire tracks are a major source of evidence for us. Shortly after this investigation started, they identified those tires as the same tires on your Pathfinder." Through measurements, he said investigators had been able to confirm that the tracks came from the same model of vehicle Williams was driving, and on the night Jessica vanished, a Belleville police officer had spotted an SUV parked in the field near the trees. "Okay," says Smyth, pressing Williams for an answer. "Do you have any recollection at all of being off that road?"

Williams denies being there. "No," he says. "I was not off the road. No."

Smyth mentions Comeau's name and asks a couple of other questions before telling Williams there are 60 or 70 investigators following up on anything that arises during the interview. "I'm just going to step out and see how things are going. Let me go out and see what's happening and then I'll come back and we'll hopefully continue, okay?" As Williams waits, Smyth consults with investigators who have been working with experts at Ontario's Centre of Forensic Sciences to compare footprints found outside Jessica Lloyd's home with the boots the colonel was wearing when he entered the police building.

Smyth glared at Williams when he returned to the interview room. "I told you when I came in here that I'll treat you with respect and I've asked you to do the same for me," he said, still looking directly at Williams. "We talked about the whole idea of how we've approached you...and trying to be as discreet as possible. But the problem is, Russell, every time I walk out of this room, there's another issue that comes up. It's not issues that point away from you. It's issues that point at you."

Lifting papers that were sitting on top of his leather
binder, Smyth puts photocopies of footprints found at the
Lloyd crime scene on the desk, together with images of the
boots Williams that had been wearing. Smyth invites him
to look at them. "This is the footwear impression of the
person who approached the rear of Jessica Lloyd's house
on the evening of the 28th and 29th of January," he tells
Williams, while explaining they have John Norman, a
world-renowned expert, who can give evidence on footwear
impressions similar to the analysts who compare
fingerprints. "This is a photocopy of the boot that you took
off your foot just a little while ago. These are identical,"
Smyth said while pulling out some additional images.

Williams, who was sitting with his arms folded in front of
him, hunches forward and stares silently at the
photocopies of the footprint and tire impressions on the
desk. He shuffles the pieces of paper around on the desk
while intently studying the images. Moving his arms back,
he looks briefly at Smyth before putting his right hand on
his knee and refocusing his attention on the photocopies.
With his head nodding, he picks up the copies of the
images and again takes a fleeting glance at Smyth before
taking more time to concentrate on the evidence found
outside Jessica Lloyd's home.

"Your vehicle drove up the side of Jessica Lloyd's house.
Your boots walked to the back of Jessica Lloyd's house on
the evening of the 28th and 29th of January," the detective
sergeant said, pausing briefly to give Williams the
opportunity to reply. Instead, he sat silently gazing at the
images on the table. "Okay, you want discretion. We need
to have some honesty, okay, because this is getting out of
control really fast, Russell. Okay. Really, really fast." Still
Williams says nothing and Smyth continues: "This is
getting beyond my control, all right? I came in here a few
hours ago and...I wanted to give you the benefit of the

doubt, but you and I both know you were at Jessica Lloyd's house and I need to know why."

Continuing to look down, Williams struggles to speak: "Well, I don't know what to say. It's…" His voice trails off. The time is now 6:05 p.m. and he's been in the interview room for just slightly more than three hours.

"Well, you need to explain it right now," the detective sergeant continues. "There's a warrant being executed at your residence in Ottawa. Okay, your wife now knows what's going on. There's a search warrant being executed at the residence in Tweed and your vehicle's been seized. Okay. You and I both know they're going to find evidence that links you to those situations. Okay. And you and I both know that the unknown offender male DNA on Marie-France Comeau's body is going to be matched with you, quite possibly before the evening's over. All right, this is a major investigation. The Centre of Forensic Sciences is on call 24 hours a day helping us with this. Your opportunity to take some control here and to have some explanation that anybody's going to believe is quickly expiring."

Williams was nodding slightly and looking down as Smyth spoke, but looked directly at the detective sergeant when Comeau's name was mentioned. His jaw moves involuntary from side to side while gazing at the floor. But as Smyth continues to speak, Williams straightens up in the chair and again folds his arms in front of him.

Smyth continues building pressure. "We're applying the investigators now. Applying for a warrant to search your office. These aren't decisions that we can say yes or no to. This is a practical step in an investigation like this."

Williams looks vacantly to his left before looking back in Smyth's direction. His arms unfold and he touches his collar with his right hand. He appears to be trying to get a grasp on what's happening. He sighs and slumps forward, but his head snaps up when Smyth calls out his name.

"Russell. Russell, listen to me for a second, okay. When that evidence comes in and that DNA match. When that phone rings and somebody knocks on this door...your credibility is gone. Okay. Because this is how credibility works. All right! And I know you're an intelligent person and you probably don't need to hear this explanation, but I also know your mind is racing right now. Okay, 'cause I sat across a lot of people in your position over the years. The bottom line is that as soon as we get that piece of evidence that solidifies it...DNA...as soon as the expert in footwear impressions, the expert in tire impressions calls me (and says) yes, I examined those and they're a match. It's all over. Because as soon as that happens, where's your credibility? Where's your believability?"

Williams acknowledges the words being spoken by the Ontario Provincial Police investigator by nodding his head and saying "mm hmm," but he appears to be searching for some way to escape the cage he's now trapped in.

"What are we going to do, Russell?" Smyth asks. "You know there's only one option."

Lifting his head and looking directly at Smyth, Williams hopes for a solution. "What's the option?" he says, while realizing at that moment he's going to have to confess. But Williams continues to remain silent.

"I don't think you want the cold-blooded psychopath option," says Smyth, as Williams continues to contort his face while staring mostly toward the floor and avoiding any eye contact with his interrogator. "I might be wrong...I've met guys who actually enjoy the notoriety. Got off on it. Got off on having that label. Bernardo being one of them. I don't see that in you. If I saw that in you, I wouldn't even be back in here talking to you...but maybe I'm wrong. Maybe you got me fooled, I don't know. This is over and it can have a bad ending, where Jessica's parents continue to wonder where their daughter is lying."

Smyth pauses, waiting for Williams to respond, but the colonel keeps looking away. He sighs and is obviously tormented, but doesn't utter a word.

"I don't know. I mean obviously there's a huge search underway and it will continue," Smyth persists. "It will continue until her body is found. That may even happen tonight for all I know. Once that happens, then I don't know what other cards you would have to play. What are we going to do?" Smyth doesn't say anything for almost 30 seconds, while waiting for Williams to speak.

"Russell, what are we going to do?"

"Call me Russ, please," says Williams, an obvious sign there's no longer a separation by rank between the two men and he's planning to surrender information that the police need.

"Okay, what are we going to do, Russ?" says Smyth, while continuing to prod for an answer.

Williams, in obvious anguish, tugs at his throat with his right hand. He then rubs the side of his face and holds his cheek before glancing at Smyth. Almost defiantly, Williams again folds his arms across his chest and sits in silence.

There's a noticeable pause before Smyth continues his questioning. "Is Jessica somewhere we can find her easily?" he asks. "Like is it somewhere where I can make a call and tell someone to go to a location they are going to find her, or is this something where we have to go and take a walk. Which direction are we heading here?"

Nothing is said for another 42 seconds. Williams is breathing heavily. His head is tilted to the left and his eyes are transfixed at a spot on the wall below the level of the desk.

"Russ, maybe this would help. Can you tell me what the issue is you are struggling with?"

More silence. This time for 24 seconds.

"What's the use of you struggling now," adds Smyth, who is looking directly at Williams.

There is a sigh while the clock ticks for just over a minute. Then Williams breaks the silence: "It's hard to believe this is happening," he says, while pulling his head up and folding his arms in front of him.

"Why is that?" queries the police officer. "Why is it hard to believe?"

His arms still folded, Williams looks at Smyth as he's speaking and then turns away. There's another sigh and 15 seconds of silence before Williams essentially repeats the words he spoke a few moments earlier. "It's just...it's just hard to believe."

Detective Sergeant Smyth kept prodding Williams for more information and encouraged him to help investigators locate Jessica, who had now been missing for nine days. Williams hadn't said she was dead, but knowing the colonel was involved, Smyth didn't think there was much hope she would still be alive. At this point, however, his main concern was finding Jessica.

During the interview, Williams was asked who issued a directive telling base personnel they were not obligated to speak with police and to seek legal counsel before answering any questions. "I don't think that was issued," he said. "That is news to me. I have a legal officer that reports to me who may have given that direction...but that's the first time I've heard it. If that's true, that's the first time I've heard of that."

Williams admits he has two immediate concerns. He wonders what his wife is going through after learning that her husband is under suspicion for some serious crimes. He's also worried about the impact it will have on the Canadian Forces. He had been sitting with his arms folded in front of him, but he lifts his left hand to his cheek while turning his head away. Williams appears to be crying and just sits silently.

"Where do we go Russ?" Smyth asks. "Is there anything you want from me? Is there anything you want me to explain? Is there something missing you're struggling with that I can shed some light on for you?"

"I'm struggling with how upset my wife is right now," Williams replies, trying to dismiss the level Smyth is probing into his soul. The detective sergeant is hoping the Colonel will realize he's been caught in the snare and provide details where Jessica can be found. "Russ, what are you looking for?"

Williams tells Smyth that he's concerned police are "tearing apart" his wife's brand new house.

"So am I," the investigator says. "But if nobody tells them what's there and what's not, they don't have any choice." Increasing the pressure, Smyth explains that police are prepared to make use of any resources that are available to obtain evidence that will help identify the killer of Marie-France Comeau, the two sexual assaults and the disappearance of Jessica Lloyd. Several times through the interrogation, Smyth has left Williams alone in the room to think while he is briefed about what police have uncovered during the various searches. He comes back and talks about the steps that could be taken if investigators believe evidence may be concealed on a computer. "Computers have been brought to Microsoft," he says. "They will be picked apart. You can't erase ink from computers. It doesn't happen. I'm sure you've seen that. I'm sure that's pretty common knowledge these days...it just doesn't happen. They sell programs that try and help people clean their computers...but our guys are pulling that stuff out all the time. The FBI's pulling that stuff out all the time."

Smyth estimates the investigation that he's involved in will cost more than ten million dollars. "They will say no to nothing," he tells Williams. "Any request this major case manager makes on this case, they've already been told it's approved. Don't even bother asking." Smyth sits silent for 33 seconds, with his left elbow on the desk and his hand cradling his head. He stares intently at Williams who rubs his forehead. He has his head down and his eyes are focused on the floor. "So what am I doing Russ?" asks Smyth. "I put my best foot forward here for you, bud. I really have. I don't know what else to do to make you understand the impact of what's happening here."

Williams shifts his body to look directly at Smyth and then turns away, again sitting silently for 20 seconds. He still seems to be trying to grasp the gravity of his predicament.

"Do we talk?" asks Smyth.

He continues holding his head down when he starts to speak, but then looks directly at the interviewer. "I want to minimize the impact on my wife."

"So do I," responds Smyth.

"So how do we do that?" Williams asks.

"Well, you can start by telling the truth."

Another 28 seconds passes. "Okay," says Williams.

"All right, so where is she?" Detective Sergeant Smyth demands. After another pause of several seconds, Williams asks for a map. "Is she close to where she lives?" says Smyth. "I've got maps of that general area. Which town is she near? Why don't we start there."

Williams requests a map covering an area from the tiny hamlet of Kaladar on Highway 7 to south of Tweed, but he can't seem to pinpoint the location on the one Smyth unfolds. "I need more," he says. "I need a real map." He also says they will find Jessica outside, indicating that she's dead. He then uses the map provided by Smyth to show the general area where the body was dumped, but insists on a more detailed map to pinpoint the exact location.

Williams says Lloyd's body is close to a road, while poring over the diagram of the Tweed area that Smyth was carrying in his leather portfolio. He also tells him she wasn't buried and would be easily seen by anyone walking over the site. Williams then points to a location in a rural area east of Tweed. He doesn't know the name of the road. "I'm not sure."

As Smyth prepares to leave the room to get a more detailed map, he asks Williams some critical questions to confirm that he was the person responsible for the killing.

"How long has she been there?" he asks, standing casually and slipping his hands in his pockets.

Isolated spot behind rock where Jessica Lloyd's body found

"A little over a week," says Williams. He also asks for a drink of water.

Smyth: "Was it fairly quick from the time she left?"

Williams: "Friday night."

"So where does she go between Thursday night and Friday night?" Smyth says.

Williams: "In Tweed."

Smyth: "With you?"

Williams: "Yeah."

"How long was she alive for?" Smyth asks, while scratching the side of his head with his left hand.

"Almost twenty-four hours," says Williams. "Not quite."

"Okay Russ," says Smyth, standing and extending his hand like the victor in a chess game. "You're doing the right thing here, okay."

The two men shake hands.

"Well, again, my interest is into making my wife's life a little easier," said Williams in a faltering voice. "And with her family as well."

"Oh, we share that," says Smyth, knowing that investigators on the team will soon be at the home of Jessica's mother with the heartbreaking news that her daughter is dead.

As Smyth was about to pick up his binder and leave the room to get a detailed map of the area, Williams says he doesn't want police wasting their time at his Ottawa home. "I'll tell you where the memory stick cards are," he says.

"Where are they?" asks Smyth, who continues standing casually with his hands in his trouser pockets while looking directly at Williams, who is sitting with his arms folded in front of him and his head slightly bowed. He says there are some memory sticks in camera bag and a couple of memory cards in his desk drawer. "I have erased them but I expect you'll be able to draw images of Jessica and I," Williams volunteers.

"What about Marie?" Smyth inquires.

Williams sits silently for a few moments before raising his head and glancing directly at Smyth, then looks back down. "There may be images on there as well," he says.

"And the two women from September?" asks Smyth.

Williams nods his head a couple of times while rocking back and forth slightly in the chair. "Yep," he says, and when asked if the images have been stored anywhere else, he mentions two hard drives that he's hidden in the house. He offers to draw a diagram to show where they are concealed.

"Do you want to do that while I...while I'm out getting a map?" asks Smyth, as he pulls a pen from his pocket and rips a page from the binder. While positioning the paper in front of him, he asks Williams if he wants anything to eat. "I'll leave that right there, okay," he says.

As Smyth is picking up the now closed binder and preparing to leave the room to get the detailed map, Williams again turns toward him. "I do want to talk to you, Jim," he says.

"That's the plan, okay," Smyth replies. "I'll be right back."

Smyth has now heard Williams confess to killing Jessica Lloyd and Marie-France Comeau, and to sexually assaulting Jane Doe and Laurie Massicotte. The task force that had been pulled together three days earlier had found the serial predator and solved the four cases they had been assigned to investigate.

Coming back to the interview room, Smyth hands Williams some water and tells him he's got someone looking around for an actual map. He has also generated one from a computer. After taking a gulp from the Styrofoam cup, Williams studies the area around Tweed and then moves his finger across the page. "Point seven," he says. "A kilometer from this intersection on this side of the road."

Smyth notes the location is Cary Road and mentions East Hungerford to confirm the spot for Williams, but also to tell nearby officers monitoring the conversation where

Jessica's body can be found. An investigative team is already standing by in the Tweed area in order to reach the site as quickly as possible after it is pinpointed by Williams. "How far off the road is she?" Smyth asks nonchalantly, as Williams slumps back on his chair, arms folded in front of him and his legs stretched outward.

"Forty feet," he replies.

Smyth starts to ask if she's buried, but then remembered that Williams already indicated Jessica's body is out in the open. "Is she covered with anything?"

Williams says she's wrapped up. "She's on the surface, just a grey something or other cover."

Smyth has drawn his chair close to Williams while questioning him about where the victim's body was dumped. To make sure the killer was now fully cooperating, the detective sergeant said there was a very obvious question he had for him. "When they go there, and they'll be there shortly...they are going to find her?"

"Oh, yeah," he replies. It was now two minutes to seven in the evening. The interview had taken four hours and 55 minutes to this point.

As Smyth prepares again to leave the room, he gets the impression that Williams wants to say something.

"Just that this place my wife has ... it's been a dream for the better part of the year ... so I'm keen to get them what they need so they can leave her alone," says Williams. As he's opening the door to make sure police are on the way to find Jessica's body, Smyth tells Williams the team will be doing it's best to keep things as low key as possible at his wife's home.

Returning to continue the interview, Smyth asks Williams what he wants to talk about.

"I guess it's pretty wide open now," says Williams. "What do you want to know?"

Smyth asks if he wants to work forward or backwards and when Williams says it doesn't matter, the investigator suggests they start with Jessica.

"Well, I saw her in her house on her treadmill," he says, still sitting with his arms folded in front of him and his head down. There were long pauses between sentences and he began recalling details from the time he broke into Jessica's home to her eventual murder. "I noticed she wasn't there Thursday, so I got in the house to look around. Then I left," he said. Noticing later that she was at home, Williams told how he entered through the back patio door while she was asleep. "I woke her up. I didn't hit her. I only hit her once Friday night."

He told about raping her at her home before forcing her to his vehicle and driving her to his residence in Tweed. "I spent the day in Tweed and I hit her as we were walking. She thought we were leaving. I hit her on the back of the head. I was surprised it...her skull gave way. She was there and immediately unconscious. Then I strangled her."

Smyth asks what he struck her with and Williams told him a flashlight. He admits the attack took place inside his house near the fireplace and, although he had cleaned the floor, he was sure that police would be able to find traces of her blood in the grouting of the tiled floor. There were long pauses between his sentences.

"There's quite a bit of blood," he said. "I hadn't expected it....I'd expected to knock her out ... but obviously it

generated a lot of blood. You wouldn't see it. Not at
all...but the right science ... will show it. I'm sure."

He tells Smyth that Jessica was fully dressed when he
clubbed her on the head and was in the same clothes
when he dumped the body.

Williams is asked about Marie-France Comeau.

"There was an open window in the basement of her house.
When she was away I went in there a couple of nights
before she came home. Looked around. I went back there
late at night when she was home. Was on the phone in her
bedroom. She actually discovered me in the basement.
She was trying to get her cat to come upstairs and the cat
was in the basement. It seen me and was fixated on me in
the corner. She couldn't get the cat up, so she came
downstairs to try and get the cat. I'm not quite sure why
she came over to me. I guess the cat was staring at me
and she was wondering what the cat was staring at. The
lights were on so when she spotted me I had the same
flashlight. I subdued her...tied her up ... brought her
upstairs and ... strangled her later in the morning. Well
more suffocated her, right. Some tape. Left her there."
There were long pauses as he spoke and it took two
minutes and six seconds to recount the details of his
confrontation with Comeau in her basement.

Williams said he was hiding behind the furnace and was
spotted immediately when Comeau approached. "I had the
same flashlight and it was ... she saw me right away ... so
it was just ... I hit her a couple of times ... around her
head ... to try and knock her out. It didn't, but she was
bleeding a little bit. Eventually after a struggle...subdued
her." He said there wasn't a lot of blood, but the flashlight
had broken her skin. Williams also said Comeau didn't
recognize him because he was using a cap pulled down
over his forehead and a headband which covered the lower

part of his face. The way he was masked left only his eyes visible.

"So you go upstairs and you said she suffocated?" says Smyth.

"Well, I suffocated her," says Williams. "I put tape on her. I put tape on her mouth and then I put tape on her nose and held it there so she couldn't breathe."

After Comeau died, Williams said he removed the duct tape from the victim but couldn't remember what he did with it. "I probably threw it in the garbage." He told Smyth that the metal flashlight, which is red with three D-size batteries, is still at his home in Tweed. When asked if he took anything from either victim, Williams mentions stealing some of their underwear.

He told Smyth the garments are in boxes in a basement storage room at his Ottawa home. Williams acknowledges that police will find sixty pieces of underwear belonging to Jessica and Marie-France.

"So you took 60 pieces from between the two of them?" Smyth inquires.

"Yeah," Williams responds.

"Does any of the underwear in those boxes belong to anyone other than Marie-France or Jessica?" asks Smyth.

"Yeah. There's some from each of the other two women," Williams replies, while glancing at Smyth – appearing to look for a reaction.

"Okay," says Smyth. "Why don't we talk about those two women."

Williams said he spotted his first victim while out boating. "I got into the house while she was asleep. She was alone and I just hit her with my hand while she was sleeping. Subdued her mostly just with my weight on top of her. Had her take off her pajamas. Took some pictures. Took some of her underwear and left."

While looking up and rubbing his chin, he said it was much the same with the second victim. "I went through the back of the house. She was sleeping. Not in her bedroom, but her, you know, in front of the TV. Very much the same story. Not much difference at all. I did have the flashlight. That time I hit her." He said the blow didn't knock her out, so he also used his weight to pin her down. Williams said he removed her clothing and took some pictures before leaving.

"Why do you think these things happened?" Smyth asked.

"I don't know," says Williams.

"Have you spent much time thinking about that?" the interrogator continues, as Williams tilts his head and looks directly at him with an almost quizzical look on his face.

"Yeah, but I don't know the answers," says Williams, again looking down. "I'm pretty sure the answers don't matter." When asked if he liked or disliked the women, Williams told Smyth he didn't know them. "I have met Marie-France that one time in our airplane." He also described Jessica as a very nice girl, but when asked why he killed her, Williams said she knew he was taking pictures and police would have connected the attack to the two cases in Tweed.

"So if you didn't take pictures, what would you have done with her?" Smyth asks, continuing to sit with his left arm leaning on the small desk and both hands folded together.

"I don't know," Williams replies, as he again looks directly at Smyth.

"I mean she's right at your house," Smyth says. "Let me ask you this. Two lived, right, and two died. What was the difference in your mind..."

Williams interrupts, saying there was a lot of focus "for obvious reasons" on photographs being taken of the first two women. "So anybody else telling stories about pictures, right, would have been a straight line."

Smyth asked if Williams believed he was considered a suspect in the Tweed assaults at the time Marie-France Comeau was murdered, but he shook his head and said no. However, because she was serving with the military, he suggested it would have drawn a direct link to him and the Tweed attacks if she told about being photographed. "It would have been ... difficult for investigators to ignore that connection."

Smyth acknowledges that his comment made sense and then asked Williams about the first time he saw Jessica. "You see her on the Wednesday night, right, on her treadmill. How did you see her?" Williams tells him the basement window was open as he drove past her home. "Okay. Did you stop to look at the house or how does that catch your eye as you drive by?"

"I was looking to see who was ... who was where," Williams replies. "Don't know that area very well, so I was just keeping my eyes open."

When asked if he stopped and went for a closer look, Williams told Smyth he just kept driving, but went back the following night. He has been looking down with his arms folded in front of him, but suddenly stands and grabs the cup of water from the table and walks three paces before leaning against the wall. "She was out," he said as the video camera continued recording all aspects of the interview, just like his cameras had taped the sexual assaults and murders. "Got in through the kitchen window." He acknowledged looking around to determine if she lived alone.

"I left the house and … then … she came home," Williams said. "Hadn't been in the house very long, so I watched for a little bit to see if she was alone. She was and I went in…when she went in to sleep." Williams continues leaning against the wall and Smyth presses for more details. "Well, I snuck up to the side of her bed…expecting to try to knock her out. She woke up but … she did as I said … I didn't hit her." He ordered her onto her stomach and tied her up with a rope he'd brought with him. After binding her hands behind her back, Williams says he removed the track pants and top she was wearing.

"Okay … and then what happened?" Smyth asks, as Williams walks, then slumps back into the chair.

"I raped her," he says in an almost inaudible voice, after another long pause.

"A rape can mean a lot of different things," states Smyth. "What kind of sexual act took place?" When Williams says vaginal and oral, his interrogator asks for a more precise explanation of what happened and who was performing oral sex.

"Me on her and her on me," Williams responds, while looking vacantly across the room. He also tells Smyth he didn't use a condom. "I started with oral sex...then I raped her...and later on I made her perform oral sex on me." He also told about putting a plastic zip-tie around her neck and telling her that it would be pulled tight if she didn't do what she was told.

When asked what happened next, Williams said he continued to rape the victim and then had her put on some of her underwear. "I took some pictures," he said. "Lots of pictures...then got her dressed and walked back to the truck." He couldn't recall at what point he decided to abduct Jessica. "I'm not sure. That wasn't necessarily always the plan, but at some point," he said. "I was there for three hours...three and a bit."

Smyth asked if he remembered the conversation as they were preparing to leave. "What was she saying?" When Williams said she was certainly cooperative, Smyth interrupted. "Cooperative can mean a number of different things," he said. "Was she excited about leaving with you...and I don't want to be sarcastic, but did she try and negotiate with you at all or what did she say?"

Williams had interrupted Smyth's question to say "she just didn't put up much of a fuss" – then added: "Well...I told her that I would let her go later on." He said her hands were bound behind her back when they left the house and she was wearing brown suede shoes that were part of the description when she was reported missing. It is obvious that Williams has read all news reports of the disappearance. He told Smyth about leading her to his truck and putting her in the front passenger seat before driving straight to his home in Tweed. He thought they arrived sometime between 4:30 a.m. and 5:30 a.m. But he didn't know the exact time.

No one had come to Jessica's house while he was inside with her, but Williams recalls someone did drive up to the house while he was waiting for her to get home. "I thought it was her," he said. "But then they left. I was outside at the time." He couldn't clearly see the person and had no idea what type of vehicle they were driving. Moments after the vehicle left, Jessica pulled into her driveway. He had no idea while in the backyard that a police officer from the Belleville Police Service had stopped to check the home and had noted some details about his vehicle in the field. "I just saw lights," Williams said.

He said Jessica needed to use the washroom and he also gave her a quick shower before taking her to his bedroom, where she slept for a while. She remained tied up and Williams told Smyth he covered her eyes "from the beginning" with duct tape so that she couldn't see him. He admitted removing the tape from her eyes after she was killed, but said he used the remainder of the duct tape to secure the grey covering that was wrapped around her body before she was dumped.

Smyth continued pumping Williams for answers. "You said who went to sleep when you came home." He also seemed a bit puzzled about the shower that had been mentioned.

"Well, we both went in. I washed her off after she'd been to the bathroom," William replied. "We both went to sleep, but she was tied up. I tied the rope, you know, so I could fall asleep a little bit ... and she could move without waking me up."

"I'm trying to picture how that would be so the rope's tied to what on her?" asks Smyth.

"It's tied in her hands ... behind her back," says Williams. "Then the rope just wrapped around me a couple of times so there was no slack." He told Smyth he'd slept a couple of hours but didn't know if Jessica had fallen asleep. "I mean … we were up and down so it wasn't two hours straight. It was two hours in bed, but there wasn't much sleep … just lying there probably." Williams takes a deep breath and then mentions that she had a seizure. "She felt it coming on," he said.

"She'd had some before … lasted … well quite a while. Got her dressed … into the family room … and anyway, she recovered." He said the seizure lasted about 15 minutes and she told him it was brought on by stress. "She suggested it was stress … she felt herself, you know, starting to tense up. She thought she was going to have a seizure. It's, you know, convulsions…is what she was having." Williams said he stayed with her, talked her through it and made sure she didn't bite her tongue.

Following the attack, he said Jessica was exhausted and lay on the floor. He covered her with a blanket and she slept for at least an hour. "I told her earlier that…before I let her go…I wanted to take some pictures of her … in her underwear … and … have sex with her," Williams told Smyth. "After she'd had a rest for an hour or so … I had her put on a number of different things she had." He pauses often while speaking and took deep breaths before starting and finishing what he was saying. He knew his words were leading him to a penitentiary cell. He admitted taking numerous bra and panty sets from Jessica's home. "She put those on and I took pictures."

Smyth wants to know if Williams was in any of the photographs and what was depicted on the images.

"Well, I am with her," he says. "They're on the hard drives. You'll see there's video as well. There's a video of … you know … almost four hours, I guess. Initially at her place … of … me … raping her … and then … I was running the video and then taking still pictures. The video pretty much covers everything."

Smyth asks if Williams made video recordings at any of the other crime scenes.

"At Marie-France's, as well," he says.

Smyth: "The same type of activity?"

"Yeah," says Williams, adding that he didn't have her putting on underwear for poses, but he did take digital images and video, which show what was going while he was inside her house.

Smyth steered the conversation back to Jessica's killing and Williams said when he finished taking photographs of her, he helped her get dressed. "She thought she was leaving. She had a bite to eat...some fruit...and then as we were walking out...I struck her on the back of the head."

"Okay," said Smyth. "When did you decide to do that?"

"Well, I was pretty sure that I wasn't going to let her leave," Williams said. "But, you know, the idea of striking her on the head was developed in the afternoon. I thought I would be able to knock her out and then I was...I was going to strangle her."

When asked what happened when he actually clubbed her, Williams said it felt like her skull gave way a little bit. "There was a lot of blood. I think that's what happened. She was immediately unconscious." Williams sits silently for more than 10 seconds before saying: "And then I strangled her."

He admits to having used the rope that had been binding her hands and pulling it tightly around her neck.

"How did you know she was dead?" Smyth asks.

Williams takes a deep breath and then responds. "Well ... er... her body stopped moving."

The interview was entering its sixth hour.

When asked what he did after the slaying, Williams told Smyth that he bound Jessica with duct tape, left her in a fetal position and cleaned the blood from the floor before carrying the body from the house. "I put her in the garage," he said. "It was very cold ... and then I went to the base." Williams explained during the interview that he left Tweed sometime between 9 p.m. and 10 p.m. and the following morning piloted an aircraft to California. He returned later that evening and drove to his home in Ottawa. Williams told Smyth he didn't get home until just before midnight because he got a bit of sleep in his vehicle after stopping at a donut shop in Brockville, 109 miles from the base. Sunday, Monday and part of Tuesday were spent in Ottawa before Williams returned to Tweed. The video of the interview shows him taking a deep breath. "I took Jessica's body to that spot," he said. "It was pretty late. It was midnightish. I'd say between midnight and 1 a.m. on Wednesday."

He drove almost half a mile or point seven kilometers on the odometer of his vehicle and tucked her body behind a large rock that was well off the roadway. Williams didn't know why he precisely measured the distance and selected that exact location, but it's part of his psyche and provides some insight into why he is so methodical and was compelled to document his crimes in detail. "That's just the way I am," he said. "Numbers, I have to know the numbers." Williams also told Smyth that he wrapped a couple of towels around Jessica's head while binding her body with duct tape and had never gone back to the spot where she was dumped.

He acknowledged vacuuming the house and washing the floor in an attempt to clean up any evidence that a murder had occurred. Williams also admitted cleaning his truck. "It was a mess," he said.

Smyth began getting details about Comeau's killing.

"When did it first occur to you to go to her house?" he asked.

"Probably in October … November," Williams says after pausing a lengthy time and shaking his head before answering. "I'm not quite sure, but somewhere in that time period. He knew she lived alone but didn't know why he targeted her.

"I'm just trying to understand … like why her versus, you know, the dozens of other women you've probably come across on a daily basis," Smyth asked.

Williams sat silently for a few moments and then struggled to give an answer. "I don't know," he said. "You know … I … you know … I went out there when she wasn't home just to see where she lived …" He said nothing more and Smyth's question went unanswered. But he did give details about entering her home while she was away, two days before she was murdered. Williams said he broke in through an unlocked basement window after pulling away the screen. "I looked around and made sure that she was living there alone," he said.

"Okay," Smyth says. "So you go in and…you're in her house figuring out if she lives alone. Do you do anything else that night?"

"Yeah," Williams replies.

"I was playing with her…underwear."

"What do you mean playing with her underwear?" queries the detective sergeant.

"Well...wearing it," says Williams. When asked if anything was stolen from the home, he admits taking "a few pieces" of her lingerie from a drawer. Williams also said it was the only time he was in her home prior to the murder.

Now convinced that Marie-France Comeau lived alone, Williams said he went to her house sometime between 10:30 p.m. and 11 p.m. on November 23, 2009. After parking his Nissan Pathfinder on an extension of her street, almost half a mile away, he cut through a field to her home. While in the backyard, he saw her through a window, talking on the telephone. Williams said that he could see she was on the phone and hear her voice, but couldn't make out what she was saying. The interview has been going on for six hours and 13 minutes. Williams again pauses and fidgets in his chair before standing up and leaning against the wall just prior to continuing his answer. He tells Smyth he entered the house through the same basement window and was hoping to wait until she went to sleep.

He's standing against the wall with his hands tucked into his belt behind his back while continuing his confession.

Williams told Smyth he wore a sweatshirt, Dockers and the same two-piece mask that was used to cover his face in the previous sexual attacks, adding that the items he took with him into the homes would be found at his house in Ottawa. When asked about his plan after getting into Marie-France's house, Williams said he made his way over to the furnace. "I was waiting for her to go to bed. "Well, she didn't. She came down looking for the cat," he said, while walking to the desk where he took several sips of water before sitting back down. "As I described, I subdued her. Hit her with the flashlight ... essentially wrestled her to the ground and tied her up." He used a 20-foot piece of green rope that he brought from his boat to bind her hands behind her back. When Marie-France came down to the basement, she had a shawl around her shoulders, but it fell off when she got into a defensive stance after spotting him. "She called out ... you bastard," he said. "Then I subdued her as I described. They were more glancing ... glancing blows that cut her skin but weren't doing much else. She fell over, then I subdued her when she tripped. Then I took her upstairs."

Smyth asks if she was able to walk upstairs on her own. "No," replied Williams. "She passed out ... on the stairs. Then I carried her up." He suggested she was probably woozy from the blows to her head. She was taken to her bedroom and placed on the bed. "I think she's on the bed," Williams said, when asked by Smyth what happened. "I raped her over a period of time."

Williams says he didn't wear a condom, but also told the interviewer that he didn't reach a climax. He answered "no" when asked if he ejaculated at any point while with the victim. The sexual assault took between 90 minutes and a couple of hours and after that Williams said he suffocated her with duct tape.

"Why did you decide to use that method versus something else?" Smyth asks.

"I don't know," he said, shaking his head. "I just did. I had thought about strangling her earlier. It's on the video. It was a short ... short-lived attempt. She struggled quite a bit. I decided that I needed to suffocate her." He explains the video will show him putting his hands on her throat and Marie-France fighting him off very aggressively.

Again moving from the chair and positioning himself against the wall, Williams estimates he was in the house about four hours. He thought he spent 30 or 40 minutes in the basement before the victim came down, but it could have been close to an hour. "I didn't have a watch on so I'm not sure," he said, while going over and putting the now empty Styrofoam cup on the desk. Apart from calling Williams a bastard, Marie-France didn't say anything else, he said. "I taped her mouth. There's no conversation." He told Smyth he put gray-colored duct tape over her mouth as soon as he brought her upstairs. He said she was quite aggressive. "I was confident she would have screamed ... given the chance." Williams said she had yelled in the basement. "When she discovered me she was very vocal," he said. "She screamed quite a bit until I subdued her."

After collecting some of her underwear, Williams said he left the residence through the rear patio door. In an effort to cover his tracks, he had turned off his BlackBerry communication device when he left Trenton so that his route couldn't be traced. Before leaving the victim's house, he took time to wash the sheets from her bed in order to destroy any physical evidence or DNA that might have been left. He told Smyth he didn't wait around to watch the laundry complete the entire washing cycle. "I just put them in and put a whole bunch of bleach in and let it go."

Williams left the Brighton home sometime between 4 a.m. and 4:30 a.m. and drove to Ottawa to attend a vital meeting later that morning. It dealt with the acquisition of giant four-engine Boeing C 17 Globemaster transport aircraft which were purchased to replace Canada's outdated C 130 Hercules cargo and troop carriers.

Continuing the interview, Detective Sergeant Smyth asks Williams to recall details the night of September 24, 2009, when he first entered Laurie Massicotte's home on Cosy Cove Lane. "I knew she lived alone," he said. "She lives three doors down and ... I didn't know her, but knew she is pretty (much) alone." Williams said she had a boyfriend, but he didn't seem to be around. "She told me that they were fighting ... so that's why he hadn't been there." A couple of nights earlier, Williams had entered Laurie's home to make sure she still lived alone. "I looked around to see if there were any permanent signs of her boyfriend," he said. "I guess I took one or two pieces of her underwear."

Smyth asks him to recall the night of September 29 and the early hours of September 30 when he attacked Massicotte. "It was pretty late," he says. "I probably got into the house around midnight. She was asleep on the couch ... though I didn't know that, but I knew she was in there." He told of entering through a rear window leading to a sun room. "I had to remove the screen and slide it up. I got into the house and she was asleep in front of the TV." Williams was wearing the same covering on his face, the headband and cap. He also wore a dark sweatshirt and pants.

"We have been through this," he says with a smile, while looking directly at Smyth. "I struck her with the flashlight...thinking it would knock her out. It didn't. I subdued her ... took some pictures ... left. Was probably in the house about two and a half hours."

"That's a pretty short description for two and a half hours," Smyth suggests.

"Well, we talked. I told her I wasn't going to hurt her," Williams says. "I told her that there were other guys in the house ... robbing her. My job was just to control her." He said she was frightened and thought she'd be seriously hurt. "She said that she was worried she was going to be killed," he told Smyth. "I said I'm not going to kill you." He said he took pictures with a Sony digital camera of the victim both clothed and unclothed. No video images were taken. Before leaving, Williams told her to either count or wait a number of minutes before calling the police. He made his way out and went directly to his home about two hundred feet away. After sleeping for a couple of hours, Williams said he went to work.

"All right, do you remember how her clothing was removed?" Smyth queries.

"Because her hands were tied behind her back ... I think I cut off her top and then pulled off her bottom," says Williams, glancing first at Smyth and then looking down at the floor. He used either a folding Exacto knife or Leatherman to cut through her clothing and acknowledged using the same knife to remove Jessica's shirt and bra.

When asked about the September 16 entry into Jane Doe's home, Williams said it was the first time he'd been inside her house. "Just 'cause," he responds when asked by Smyth why she'd been chosen as a victim. "I'd seen her ... and she was cute," Williams replied, scratching his left shoulder with his right hand and looking down at the floor. "That's it."

He entered through an unlocked side window after cutting the screen. Williams, who wore the same clothing he was wearing when he broke into Laurie Massicotte's house, went to the bedroom, where Jane Doe was sleeping. "I stood over her for a while and then I ... hit her on the left side of her head. Just with my hand. Just woke her up," he says. "We struggled ... then I just lay on her and...very much like I described a little bit ago ... pulled her top down ... took off her pants ... took some pictures and left."

Smyth asks if the victim said anything to him.

"Well, all kinds of things," Williams said. "She had a young baby just next door in the other room ... eight months old

... so obviously concerned about the baby. Concerned for herself. I assured her I was not going to hurt her ... physically anyway." He admits taking some of her underwear just like he had done at Massicotte's home. He explains they will find it stuffed in a green duffle bag in a cupboard off the laundry room at his house in Tweed.

After chatting a little more about the photographs that had been taken of the underwear, Smyth tells Williams he has only a couple more questions.

"I guess what's on my mind right now, Russ, is what made you decide to tell me this tonight?" he asks.

"Mostly to make my wife's life easier," Williams replies.

"How do you feel about what you've done?" Smyth asks.

"Disappointed," he tells him.

"Okay, let me ask you this," Smyth says. "If this didn't come to the point it's at right now ... if for whatever reason you didn't end up on our radar, so to speak ... do you think it would've happened again?"

"I was hoping not," Williams replies, "but I can't answer the question."

Smyth leaves the room, but returns a short time later to get additional information about the slaying of Marie-France Comeau. "Russ, just a few details that I wanted to cover off," he says. "There's a hole in the drywall...do you recall how that happened." When Williams says he cannot remember, Smyth asks if some clothing had been used to tie her up in the basement.

"Yeah, I tied her up against one of those poles in the basement, initially," Williams responds. "I went outside to put the screen back on and secure the window." He explains it was shortly after she was subdued that he tied her up. It was at that point he put duct tape on her mouth … not when he got her upstairs. Moving his head as though he's picturing the events as they unfolded, Williams said he went outside to put the screen back on the window, so that no one would know how he got into the house.

Smyth then asks about some blood in the upstairs bathroom. "It looks like something's occurred there," he says. "Do you remember that?"

"Yep," Williams replies. "She had passed out on the bed and I had gone to look out the front window to see if anybody was coming. She got up and closed the bedroom door and raced into the bathroom trying to get somebody's attention, but her mouth was taped and her hands were tied."

"What did you do as a result of that?" asks Smyth.

"I just got in and subdued her again," he says. "I got her back into the bedroom. Didn't do anything, just regained control of her."

"If I remember correctly … there's a little bit of blood in there," says Smyth. "Do you know … how that would have occurred?"

"All the blood was from the initial hits as I was trying to subdue her," Williams tells his interrogator. "Her skin breaking with the blows to her head." He didn't recall seeing any blood, but explains that the light hadn't been turned on. He told about removing the duct tape after she died, moving her to the bed and covering Marie-France with a duvet. When he couldn't explain why he did that and had recounted all the details about the two homicides and sexual assaults, Detective Sergeant Smyth tells him that news of his arrest has spread through the Ottawa Police headquarters building and one of the city detectives had mentioned a number of unsolved incidents that have occurred in recent years.

"I was going to get into that," Williams said casually, but at that point he told Smyth he couldn't continue because he desperately needed to use the washroom.

When brought back to the interview room, he began recalling what he remembered about numerous burglaries in Ottawa and Tweed. It was 1:33 a.m. when the interview officially ended.

The startling revelations uttered by Russell Williams during the interrogation focused worldwide attention on the crime spree and the senseless deaths of Marie-France Comeau and Jessica Lloyd. Print and electronic media outlets across North America and in other countries carried articles about the colonel's arrest, and coverage continued until his incarceration. Major United States television networks produced news specials for public affairs programs and on July 21, 2012, the U.S. Lifetime Network broadcast a docudrama on the Williams' case. The production – An Officer and a Murderer – starring Gary Cole, Laura Harris and Rossif Sutherland, was based on the crimes of Russell Williams, but has a detective in a rural community teaming up with a Toronto homicide investigator to bring the perpetrator to justice.

Chapter Ten

Williams had been in the interview room almost ten and a
half hours when Smyth got word that members of the
investigative team were unable to find the body of Jessica
Lloyd. They were at the precise location on the map that
Williams had marked, but they couldn't find her remains.
He had agreed to fully cooperate with police and had
already given a sample of his DNA, an impression from the
tread on the boots he wore to the police station and had
handed over his BlackBerry communication device so it
could be analyzed by technical experts.

Arrangements had been made to have a number of
specialists available to quickly assess any evidence
obtained during police searches and make immediate
comparisons of any evidence obtained from the suspect.
Results were immediately given to Smyth to assist with his
questioning.

The first concrete evidence came when experts concluded
that the pattern on Williams' boots matched footwear
impressions found near a fire pit behind Jessica's home. It
also meant the person in the interview room was
responsible for the woman's disappearance and Smyth
was able to greatly increase the pressure on the colonel. It
was 6:21 p.m. when Williams was told his boots had been
linked to the murder scene and police were preparing to
search his homes in Ottawa and Tweed. It was an hour
and twenty minutes later when he confessed to murdering
Jessica and asked for a map so that he could show where
her body was dumped.

Police were directed to a spot on Cary Road, six miles east
of Tweed, between East Hungerford Road and Marlbank
Road. Jessica was supposed to be behind a rock about

forty feet from the road, but the officers searching the area in the darkness found no sign of her. Williams had been forthright in every other detail he provided and Smyth found it hard to believe he wasn't telling the truth regarding where her body had been left. The interview concluded at 1:33 a.m. when Williams agreed to go with Smyth to pinpoint the spot where he had dumped the victim's body.

Before leaving the Ottawa Police building, Williams was formally arrested for killing Marie-France Comeau and Jessica Lloyd, breaking into the homes of Jane Doe and Laurie Massicotte and sexually attacking the two women. Although the crime spree had been going on since September 2007, this was the first occasion that police had enough evidence to positively identify and apprehend the culprit. At this point it was also necessary to assign investigators to gather evidence on the burglaries of homes in Ottawa and Tweed, since many were never reported to the authorities.

Smyth and Detective Sergeant Coburn drove with Williams to Cary Road, and at 3:47 a.m. Jessica's body was located behind the rock that had been described in the interview. They noticed her head was wrapped with towels and bound with duct tape, as had been earlier mentioned by Williams when interrogated by Smyth. The crime scene was sealed off and forensic investigators painstakingly spent the remainder of the night and early daylight hours collecting all possible evidence before the body was taken to the morgue at the Centre of Forensic Sciences in Toronto.

The same pathologist who performed the autopsy on Marie-France Comeau, Dr. Michael Pollanen, the director of the centre, conducted a post mortem examination on the body of Jessica Lloyd. He determined she died from strangulation, but also noted other injuries, including significant blunt impact trauma to her head. There was a laceration on her scalp where she was struck with a flashlight and there was bruising and abrasions to her forearms, wrists, legs and on her back. He also observed ligature marks where her arms had been tied together with a rope.

Constable Jayne Pellerin, an identification officer with the Forensic Identification Unit at the OPP's Belleville District Headquarters, attended the autopsy. She took swabs from the victim's vagina and fingernails on her right hand, hoping to obtain a genetic fingerprint from DNA which would identify the attacker. Analysis later showed Williams could not be excluded as a suspect, but the findings weren't narrow enough to confirm that he was the person who had sex with Jessica Lloyd or was responsible for physically assaulting her. However, his confession, and the photographs and videos he took during the attack were "proof positive" that he was responsible for her death.

Although the interview with Williams began at 3:03 p.m., it wasn't until 5:36 p.m. that police knocked on the door of his house at 473 Edison Avenue and presented a copy of their search warrant to his wife. Investigators had been hoping that in the first two and a half hours, Williams would have realized the untenable predicament he was in and would provide information as to where specific evidence could be found without the necessity of combing through his home or the cottage in Tweed. To that point during the interview, Williams had denied any involvement and insisted it would be impossible for his DNA to be at any of the crime scenes. He told Smyth he'd never been unfaithful to his wife and didn't have any sort of personal relationship with any of the victims.

About three hours later, Detective Inspector Quigley, one of several investigators monitoring the interrogation, contacted Detective Sergeant Brian Mason, the officer who was supervising the team hunting for evidence at the Williams home and told him to stop the search. Mason was told that Williams had admitted killing Jessica Lloyd and an application was being made for a new search warrant which would identify specific items to directly link him to all four incidents. Police remained at the home until 1:10 a.m. cataloguing and photographing the items collected in the initial search. When they left, guards were posted to protect any evidence that Williams mentioned during the lengthy and intense interview.

Several days later, Lieutenant Commander Stephen Merriman, the senior chaplain from the Canadian Forces Base at Trenton, delivered a message to police from Williams – telling them about additional evidence that was hidden at 62 Cosy Cove Lane in Tweed. The chaplain had been informed during a pastoral visit on February 9, 2010 to the Quinte Detention Center in Napanee, where Williams was being held, that investigators would find video tapes and a memory card inside the piano at the home. Williams told the chaplain he hoped the additional evidence would allow police to end the search in Ottawa so that his wife could return to the home.

Two Hi-8 video tapes and a SanDisk memory card were located in the piano. There were 325 digital images and two video recordings covering a 19-hour period, starting at 1:19 a.m. on January 29, 2010, which depicted the rape and murder of Jessica Lloyd.

During searches of the Ottawa home, police discovered two 500 gigabyte Lacie hard drives that were concealed above an electrical panel in the basement. The drives contained duplicate copies of the evidence police found hidden in the piano. The crimes involving Jessica Lloyd had been transferred onto the computer on February 1 and were in three main folders, each containing various subfolders. The videos, identified as JEL1 and JEL2, were in separate files and graphically showed Jessica's attack and slaying. The third main folder contained duplicates of the 325 digital images that were on the SanDisk card.

One of the subfolders, containing 45 photographic images dated February 6, depicted various pieces of lingerie taken from Lloyd's home. There were also copies of four-by-six-inch photographs of Jessica and some of her friends that were taken by Williams while he was inside the victim's house. Among the images was a copy of her student card.

Another subfolder held 53 photographs of computer screens that showed websites from police services, media outlets and chat lines which were highlighting Lloyd's disappearance. Experts from the OPP's e-crime section, who traced histories permanently stored in the computer that Williams was using, learned he was reading an article from the Belleville Intelligencer about the hunt for Jessica being called off while at the same time watching a video on another computer of him sexually assaulting the young woman.

There were 34 photographs of websites from several news organizations taken January 31, plus some Facebook pages with information about the disappearance and appeals being made for her safe return. Another subfolder had three images of home pages, which showed websites containing chat lines of people talking about the missing woman and wondering what might have happened to her.

In addition to the initial search warrants, police obtained permission to examine the Nissan Pathfinder that Williams owned, search his office at the Trenton military base, look through his financial records, a safety deposit box at a Bank of Montreal branch in Ottawa and to obtain medical records on file with the Canadian military. The searchers were also authorized to get copies of all records from Rogers Communications, a Canadian-based wireless provider, which pertained to his cell phone and other communication devices, including the BlackBerry which he carried.

Five minutes after the interview with Williams began, officers entered his property in Tweed, hoping to rescue Jessica or discover evidence of where she might be located. She wasn't there and a team of officers from the Belleville Police Service and the Ontario Provincial Police spent from 3:08 p.m. until 9:35 p.m. looking for any clues that would reveal the victim's whereabouts or any sign that she had been harmed. A forensic team led by OPP Constable Pellerin and Constable Warren Easby of the Belleville Police Service discovered red stains on the living room floor and found a Leatherman knife on the dining room table. They also seized a quantity of camera and video equipment.

The initial visit by police to the Ottawa residence yielded nothing of significant value. But when the updated search warrant was issued four days later, investigators spent seven days in the house and located numerous items that Williams had mentioned while confessing to his crimes. Police there, led by Constable Pellerin, began combing through the two-storey home at 12:32 p.m. on February 11, 2010 and finished their hunt for evidence at 3:04 p.m. on February 18. That forensic team collected and catalogued an array of items linking Williams not only to the murders of Jessica Lloyd and Marie-France Comeau, but the two sexual attacks in Tweed and the numerous break-ins that took place near the homes Williams owned.

Among the items found at the Ottawa house was a Sony digital camera which had been used to take pictures of the victims, a black skull cap Williams had used to conceal the upper part of his face when confronting them, a variety of computer equipment, including the two Lacie external hard drives containing photographs as well as videos of the sexual assaults and homicides. The searchers found a book – 'LSI Guide to Lock Picking' – numerous photographs that were stolen from Jessica Lloyd's house, her student identification, plus a duffle bag that held the rope, tape and other items that Williams used to tie up his victims.

The exact location where each item was found was methodically catalogued and photographed. Forensic officers also made sure that all physical evidence was preserved to accommodate further analysis by experts at the crime lab. The search was thorough. Nothing was overlooked.

Other items seized included some of the suspect's flight suits and what seemed to investigators to be a mountain of women's undergarments and other clothing. They found one bag containing 34 bras, 14 pairs of panties, two camisoles and a slip. A pillow case in the garage was stuffed with five pairs of panties, pajama bottoms, a bra, a slip, two pair of children's panties; plus a vibrator. A camera bag containing a Sony camera also included a pair of women's underwear. In a box that had contained an Epson printer purchased by Williams, investigators found a bag filled with 13 pairs of women's panties, lubricant jelly and three bras. Another bag held eight photographs of Jessica Lloyd along with four camisoles, a pair of grey sweat pants, 22 pairs of panties and 10 bras.

In a spare room in the basement, police found a plastic bag in a KRK Systems box containing a quantity of underwear and some lubricants in a separate zip-lock storage bag. Searchers also discovered two other bags. The first containing four vibrators, several sex videos and batteries; the second one was stuffed with 34 bras, two camisoles, a slip and 14 pairs of panties.

During a subsequent search of the cottage on February 11, 2010, a team of OPP and Belleville Police Service officers led by Constables Dave Tovell, Gord Lefebvre and Nicole Burley discovered possible blood stains on a set of drawers in the master bedroom, similar stains on a wooden chair and a cushion in the living room, plus blood in the bathroom. They also located the two Hi-8 video tapes wrapped in black electrical tape, which Williams had admitted hiding in the piano, plus a four-gigabyte SanDisk memory card.

Also seized during the search was some rope, a quantity of electrical and duct tape and a military duffle bag filled with eight plastic garbage bags. The contents of the first bag were listed by police as 93 pairs of women's panties and a slip. The next one held four camisoles, six tops, a t-shirt and 13 dresses. Bag three contained two bathing suits, two bathing suit bikini bottoms, eight pairs of panties, a pair of tights, a garter and garter belt, plus a pair of fishnet stockings. The fourth bag contained a nightie, a slip, a pair of panties, a camisole and a panty-camisole outfit. There were 51 pairs of panties in the fifth bag and 35 pairs in the sixth bag. The seventh bag contained a bathing suit bottom, three bathing suit tops, two bras, two unmatched socks and 67 pairs of panties. In the final bag, police located 49 bras, several sex toys, some black zip-ties and photographs of Jane Doe on vacation with friends. Investigators also seized some computer equipment.

Ironically, Williams told Smyth during the interview that he was planning to take all the underwear from his Ottawa home to Tweed on the day that police asked him to come in and give a statement.

He had already burned some of the stolen lingerie at the Tweed dump and was planning to dispose of his later haul in a similar way. Because police called him on that

Sunday, investigators were able to seize evidence that was destined to be destroyed several hours later. Also, before leaving the Ottawa house on February 7, 2010 to give a statement to police, Williams detached the two Lacie hard drives that he was using to store photographs and images of his various crimes – and hid them in the ceiling above an electrical panel in the basement. Detective Sergeant Jim Falconer and other members of the Ontario Provincial Police e-crimes section duplicated the various files from the computer and, in a follow-up interview on March 4, 2010 at the Hastings County Jail in Belleville, Williams divulged details of the various break-ins.

He told Smyth his burglary escapade began in September 2007 around his cottage residence in Tweed and later in the Ottawa neighborhood, where Williams and his wife owned a house on Wilkie Drive. It continued in Ottawa's west-end after they purchased what was described as her "dream home" on Edison Avenue. In addition to details about the enteries, Williams revealed the location of the secret files that detailed the sexual assaults and murders. He had intended the horrendous images to remain hidden in the computer's memory so that no one, including his wife, could ever find them – other than him for his sexual pleasure. In the complex series of subfolders, which computer experts confirmed were deeply buried in the computer, Williams provided information that directed investigators to a folder with information and photographs related to the sexual molestation of Jane Doe. They also found a two-page typed document dated September 20, 2009, on which Williams describes the attack in great detail, plus a file containing nine photographs in one subfolder. Inside the other file, police discovered four photographs showing a baby's receiving blanket, a sheet, a bassinette blanket and a shirt that were stolen by Williams from the victim's residence. Two other photographs which police found on the computer depicted the four items along with a printed sign which indicated they had been discarded on September 19, 2009.

Williams told investigators he had so much underwear and other clothing at his home that on several occasions he had to throw things out. On June 21, 2008 and on March 29, 2009, he took items to different fields on the outskirts of Ottawa and set them ablaze. He said he brought undergarments from the break-ins to his homes in Tweed or Ottawa, where he would take photographs and add to a catalogue that detailed what had been stolen. On many occasions, he would put on some of the lingerie and take pictures of himself, or hold the clothing while masturbating. After being photographed, the clothing was placed in boxes and bags. During one of the interviews with Detective Sergeant Smyth, Williams said from time to time, he had to dispose of the accumulated items because there was no longer any space left at his Ottawa home to store them.

Police continued to press Williams for details about the various cases and insisted on getting his cooperation to retrieve photographs and other evidence that he stored on the hard drives found in his Ottawa home and at the cottage residence. There were four main folders containing several subfolders detailing the murderous assault on Marie-France Comeau. One contained a file called MFC.mov, which showed video images from the HD-8 video tape police seized at the Tweed house. It was transferred onto the hard drive on November 30, 2009, six days after the victim was suffocated in her home. The digitalized video recording covers a lengthy span of time and details both the sexual attack and Comeau's murder.

Another folder containing 67 still images taken on November 24, 2009 between 12:21 a.m. and 4:23 a.m. depicted graphic details of Comeau being raped. The third folder with 11 digital images taken on November 29, 2009 showed numerous undergarments from her home that had been spread out on a flat surface and photographed separately. Next was a folder with seven photographs taken of a computer screen that featured news media sites with articles detailing the slaying. Another folder contained 33 photographs of other news articles, plus copies of Facebook pages which paid tribute to Comeau. The images in those folders were taken on January 9, 2010 and transferred onto the computer on January 31. Articles and reports from media, plus police websites, were stored in a sixth folder, which also contained a copy of a condolence letter sent to Comeau's father by Williams in his capacity as the commander of the Canadian Forces Base in Trenton.

The official letter of condolence, dated December 1, 2009, to Ernest Comeau, reads:

Dear Mr. Comeau,

I would like to take this opportunity on behalf of the men and women of 8 Wing Trenton to express my sincere condolences on the tragic death of your daughter.

Marie-France was a professional, caring and compassionate woman who earned the respect of all with whom she came into contact. She set high standards for herself and others and was devoted to the well-being of those around her.

Marie-France made a lasting impact in Trenton, and will be sorely missed by her many friends.

Please let me know whether there is anything I can do to help you during this very difficult time.

You and your family are in our thoughts and prayers.

With our deepest sympathy,

D. R. Williams Colonel Wing Commander

This is the note Williams scribbled to Laurie Massicotte while being interrogated by Detective Sergeant Jim Smyth about the murder of Corporal Marie-France Comeau at her home in Brighton and the disappearance of Jessica Lloyd from her residence in Belleville.

Chapter Eleven

Russell Williams selected Laurie Massicotte as his second victim because she lived alone. In fact, she resided only "a few doors down" from the white frame bungalow that Williams owned northeast of Tweed on Cozy Cove Lane south of Sulphide Road, which is also known as Highway 39. It was in the normally tranquil refuge on an inlet off Stoco Lake that Williams and his wife bought what some people refer to as a cottage in the summer of 2004. He had just been promoted to lieutenant-colonel and placed in command of 437 Squadron at Canadian Forces Base Trenton.

Massicotte had bought a neighboring house several years earlier.

"She had a boyfriend and I knew he hadn't been around," Williams coolly told Detective Sergeant Smyth, while confessing to the attack on Massicotte and other crimes in the neighborhoods where he lived in Ottawa and Tweed. Portions of the video-taped confession were played in the Hastings County courthouse in Belleville after Williams pleaded guilty to raping and murdering Marie-France Comeau and Jessica Lloyd, the sexual assault on Massicotte and a similar earlier attack on a woman, who can only be identified as Jane Doe. Massicotte, who was sexually molested but not raped, made a formal request for removal of a ban mandated by Canadian law to protect sex assault victims from being publicly named. Many people in the area already knew she was one of the women that Williams had assaulted and she wanted to speak publically about the attack.

He confessed to entering the 47-year-old woman's home several times before her September 30, 2009 attack. "I looked around to see if there were any permanent signs of her boyfriend," he said during the February 7, 2010 police interrogation. While giving details of the sexual assault on Massicotte, Williams said he let himself into her home around midnight, after removing a screen and forcing open a rear window. His victim was on a couch in the living room. She had fallen asleep watching television.

In an interview for this book, the slender former accountant, ex-telemarketer and mother of three daughters – twins, who were aged 17 at the time and attending separate high schools, plus a 19-year-old who was just settling into university – described what she remembers of that nightmare. She also recalls her strange, occasional feelings of sympathy for the man who put her through such a hellish ordeal.

Laurie Massicotte had been watching her favorite program, Law and Order, curled up on a couch after spending the day alone, "minding my own business," as she describes it. Sandwiched between two halves of a comforter, her sleep was literally shattered by a wallop from the flashlight that Williams wielded. The blow, however, did not knock her out.

"I remember waking up around one o'clock," she recalled.

Massicotte learned only later, from the confession Williams gave to police, that a flashlight struck her head. "I thought it was his fists," she said. "I was seeing stars. I think I was disoriented for a long time."

Williams told Smyth that he had struggled with his victim, but promised Massicotte she would not be hurt. She remembers that promise, which only partially calmed the frightened woman. "He cut off my breath," Massicotte said. "He subdued me for about 20 minutes ... then he let me breathe. He was probably leaning on my chest. He was a big guy."

She was unable to see, since he had covered her face with the comforter. Massicotte remembers Williams uttering his first of several chilling warnings, when he intoned: "You do not want to see me."

Finally, when allowed to sit up, she assured him: "Oh, I don't want to see you." Her unknown attacker insisted other men were in the house robbing her, "cleaning me out," she said. "I always thought the others were going to join." Massicotte feared at the end of the day she wouldn't be left alive.

She later learned, after his confession was made public, that the threat of other intruders was merely a ploy to control her. As part of his routine, Williams began taking photographs, first while Massicotte was clothed, then of her partially disrobed. "He held the knife as if he was going to slice the pajamas off," she said, adding her attacker then helped slip off the cut pieces of night clothing. Williams also blindfolded her, using strips of cloth from a pillow case taken from the couch. When Massicotte heard a strange sound and asked if he had brought a firearm, she remembers him saying: "No Laurie, I don't have a gun."

"He let me feel the camera strap on my face," she said. "I asked what he was doing and he said he was just recharging the battery, so I feel it was the video." Although Massicotte was told by the prosecutor in Belleville that her tormentor did not make a video recording of her attack, "I believe he was running a video all the time." (No video was found which showed the attack on Massicotte and Williams told police he didn't record the assault. But investigators did discover that something had been erased when one of the high definition cassettes was used to document one of the attacker's subsequent murderous assaults.)

Massicotte said she felt humiliated while enduring Williams' repeated demands for her to pose for him and to submit to his intimate touches. The worst demand, she said, was for her to get on her hands and knees so that he could photograph her intimately. "I was sweating and shaking. I was trying to cover up with my hands and he had to pry them away. I was, like, shaking."

As the minutes and hours ticked by, Massicotte said Williams appeared to open up to her, whether truthfully or as part of a diversionary game, she will never be sure. She also thought that he showed some compassion when he led her from the bathroom, with her hands tied behind her, after helping her get Tylenol and some water. "He touched my head and he said he was sorry for hitting me so hard," she said. "He even admitted he was surprised I had rallied back ... so he believed I was unconscious for a while."

She mentioned Williams adjusting the blindfold that prevented her from seeing his face and thought he wanted to help her relax. She said he allowed her to fix her hair and then there was some small talk between them, including "conversations about my cat." She told him about her three daughters and suggested he had likely seen their photos on the wall in the hallway of her home. "Yes," Massicotte quoted Williams as saying. "They're pretty."

"He asked at one point where they are and I said they don't live with me," she said, while recalling the events after being confronted by the intruder who broke into her home. "He asked me if I was married and I said no. I was having a hard time keeping up with him. I was playing a mind game. I was trying to be smart."

Describing herself as someone with empathy for other people – able to read nuances in their tone of voice and inflections – Massicotte said she even asked why his breathing had taken on a heavy inflection. She didn't realize the sexual satisfaction that he got from his escapades with helpless women. "I said what was wrong? He didn't answer and I said you're breathing differently ... what's wrong? I had no idea what was going on."

She remembers him sitting on the couch beside her. "I said to him ... do you have a wife and children, and he said no. I said do you think you'll have a wife and children some day, and he said no. I asked him why and he said too young."

It felt like she was gaining his trust. "I felt if I was being respectful of him ... I thought he'd be respectful of me. I felt sorry for him. I really did. I didn't want to tell him that. I knew he was one sick individual."

Massicotte, a fan of Criminal Minds, the popular television series featuring a Federal Bureau of Investigation team that profiles and hunts serial killers plus sex fiends, was enduring a real-life version of the show. "I guess I was profiling him," she said. "I didn't think I could ever do that. I guess I was having empathy for him ... not realizing it."

She remembers Williams telling her that she seemed like a nice lady. "He asked me if I worked and I said no." During the conversation, Massicotte told him about her past jobs.

When he was leaving, she said he asked if anyone would find her if she was left tied up. "I said no, no, no one will find me...please don't do that...and he didn't."

She said thoughts were racing constantly through her head about his motives throughout the ordeal, including whether her attacker was part of an outlaw motorcycle gang such as the Hell's Angels.

After ending his photo-fetish and fondling, Williams systematically began wiping any objects that he had touched, including the headache tablet bottle, to make sure police wouldn't find his fingerprints. When Massicotte discovered what he was doing, she suggested he wipe off the coffee mug in which he had brought her the water.

"Thank you," he said, then told her he would soon be leaving.

While sitting and waiting – not knowing what might happen next – Massicotte had all sorts of thoughts flooding through her mind. She worried about him posting the photographs of her on the Internet. "Would my daughters see them?"

Since he also warned her not to immediately try to get help, she waited about 30 minutes before fumbling around and finding the telephone to call the 911 emergency number. When dialing for help, Massicotte still did not know if she was doing the right thing. He hadn't told her not to notify the police, but she was petrified. She had no idea what would happen while waiting for help to arrive.

When the first two officers reached her home, they found the still-bound victim sitting on the living room couch covered with a blanket. Massicotte said she had been told by the police to remain under the comforter and not move while they looked around outside for the intruder who had attacked her. She said it was five hours before they let her get up. During that time she was forced to sit motionless on the couch with two officers standing nearby. She said the police told her she had to wait until forensic officers got to the house before her hands could be untied.

Massicotte said an investigator, who identified herself as Detective Anne Marie Brock, came in from time to time to talk with her about the assault and at one point brought her a bathrobe. She said when Brock finally took her outside, they sat in a police car while Massicotte provided details for an initial statement about the attack. "They kept me in the dark," she said. "Throughout the whole process ... even when I got out to the car, they were telling me, they felt this was a person ... someone who would never return. It was like a random thing. They felt it was a transient person ... that was the word. They felt this would never happen again."

While Williams was in her home, Massicotte said she had the impression somehow that her ex-husband was involved. She said that she had been forced to call the police previously about what she described as his unwanted attention. Massicotte, who has filed a lawsuit against police for keeping her tied up, claims the officers treated her as if she was lying. She said friends who monitor police calls on scanners told her they had heard officers expressing their doubts. "They felt I was crazy," she said. "There were some domestic calls before. I felt betrayed ... let down and I lost trust in the whole detachment." Massicotte said there were suggestions that she was trying to cash in on the earlier attack on Jane Doe, even though only limited information had been made public by the police about that assault.

When interviewed later in the evening, Massicotte said officers at the Ontario Provincial Police detachment asked her if she knew the person who had been attacked earlier in the neighborhood, or the woman's boyfriend. "I said no," she said. "They had only been there three weeks. They had only rented that place at the first of September." Massicotte said it was at the police station where she learned most of the details about the attack on Jane Doe. Until that point, police hadn't disclosed very much.

When Massocitte's then-boyfriend picked her up at the police station and drove her home, they discussed getting an alarm system. It was put in the following week. "I had it expedited," she said. With word then out in public about both attacks – alarm companies were being deluged with requests – and "there were numerous women ahead of me." She also borrowed a two-year-old German Shepherd from a friend for protection. They went everywhere for awhile, including to parks, but she found the dog too much to handle and finally gave him back.

When called to provide a DNA sample at the police station about two weeks after the attack, Massicotte spotted a young woman in the waiting room. She had a baby and concluded the mother was the other victim. "I wanted to talk with her," she said, but a detective discouraged her, suggesting any conversation might compromise the investigation. "I was just sick. I couldn't even imagine a 21-year-old going through that. When you look into someone's eyes ... you know when something was taken from them, too. It hurts."

In mid-October, Massicotte placed a telephone call to the detachment, which she now deeply regrets. She thought she had finally recognized her attacker's voice and told them it might be Larry Jones, a long-time resident of the area. Massicotte said she made the call after being pressured by a friend. Her allegation touched off a major investigation that led to Jones, a retired Ministry of Natural Resources surveyor, becoming a prime person of interest. After being hauled in for questioning, his home was searched. The 65-year-old man was not charged, but remained under a cloud of suspicion until Williams was arrested in connection with Massicotte's attack.

Before the colonel's arrest, Jones was shunned by many people in the area, and is now one of several people who have launched lawsuits.

In addition to the Ontario Provincial Police, Massicotte's claim in late September 2011 named Williams, his wife, and the Department of National Defence. She is seeking $7 million in damages for pain, suffering, mental distress and anxiety disorders. Massicotte is alleging that police breached their duty of care by not warning her that a previous sexual assault had taken place 13 days earlier on the same street where she lived. Her suit also accuses the OPP of dereliction of duty for not having paramedics or a doctor brought to her house to determine if she had any emotional issues or physical injuries. While there is no evidence of rape, Massicotte expressed doubts when interviewed two years later. She says she lapsed into unconsciousness at the start of the ordeal and has no idea what occurred during that time. The other Tweed victim, Jane Doe, brought a lawsuit against Williams and his wife in May 2011. She is seeking $2.45 million in damages.

Massicotte and several other village residents have publicly questioned why it took police so long to warn people. They suggest an alert would have prompted women in the tight-knit community to be more cautious. It wasn't until October 1, 2009 that the OPP first issued a notice to residents with the heading: Public Safety Concern.

"The Ontario Provincial Police, Central Hastings detachment, is investigating two break-ins that occurred, in which a male suspect entered the home while residents were sleeping," the alert read. "On September 17 and again on September 30, 2009, both in the early hours of the morning, an unknown male entered Tweed residences. During both separate incidents, the suspect struck the female victim, tied her to a chair and took photos of her. The suspect then fled the scene. The OPP want to remind everyone to ensure all doors and windows are secured and to practice personal safety. Please report any suspicious activity to the police immediately by calling 911. OPP officers are following up leads to identify the suspect. If anyone has information about these incidents, they are asked to call the Central Hastings OPP."

The alert made no reference that the attacks were sexually motivated or that explicit photographs had been taken of the victims.

After the arrest of Williams, several Brighton residents also expressed concern that police had not issued a warning to women after Comeau's murderous attack. The Northumberland OPP detachment sent out an alert on November 27, two days after her slaying, which urged residents to remain calm. "Police investigators are advising area residents that there are presently no issues with regards to public safety," stated the notice.

Massicotte still wonders why she felt sympathy for Williams when she was his prisoner – while at the same time realizing he was one badly-warped individual. Experts might call that double-attitude similar to the Stockholm Syndrome, a term coined after psychologists analyzed a number of people who were taken hostage in Sweden's capital in 1973. Several sympathized with their captors during their six-day ordeal and refused to testify against them.

Massicotte says she continues to relive the nightmare of the attack. "I'd never been sexually assaulted," she says, before whispering that "the other girls have gone home." She was referring to Comeau and Lloyd, who were killed by Williams, and suggests they are no longer suffering. "I'm grieving," she added. "I feel I'm living my own death."

In public statements, Massicotte said she has forgiven Williams. She has also apologized to Jones for telling police that he might have been her attacker.

Massicotte admits to having thoughts that suicide would allow her to escape the trauma she continues to go through, but acknowledges it wouldn't be an option since that would mean Williams had totally defeated her. "There are days when I don't feel like getting out of bed," she says. Each day "I try to keep it simple … just baby steps." Sometimes she feels quite depressed and admits finding relief with an "over-indulgence" of wine and medication. "I chose to live," she says. "I talk to myself all the time. Whatever it takes."

Massicotte said she's saddened that in the aftermath of the attack, she has lost girlfriends, her boyfriend and even the great relationship she previously had with her mother. "They just can't handle what happened," she said, adding her mother went to the courthouse to watch Williams being sentenced, but then wouldn't talk to her about the case. "I've lost girlfriends over this," she said. "It's ripped my whole family apart." Massicotte said her daughters continue to be close to both her and their grandmother, but sometimes she feels they are trapped in the middle of a nightmare. She didn't find counseling sessions helpful, but does get relief from reading books about others who have gone through the same experience, including the story of a woman who was raped in the mid-1980s, after Toronto Police failed to issue a warning that a sex offender was scaling balconies to get into the apartments of unsuspecting victims. A judge who reviewed the case found that police had deliberately not alerted women to the danger and basically used them as bait, hoping to catch an attacker who eventually became known as the Balcony Rapist.

"I think it helps with the healing process," Massicotte said, adding those type of books give her a better understanding about police investigations, trials and the justice system. "I hope someday to write my own book" she said. "I try to stay in the moment … tomorrow may never come." Despite the negative memories and fluctuating emotions of not only the attack, but dealings with police, her family, friends and the decision she made to make her name public and speak about her ordeal with the media, she is convinced the way she behaved with Williams in all likelihood may have saved her life. She said it also saved her children from finding her tied up, naked on the couch – or worse. She reflects back and thinks about the other victims: Comeau fought him; Lloyd co-operated. Both died. Jane Doe said she gave in, fearing her baby would be killed. Massicotte fought at first, then engaged Williams in conversations about himself, while asking for reassurance that she would not be harmed. No one may ever know for sure why she survived.

Chapter Twelve

The neighborhood which Marie-France Comeau called
home for 14 months was built about two years before her
murder. Nestled on the south side of Brighton, Ontario, a
town of 10,250 residents and a 15-minute drive west of
Canadian Forces Base Trenton, her bungalow is in an area
of relatively new homes. An agricultural community,
Brighton is mostly a peaceful place, where young couples
raise children and seniors settle. It is also home to many
military families.

Born in Quebec City on April 19, 1972, Marie-France
Comeau was a slender, attractive and cheerfully outgoing
37-year-old woman. She joined the military in 1997, first
with the army and later transferring to the air service,
which in 2011 was renamed the Royal Canadian Air Force.
In 2002, Comeau was part of Operation Apollo, Canada's
first wave of military personnel to arrive in Afghanistan as
part of the International Security Assistance Force
organized through the United Nation's Security Council to
protect the region around Kabul from Taliban fighters. It
was all part of a strategic effort in both Afghanistan and
Iraq to crush al-Qaeda terrorists responsible for the
deaths of more than 3,000 people on September 11, 2001,
when hijackers flew passenger jets into the World Trade
Center buildings in New York City and the Pentagon in
Washington. The same day other terrorists deliberately
crashed a jetliner into a grassy field in Shanksville,
Pennsylvania after passengers fought to gain control of the
hijacked aircraft. Their struggle was the first battle to be
fought in the war to combat modern global terrorism and
most likely prevented the plane from being flown into the
U.S. Capitol building in Washington.

Comeau was assigned to the secret non-combat facility known as Camp Mirage in the United Arab Emirates. It opened in December 2001 at the Al Minhad Air Base near Dubai and was vacated by Canada's military nine years later. She spent long hours with forklift trucks, moving cargo aboard large, four engine C-130 Hercules transport aircraft which ferried supplies to the troops serving in Afghanistan. Camp Mirage, which Russell Williams commanded from December 2005 to June 2006, was also the last stop in the Middle East for the bodies of the 158 Canadian soldiers killed in the war as they were flown home to Canada. The remains were actually brought to the base at Trenton, where they were received with full military honors before being driven along a section of Highway 401 known as the Highway of Heroes, which passes Comeau's community on the road leading to the coroner's building in Toronto.

Camp Mirage was extremely hot and dusty, with temperatures at times reaching more than 120-degrees. While there, Comeau and her colleagues were forced to work mostly at night to escape the sweltering heat. She later worked at the Canadian Forces Base in Bagotville, Quebec before being transferred in 2005 to a base at Cold Lake, Alberta. Comeau moved to Trenton two years later.

In 2009, she was assisting in the transition of Canadian troops in Afghanistan from Kabul to Kandahar. In July of that year, while working with 8 Wing in Trenton, Comeau applied to serve as a flight attendant aboard the military's VIP aircraft. It was shortly before Williams took over as commander of the base. Her duties in the 437 Transport Squadron had her on globe-trotting flights with Stephen Harper, Canada's prime minister; Governor General Michaelle Jean, the country's official representative of the Queen; and General Walt Natynczyk, Chief of the Defence Staff, the commander of all Canadian Forces. Williams was the pilot on at least one of the corporal's flights to Germany in the autumn of 2009.

In September 2008, Comeau moved into the bungalow at 252 Raglan Street, between Ontario Street and Prince Edward Street. She had lived elsewhere for four years with Alain Plante, a basic training instructor at the Trenton base, and his sons, Etienne and Cedric. When Plante was transferred to Quebec, Comeau decided to remain in the Trenton area. Although they had formally separated, she and Plante continued to be good friends.

On the evening of November 16, 2009, Williams broke into her Brighton home while Comeau was on an overseas mission. Her passenger on the flight was Canada's prime minister.

The intruder parked his Nissan Pathfinder SUV in a wooded area almost half a mile from the house and slipped inside through a basement window. With plenty of time to explore, the colonel took photographs of himself wearing some of Comeau's underwear, plus a couple of pictures of her military uniforms and some sex toys in a drawer beside her bed. When the corporal came home, she noticed that someone had rummaged through her dresser drawers and blamed her new boyfriend, Paul Belanger. He vehemently denied her accusation.

In media interviews, Plante said he had spoken with Comeau on November 22, 2009 when she returned from the assignment which took the prime minister to Singapore, Japan and India. He also told police that she was excited to have been on the trip and always enjoyed seeing new places. Neighbors in the Brighton suburb where Comeau lived said she was rarely home, but considered the house a place of rest and refuge when not at the base or flying around the world. "She kept to herself," neighbor Terry Alexander recalled in an interview

Neighbor Terry Alexander lives across from Comeau's home

for this book. "She was French and there were no other French people here ... but she spoke some English." During the brief time she lived across the street, they would sometimes see her sitting with one of her cats, said Alexander, who moved to Brighton with his wife in 2007 after retiring. "I would just say hi," he said.

Shortly before 1 p.m. on November 25, 2009, the couple spotted Belanger scurrying from Comeau's bungalow. He was obviously distraught and appeared dazed. Something was terribly wrong. When he was unable to reach Comeau, who had missed a dinner date with him and hadn't shown up for work, Belanger went to her home to make sure everything was all right. After letting himself in through the back door, he found his girlfriend's blood-soaked body on her bed.

Reeling from shock, Belanger dialed the Ontario Provincial Police for help and then staggered outside. "He came to the sidewalk and asked me if I'd seen anybody around here," Alexander recalled. "Then he said she was dead. He sat down and cried."

The death of Marie-France Comeau was a homicide and word of the slaying spread quickly through the normally safe and peaceful neighborhood.

Alexander said everyone was talking. People were worried, wondering if a killer had arrived and would be terrorizing the quiet community. "Everyone said who's next," he said. "We were interviewed three times by the police."

When Comeau's murder was eventually linked with the slaying of Jessica Lloyd, he said police converged on the area and were doing spot-checks everywhere. "Then they cancelled that," said Alexander, adding the police had been canvassing residents on Raglan Street and the surrounding area. "They wouldn't give us any information," he said. A short time later, the arrest of Williams was announced. "We could walk the streets a little bit safer," Alexander said.

Another neighbor, Lorraine Traccy, also saw Belanger moments after he discovered Comeau's body. "He was so upset," she said. "His face ... he was crying. The military flight attendant was already living on the street when Tracey and her husband, Dan, bought their home. She didn't know her well. "I had spoken to her just a couple of times ... four or five months after we moved in," she said. "I'd wave to her when she drove by." Tracey also recalled chatting with her one day while she was outside doing some snow shoveling. "She told me she was heading south to Cuba for a vacation. I asked if she had space for me, I'll carry your luggage," Tracey said.

"It's so sad what happened. She was such a nice girl. She didn't deserve that."

Living directly behind Comeau's home, retired Captain Patrick "Pete" Peterson said the young corporal was always on the go. Peterson, who had duties in the first Gulf War and served on peacekeeping missions in Somalia and Ethiopia, spoke to Comeau three or four times. "She was a very pleasant person ... very friendly with everybody," he said. "I wish I'd gotten to know her better. What happened to Marie-France is an aberration."

When Comeau's father, step-mother and other relatives came to her house to pack up some of her belongings, Peterson spoke briefly with them. "We offered to help, but no ... they're a close-knit family. They spent one day cleaning up her house," said Peterson, adding Plante came later "and cleaned out the rest."

Plante spoke publicly several times after Comeau's murder, saying he had hoped they would be able to get back together. "I'll miss her for the rest of my life," he told a Canwest reporter. "She was an angel ... a flower ... and even though we were not together, I could never speak against her. She's a lovely person." He told a Canadian Broadcasting Corporation interviewer that she enjoyed shopping and loved her job. "Inside her, she was an artist, a bohemian, in love with life in general," Plante said. "I miss her a lot. I always had the hope that she'd come back to me some day, for sure. She was the most beautiful flower you could imagine."

Memorial pages set up on Facebook gave a further glimpse into Comeau's life and the affect her murder had on friends and colleagues. Comrades posted numerous photographs along with their comments. She is described as friendly, always smiling and popular. Photos show her in different countries, both in uniform and civilian attire.

"She was an absolutely beautiful person and friend," wrote Kim Hill Chornaby. "She was always so happy and positive and I am truly saddened by this horrible tragedy. Her smile will forever live on in the hearts of those who knew her and were lucky enough to call her a friend." Adam Frey, who worked with Comeau for four months, called her "a fun person who loved life and seemed to find the best about everything she did." On the website memorial, Marc-Andrew Comeau thanked the police for their efforts in investigating his sister's murder.

After Comeau enlisted at the age of 25, she spent most of her life living on military bases. Her father, Ernest "Ernie" Comeau, was a career soldier who took his family from Quebec to Lahr, Germany, where the Canadian Forces maintained a base until it was closed in 1994. He retired after serving 42 years.

On December 4, 2009, Marie-France Comeau was buried at the National Military Cemetery in Ottawa. There were hundreds of mourners, including relatives, friends and military personnel, but her commanding officer – Williams – did not attend the service. Three days before the funeral, he signed the official letter expressing condolences to her father. He even asked for the letter, written by a high-ranking assistant, to be corrected after noticing that her name was misspelled.

Ten weeks later, Williams was charged with killing Comeau and murdering Jessica Lloyd.

Marie-France was described as "brave, amiable and charismatic" at a memorial service held at the National Air Force Museum on the first anniversary of her murder. Colonel David Cochrane, who succeeded Williams as the base commander in Trenton, told the more than 100 people attending the ceremony that Comeau had a zest or life. "She was fun-loving and kept her co-workers on their toes with her mischievous ways," Cochrane said. "Her infectious smile made a positive impression on anyone who had the privilege of making her acquaintance." Lieutenant Colonel Andy Cook, the commanding officer of 437 Squadron, said Comeau was an ordinary woman who faced extraordinary circumstances. "She fought evil. She

never gave up her fight," he said. "To her killer, she had no value as a person. For us, to defeat her killer is to remember her and see her value as an individual." Cook said the courage of Marie-France made "a profound and indelible impact" on him. "I don't honestly know if I could face the same circumstances with the same courage as she did," he said. "I only hope that I would have a fraction of the inestimable valor she displayed if faced with such adversity."

Comeau's remembrance marker at the Trenton military base memorial

Although the service was held to dedicate a six-by-ten inch granite marker along a tree-lined memorial pathway honoring those who have served with the 437 Squadron, the guests who attended were asked by Cook to also remember Jessica Lloyd.

Chapter Thirteen

"Okay ... it's a little rough," the brother of Jessica
Elizabeth Lloyd told reporters who were waiting on the
steps of the Hastings County courthouse in Belleville. It
was on October 19, 2010, after the prosecutor began
revealing facts on the first day in the trial for Russell
Williams. Media representatives knew Andrew "Andy"
Lloyd from previous interviews as police continued
gathering evidence. The investigation findings compiled in
a lengthy statement of facts which was read to Superior
Court Justice Robert F. Scott after Williams pleaded guilty
to all the charges against him. The face of Lloyd, a big
bear of a man, had also become familiar in newspapers
and on television as the murders of his sister and Marie-
France Comeau, two sexual assaults and a bizarre sex
fetish by a high-ranking Canadian military officer
garnered worldwide media attention. "I don't know
anybody else that's gone through this," he said. "It's pretty
hard to go through it twice. A horrible man ... terrible
stuff."

In the courtroom that day, the prosecutor, Crown Attorney
Lee Burgess, captured Jessica's compassion and loving
nature by echoing the words she spoke to Williams before
he killed her.

"If I die, will you make sure that my Mom knows that I
love her."

Many in the court's public gallery began crying when they
heard Jessica's plea to the man who would proceed to end
her life. The heart-wrenching and haunting words only
became known because Williams was video-taping the
torment she was enduring prior to her murder. The
message to her mother was found when investigators

viewed the tape that he had concealed in the piano in his Tweed home. Burgess told the court he had no doubt Williams was laughing "as he lived the life of a community leader by day and the life of a serial criminal by night. That the victims suffered trauma at the hands of Mr. Williams is an understatement," he told the court. "They were violated...not only by this man's hands, but by his lens."

On October 20, Lloyd's family and friends were back at the courthouse, ready to deliver victim impact statements to the judge and face the stone-faced killer in the prisoner's dock. Williams was the keeper of her last words – words of love for Roxanne Lloyd, the mother who bore her and to whom she remained extremely close. Her mom arrived at the courthouse each day, clutching a framed photograph of her beloved daughter.

Having already heard that final, heart-wrenching message, the family matriarch stood in the witness box adjacent to Judge Robert Scott and faced the killer. "Because of him, I can never hold my daughter, Jessica, in my arms again, hug her and tell her that I love her," she told the hushed courtroom.

"Because of Mr. Williams' actions, my only daughter, Jessica, has been taken away from me. This is not only for this time and the immediate future. This is forever. She can never come back to me," Roxanne said. "I can never hear her voice telling me she loves me. I can never receive another hug from her, another phone call, another email. We will never go shopping, go out for lunch, go away for a weekend together, which are all things that we did do together. I can never spend another minute with her. I feel like my heart has been ripped right out of my chest."

Twelve of the 26 victim impact statements, filed with the court, were read by those most directly affected by the crimes, as Williams sat rigid in the prisoner's box. He looked towards those in the 153-seat courtroom who were expressing their anger and even hatred for the harm that had been caused, but he tried his best to avoid direct eye contact. Through most of the earlier hearing, the disgraced colonel had sat either reading a newspaper or with his head bowed and eyes cast downward. He moved his head and faced Jessica's mother when she stopped reading her statement in mid-sentence and accused him of not even having the courage to look at her.

She told how much the loss of Jessica affected her on Mother's Day. "Then it was her birthday in May. So many dreams I had for my daughter have been destroyed. I will never walk her down the aisle (or) hear that she's expecting a baby. He has not only taken away my precious daughter, but dreams of her future children, my future grandchildren. I've cried and grieved every day for Jessica."

Continuing, she said: "Jessica and I always had a close, loving relationship. I loved her since the moment I realized I was pregnant with her, the nine months that I carried her, the second she was born and every moment since. And I will continue to love her for the rest of my life here on earth and even after I die when I meet up with her again." She said Jessica didn't deserve to go through what she did at the hands of Williams. "She never, ever did anything to hurt anyone. Why did he do this to me too?" she cried. "Now I am a broken women and my life has changed forever. I will never be the same woman I was before Jessica was taken away from me."

Speaking from the heart and sharing a thought that everyone in the court room was thinking, Roxanne said: "No mother should ever have to go through what this has put me through."

Trying to find something positive, she added: "The only good thing to come from all of this is that he can never kidnap, hurt, traumatize, rape or kill another woman ever again. And it's because of my Jessica."

Although Roxanne Lloyd said people suggest that everyone should be forgiven for their sins, she could never forgive Williams. "I can never, ever, ever forgive him for taking my daughter's life and taking her away forever." She also told the court there is no punishment that can make things better. "I can honestly say I hate Russell Williams."

Jessica's brother, Andy, glared at Williams while reading the statement he had prepared. He was the last speaker. "I never imagined anything like this could ever happen. That she could be abducted and that it would attract so much national and international attention," he said. "Not only have I had to endure this grieving process, but I've had to do it in a public spotlight. Strictly because of who Russell Williams was, an important figure in the Canadian military, this case has drawn so much attention ... I am a very proud supporter of the Canadian Armed Forces. I believe the men and women that serve our country are heroes. They deserve to be led by a responsible and morally sound individual. Not someone who committed such horrible crimes."

Lloyd said his father was both a proud Canadian and a very proud member of the military. "He would be mortified if any member of the armed forces, let alone someone of such high-ranking and importance, could commit such terrible crimes against his daughter. I feel for military personnel on an individual basis, knowing how much they must have been dishonored and misled by their commanding officer."

"Evil, pure evil," are the words he chose to describe Williams and imagined that he had been laughing at the family during the 11 days from her abduction to the time her body was found. Lloyd said Williams drove past his sister's home knowing exactly where the body had been dumped, while all her friends and other volunteers were out searching for her. "My sister and I were very close and because she was taken away from our family, there is only my mom and I left. Every day is a struggle to get through. I love her so much. I miss her every day."

Although the Ontario Provincial Police notified the family that Jessica's body had been found and a suspect arrested, they did not learn that the killer was Russell Williams until after his name was revealed the next day on a local radio station.

Outside the court after giving his victim impact statement, Andy Lloyd, just a year older than Jessica, said it was good for everyone to tell Williams what they thought. However, he said the family will never be the same. When contacted to help provide details for the book, he didn't want to relive things. "It's still hard to talk about this."

Born in Ottawa in May 1982, Jessica was almost 14 when her father died following a lengthy battle with cancer. After retiring from the Canadian Navy, Warren Lloyd moved the family to a home on Highway 37, in a farming area in the hamlet of Plainfield, a 10-minute drive north of Belleville. Several years later, the city annexed the rural site and the home where the Lloyd family continued to live was absorbed into Belleville. After completing studies in business administration and human resources at the local community college, the five-foot-five, 125-pound Jessica had several jobs before being hired by Tri-Board Student Transportation Services. When she finally got full-time employment, Jessica bought the family home from her mother.

She was regarded as someone who loved life, whether
sharing time with family members and friends or riding
her motorcycle. Those who knew Jessica talked about her
contagious laughter, her sincere smile and the happiness
she willingly shared. Friends said she captured people's
attention whenever she entered a room and had a gift for
the gab. She loved joking around and had a wide interest
in music. In interviews with media outlets after her
slaying, Andy said his sister was extremely witty,
sometimes sarcastic but with a great sense of humor. She
also loved the Toronto Maple Leafs and hoped some day to
have a son she would name "Tie" after Tie Domi, the now-
retired right-winger who had the reputation of being an
enforcer in the National Hockey League.

She named the black Pontiac Grand Prix that she
commuted to work in her "Black Ninja." At her February
13, 2010 funeral, which co-author Ian Robertson covered
for his newspaper, mourners remembered the impact she
had on everyone. They recalled how she loved children and
how much she enjoyed her own childhood, both as a
military brat and later a teenager in Belleville.

The obituary from the John R. Bush Funeral Home in
Belleville reads: "Lloyd, Jessica Elizabeth – of RR 1,
Plainfield at the age of 27. Cherished daughter of Roxanne
Lloyd and the late Warren (Ebb) Lloyd. Beloved sister of
Andy Lloyd of Belleville. Ever remembered by grandmother
Jean McGarvey (late Ronald McGarvey) and great aunt
Youearln Wright. Predeceased by her grandparents Keith
and Alexandria Lloyd. Lovingly remembered by aunts and
uncles Debra Lloyd (late Jim), Sharon Gerber (Bill), Terry
McGarvey (Liz), Janice Pitt (George), Janet Calnan (Brian),
Armour Watson, Keith Lloyd (Carol) and David Lloyd
(Anky). Much loved cousin of John, Sarah, Kristin, Ryan,
Melissa, Sheena, Dillon, Andre, Stephanie, Erin, Jennifer,
Brianna, Brandon, Jared, Bryana, Katie, David and their

spouses. Jessica will be greatly missed by her many friends."

The death notice gives the location, time and date of the funeral and visitation, and asks for expressions of sympathy to be made in the form of donations to the Canadian Cancer Society, Child Find or the Quinte Secondary School Scholarship in memory of Jessica Lloyd. The family also made public statements thanking the police and others with the investigative team who caught the man who killed Jessica and caused so much pain for all those in the community.

Six prosecutors took turns reading the facts of the case against Williams to Judge Scott in the courtroom at Belleville's Ontario Supreme Court of Justice. They detailed how he became "bolder" during his break and enter spree and eventually, after stripping naked, entering a home where a woman was showering. He didn't confront the victim or do anything to let her know that he'd been in her home, but Prosecutor Robert Morrison said it was a turning point. One of the other prosecutors, Joe Dart, said Williams had admitted when interrogated by Smyth that he wanted to take more risks and escalated his behavior.

Chapter Fourteen

The military has been criticized by some segments of the public for not having recognized the danger lurking within Russell Williams as he moved through the ranks of the Canadian Armed Forces. As often the case with armchair critics, it is easy to theorize after an evil-doer has been exposed, about how they could have or should have been ferreted out earlier and stopped. Those individuals are sometimes influenced by television programs such as CSI or Criminal Minds, but the scientific methods and processes seen on these shows are sometimes not completely bona-fide. Obviously a great deal more time than the allotted hour is required before evidence and clues in actual cases can be transformed into a real-life solution. There are also other legal limitations designed to protect people from having their privacy invaded.

There has been an assumption by many members of the public that Williams is a criminal psychopath, but in reality he has been classified as a sado-sexual serial killer. It is important to note that not all people with psychopathic tendencies will resort to criminal behavior and those who are more intelligent will often acquire a good education, jobs, marry, have families and generally blend into regular society.

While little has been said about methods used by the military to weed out men and women who may put others at undo risk based on psychological imperfections – from pre-existing conditions or problems that develop because of traumas suffered during active duty – checks and balances are undertaken. Lieutenant General Andre Deschamps, the Chief of the Air Staff, said Williams underwent an assortment of screenings and aptitude tests. "When this came out ... we did some serious soul searching," said Deschamps after the disgraced colonel was convicted. "His file was looked at extensively from every angle we could think of to see what we could have missed. The truth is, we didn't miss anything that was visible." He said Williams had a yearly review that assessed his performance plus promotion potential, and was also the subject of a standard criminal background check.

When killers, con artists or thieves are exposed, society is now too ready to call them psychopaths. Generally, a psychopath lacks so-called "normal" feelings, especially empathy, but all of them have a rare ability to hide their potential dark side even from psychiatrists. This was particularly driven home to Ian Robertson in 1992 during his coverage of the lengthy and high-profile coroner's inquest into the abduction, sexual assault and murder of 12-year-old Christopher Stephenson near Toronto. The lad's killer, a lifelong pedophile named Joseph Fredericks, was described as slow-witted – but had managed to avoid prison for decades by exhibiting behavior while incarcerated at mental institutions that appeared to no longer pose a threat to children. After Fredericks was released from prison, he spent several days bicycling around the city of Brampton before finding Christopher at a local shopping centre and leading him away at knifepoint.

In the wake of the Williams' case, some people spouted unbelievably juvenile and unfounded accusations that Canada's military "culture" is a breeding ground for rapists. People rarely, of course, carry signs proclaiming themselves as criminals. And not everyone arouses suspicion by their appearance. Researchers can measure a person's deviances, which include manipulative and superficial behavior. Such tests, however, are designed to explore the psyches of convicted people, not those outside prisons or in institutions for the criminally insane. Senior officers with the Canadian Armed Forces say a review of

Williams, plus methods used to choose senior officers, were conducted. Conclusions were reached that too many variables existed to have accurately revealed his alter ego.

The judge who sentenced the colonel to life in prison was not among those who regard him as a psychopath. He declared that Williams will be "forever remembered as a sado-sexual serial killer." The World Health Organization says the label applies to an individual who is found to have "preference for sexual activity that involves bondage or infliction of pain or humiliation."

Williams was regarded by military supervisors as a hard-working and very skilled person, according to an evaluation written by Major Greg McQuaid in 1992, when the now convicted killer was being considered for promotion to captain. This was the beginning of his rapid rise through the officer ranks. He graduated from university with an economics and political science degree and became a major in 1999, a lieutenant-colonel in 2004 and colonel just before his arrest. McQuaid, now retired, made his findings known in an interview with Mclean's magazine shortly after Williams was unmasked. He said the younger officer could be "so focused ... sometimes it was like he could look right through you." But McQuaid acknowledged that Williams fit in well and was respected. "I saw nothing that made me think he'd be capable of something like this," he told the national weekly magazine's interviewer. Williams had also passed routine annual performance reviews.

In an interview for this book, a man living directly behind the home of Corporal Marie-France Comeau revealed that Royal Canadian Air Force officers have been required to undergo "scrutiny" since before the Second World War.

Retired Captain Patrick "Pete" Peterson said the psychological tests are designed to detect bipolar disorder and other mental problems that could spell trouble for the individual and others who they serve with or command. In an attempt to "weed out" anyone who could adversely affect future missions, he said military teams are also debriefed and given psychological testing before being redeployed. The military today recognizes that those involved in peacekeeping patrols or battle can experience post traumatic stress disorder. In bygone years, particularly during the two World Wars, shell-shocked and battle-weary soldiers were quite often treated with contempt and there were cases in which some faced a firing squad for cowardice if they failed to "shape up" when ordered back to the front line. "Everyone is affected by war, no matter what they say," Peterson said.

Shortly after police disclosed that Williams had been charged with the murders of two women, there was a brief outburst of anti-military sentiment. A handful of the usual type of malcontents surfaced, including some who posted ludicrous comments suggesting the forces train people to be killing machines. One person even went on a rant, alleging that other murders and rapes involving armed forces personnel had been "covered up" by the military. Except for simply glorifying in their own anonymous vitriol – as so many scream-mailers do these days on instantly-accessible comment areas of media websites and chat rooms – they did not rally supporters and the attempted smear campaign quickly fizzled.

While there were reports of people in uniform being spat upon in public and told they should be ashamed of themselves, such vile and reprehensible behavior also vanished in the wake of overwhelming public sympathy and support. People living in Trenton and surrounding communities, who have welcomed the armed forces since construction of the base began in the late 1930s, quickly muzzled the malevolent minority by responding in no uncertain terms to say that such puerile spouting was disgusting, unwarranted and unwelcome.

Area residents personally know many of the men and women who work at the base, and could not comprehend why they had become targets of hatred in the wake of Williams' arrest. Rallies were organized to show support for the 3,500 military and civilian personnel at the sprawling 960-acre base, which is the largest employer in the region. The majority of letters sent to the editors of newspapers in communities around Trenton praised the men and women in uniform, who were obviously deeply hurt by the stigma inflicted on Canada's forces by someone who was branded an "effing" monster by John Williams, the Mayor of Quinte West, an amalgamated community that includes Trenton and the base. "He's sick. He's a monster," Williams, who is not related to the killer, told local reporters after the disgraced colonel admitted to the killings in court. "In a matter of months, he's gone from being one of the most respected people in the community to being a sicko murderer. Like everyone else, I'm still in shock. He's a f...king monster."

The mayor had flown on a trip into Canada's Arctic with the colonel. They spent several days at Alert, an outpost about 500 miles from the North Pole, before returning to Trenton on September 16, 2009. He had tried talking to Russell Williams several times as they headed back home on the eight-hour flight, but there was no real conversation. "It was like his mind was somewhere else," the mayor said. "Thinking about something else." After leaving the base, Colonel Williams drove to Tweed, where he sexually assaulted his first victim. Although Mayor Williams condemned the colonel, he publicly urged his constituents to show support and empathy to military personnel and their families.

There has never been a case in the Canadian military in which a top-rank officer has engaged in such heinous behavior. Williams is an anomaly. Those who served with him have had a particularly tough time coming to grips with what he did. Experts also cannot explain what seems to have triggered Williams to move from a lifestyle of the rich and famous to a depravity which normal people can't even fathom. It is also a matter of record that most serial killers are white men with an average age of just under 30. Williams, at 44 when he began his crime spree, was at the high end of the age on the criminal profile spectrum. He was also someone who would not quickly surface as a suspect on the police radar and – as a result – would have been extremely difficult to catch.

A challenge for anyone reading this book is to select the exact moment when you could have legally arrested Russell Williams for the crimes he committed. Reading these pages, you have the ability to see the break-ins, assaults and sex-related slayings in the sequence as they unfolded and the amount of evidence that the investigators obtained. Until Williams turned up at the police roadblock and the tire impressions were found to be similar to those outside Jessica Lloyd's home, the colonel had never surfaced as a suspect. Even then, it was hard for anyone to imagine that a military commander could be responsible for the crime wave that had plagued the Ottawa and Tweed communities and spread into Brighton. In reality, the investigative team probing the murder of Marie-France Comeau, the abduction of Jessica Lloyd and the two sexual assaults, were not in a position to arrest Williams until he confessed during his interview on February 7, 2010 with Detective Sergeant Jim Smyth.

The fact that Williams was bright, had a good education and attained a trusted position, gave him an added advantage and made it easier for him to continue his "night-time hobby" without being detected. Using that term may seem trite, but in reality serial predators are as dedicated to their trophy-collecting as any hobbyist. And considering the huge quantity of women's intimate apparel he accumulated, the carefully-indexed video segments and photographs on his different computers, plus the sex attacks leading up to the slayings of Comeau and Lloyd, the pattern of an escalating sexual predator certainly fits.

A sexual deviant who ties up and photographs female victims is "the worst of the worst," said Dave Perry, a former sex crimes detective with the Toronto Police Service and now a private investigator and CEO of Investigative Solutions Network. He said very few individuals take photographs of victims. It is more likely that serial sex offenders will fantasize about assaulting someone while in their teens and gradually progress to the "Peeping Tom" stage. Perry said such individuals are capable of committing physical attacks, rape and murder.

There is a close-knit bond not only with military personnel, but among their families, and everyone was in shock, especially those at the Canadian Forces Base in Trenton. Reverend Philip Boudreau met with six other Chaplain Service colleagues after learning of the colonel's arrest, to determine the level of counseling that would be required. Most people felt that what Williams had done was a "personal act of betrayal" since, as the commanding officer, he was held in such high esteem. "It was base-wide shock and disbelief," Boudreau told reporters from the Intelligencer and the Pioneer, the local Loyalist College newspaper. People in the services also felt particularly let down by Comeau's murder because the colonel had flown with her and she was regarded as someone who was highly-personable, friendly and an outgoing young woman. Williams was also someone who had been well-liked by people on the base. Despite being a high-ranking officer, he would often stop to chat with personnel, was mostly even-tempered and took interest if anyone was ill or facing personal issues. Boudreau pointed out that people in the military place a "sacred trust" in their commanders.

The padres offered suggestions to help people dealing with a sense of guilt for not having spotted the evil behind the façade the colonel had presented while on day-to-day duties, speaking in public on their behalf or piloting planes with dignitaries. After the consultative meeting, the spiritual leaders did their best to remind people at the base that the attacks by Williams were of his making, not by those around him. Regarding the few incidents of military-bashing, Reverend Catherine Askew had the most cogent comment: "We are not aliens from another planet," she said. "We are sons and daughters of Canada. For Canada to love us as much as they always did ... that's what we need."

The telephone number for the National Defence department's Member Assistance Program was sent to all Canadian military installations worldwide and personnel were reminded it is available year-round and at all hours, if any form of counseling was needed. Canada's MAP program is similar to the Employee Assistance Program which the United States Army offers as an aid to help personnel identify and resolve personal problems. The Canadian Armed Forces operates its program in conjunction with the Employee Assistance Services of Health Canada for all regular force members, eligible reservists, cadets and relatives. Operating for more than 20 years, the free, voluntary program is confidential and provides short-term, non-therapy help to those with marital or family problems, grief, anger or difficulty with depression. It also assists with several other issues, ranging from dealing with traumatic experiences, including sexual assault, to coping with alcohol and drug addiction. In addition, a specialized Military and Family Life Consultant program provides support to personnel and members of their families who face stress when regiments are deployed to war zones or to foreign countries for peace-keeping or relief missions.

Lieutenant-General Deschamps visited Trenton to inform base members that Williams had been stripped of his rank and booted out of Canada's military. He had also ordered that the ex-colonel's uniforms be burned and made a formal request to the media to stop referring to Williams by his former rank.

"I guess we don't understand the why, and this is something that troubles Canadians at large, as it troubles those who have known this individual," Dechamps said. "How could we have known? What could we have done differently? I'm not sure we'll ever get the answers." Deschamps said there is no accurate way to predict what someone will do in the future, but he promised to seek better ways to evaluate those who serve in the military. Prime Minister Harper also commented on the Williams case, saying: "The Canadian Forces are the victims here ... as are the direct victims of these terrible events."

When announcing funds to increase support for military members and their families, Defense Minister Peter MacKay acknowledged the trauma people at Trenton's base had experienced. "You have had to deal with the reality of a monster in your midst and you've done so with courage and determination to overcome," he said, while describing the crime spree as a shocking breach of trust and an unspeakable period of violence and depravity. MacKay said the Canadian government had approved $6.9 billion to expand the number of medical and employee support centers for military personnel who are ill or facing problems after returning from dangerous places such as Afghanistan. One of the five new facilities was earmarked for Trenton, with yearly operational costs of about $4 million.

With the passage of time, since the arrest of Williams, the people of Canada and, in particular residents living in communities around Trenton, have continued to show support for the military family. The sentiment came as a direct result of the public recognizing a need to demonstrate their respect and trust for those serving with the Canadian Armed Forces as a way to help heal the residual trauma created by this case and to raise the morale of all personnel at the base. Public demonstrations of support were most visible when people, young and old, joined veterans, police officers, firefighters and paramedics on Highway 401 overpasses whenever the body of a Canadian soldier killed in Afghanistan was carried from Trenton's tarmac to the coroner's building in Toronto for an official autopsy before being returned to their family for burial with full military honors. The first leg in Canada on the route along the freeway taken by all fallen soldiers on their journey home was officially renamed – the "Highway of Heroes" – in a direct response to the outpouring of love by the people who came to stand tall with those who put their lives on the line for freedom.

Chapter Fifteen

Although some novels and a number of motion picture productions through the years have featured killers taking pictures of their torturous attacks on victims, until the sexual assaults and homicides by Russell Williams there was no known case in which an identified individual has documented a murder in its entirety with written notes, photographs, sound and video recordings.

There have been incidents in which rape and murder victims have been photographed or videotaped in the early stages of a sexual assault or after being killed. But until the arrest of Williams, homicide investigators had never encountered a killer who fully documented their crimes from start to finish. In fact, from the evidence uncovered during the Project Hatfield investigation, Russell Williams provided the law enforcement community, police psychiatrists and researchers with an encyclopaedia of information about his 29-month crime spree – which began with sexually-motivated residential burglaries and culminated with the senseless slayings of two young women.

Ironically, 14 months after Williams was taken into custody, law enforcement officers in Nevada arrested a 77-year-old man who kept a diary and had photographs of female victims murdered in a time span stretching from the early 1970s to 1994. Joseph Naso did not detail the killings to the extent Williams has, but investigators from the Nevada Department of Public Safety discovered a 23-page journal describing several homicides and sexual assaults. Also located during searches at his Reno home and of a safety deposit box was a list with the names of 10 women who disappeared through the years and numerous photographs of females, young and old. Among the pictures found by police were images of known homicide victims, including photographs of two women who appeared to be dead and wearing only lingerie. Naso is facing execution for the slayings of 18-year-old Roxene Roggasch, who was found dead in 1977 near Lagunitas, Nevada; 22-year-old Carmen Colon, whose body was discovered by a California Highway Patrol officer in 1978 near Port Costa, California; 38-year-old Pamela Parsons, who was strangled near Yuba City, California in 1993 and 31-year-old Tracy Tafoya, whose remains were found off Highway 70 in Yuba City in 1994. The victims had double initials, and detectives with the New York State Police began gathering evidence to link Naso with the Alphabet Murders, involving three young girls who were abducted and slain outside Rochester – where he lived in the early 1970s. Ten-year-old Carmen Colon, who shared the same name but is not related to one of Naso's California victims, vanished on November 16, 1971 and was found dead two days later in Riga, New York; the body of 11-year-old Wanda Walkowicz was discovered in a highway rest area near Webster, New York on April 2, 1973. one day after she disappeared; and Michelle Maenza, also 11, who went missing November 26, 1973, was found dead two days later in Macedon, New York.

The killer closest to duplicating the documentation of Williams is Robert Berdella. Dubbed the Kansas City Butcher for the savagery he committed while holding victims hostage in his home, he was convicted of killing six men between 1984 and 1987. Evidence presented at his trial revealed he had taken graphic photographs while committing sexual acts on them. Investigators with the Kansas City Police in Missouri found more than 350 photographs that showed 23 men being sexually abused and tortured, but detectives learned most were male prostitutes who had participated willingly. Berdella, who died in prison in 1992 at the age of 43 while serving a life sentence, also kept a detailed diary describing what the murdered men had endured, including having electrical cables attached to their genitals, irritating chemicals poured down their throats after they were drugged, plus devices inserted into their rectums. One homicide victim had his eye gouged out. Berdella told authorities that he had cut up the slain men and put them piece by piece into trash bins, which were picked up by the city's garbage collectors.

Armin Meiwes is the first individual known to have actually video-taped a killing, but it involved a willing volunteer who agreed to be slaughtered and eaten. This bizarre and gruesome case took place in Germany in March 2001, after Meiwes appealed through the Internet for a man who would allow him to satisfy his desire for cannibalism. Several people answered the advertisement, but Meiwes selected 43-year-old Bernd Jurgen Brandes, who was given a concoction of alcohol and sleeping pills before his jugular vein was cut and he bled to death in a bathtub. The killer, who made a two-hour videotape of the slaying, hung the victim with a meat hook – and over a 10-month period hacked pieces from the body and ate them. Meiews also fed some of the human remains to his dog. Police found the video and other evidence when they raided his home after he posted a computer appeal for a second victim. Incredibly, he was sentenced to just eight and a half years for manslaughter – because the victim had consented to being killed. The ensuing public outcry, however, forced justice officials to bring a murder charge against Meiwes and he was eventually sent to prison for life.

It was virtually impossible for someone to film or photograph a homicide through the first half of the 20th century. But with the advent of the Polaroid camera, people were able to take pictures without having them developed through a photo-finisher who would likely call authorities if any photographs aroused suspicion. In the

1970s, the home movie camera was replaced by video recorders and in the late 80s, the first cameras producing digital images that could be displayed on computer screens became generally available. It was in the latter half of the last century that law enforcement agencies began hearing rumours of "snuff films" which supposedly contained scenes of actual murders. Nothing conclusive has ever turned up, however, to prove that someone was killed during the production of such movies. There was also a suggestion that the diminutive five-foot-three Charles Manson was planning to record one of his California cult group's killing sprees for a snuff film. But police never confirmed that he had ever considered the idea. Polaroid photographs have turned up from time to time with depictions of graphic sexual attacks or images of victims before or after death, but none have ever shown a homicide in progress. Manson was imprisoned for life for master-minding the August 1969 murders of actress Sharon Tate, Steve Parent, Voytek Frykowski, Abigail Folger and Jay Sebring at Tate's Cielo Drive home in Los Angeles and the slayings of millionaire Leno LaBianca and his wife, Rosemary, at their Waverly Drive home in Los Angeles a day later. Tate was eight months pregnant when she was stabbed to death and her soon-to-be-born infant did not survive. On October 11, 2011, Manson was denied parole and won't be eligible to reapply until 2027. At that time, if still alive, he will be 92.

Former homicide detective, Tom Klatt, a partner at MKD International Inc., a leading worldwide private investigation agency based in Toronto, said it's "extremely rare" to find a case in which the culprit has taken pictures. But, he predicts it will become more common in the future. "I was involved in approximately 70 murder investigations while with Toronto's homicide squad and none of those presented any evidence of video or photographs being taken of the victims or the crime scenes," Klatt said. "Since leaving the Toronto Police

Service 14 years ago, I have been involved in several high-profile historic murder cases and numerous more current cases and, again, in none of those was evidence located of video or photographs." The historic cases referred to by Klatt include the January 1991 slaying of Dr. Carolyn Joyce Warrick in the underground garage of her Toronto apartment building; the June 1959 rape and strangulation of a 12-year-old girl that resulted in 14-year-old Stephen Truscott being sent to prison for life after a reprieve spared him from the death penalty; and the case of Robert Baltovich, who served eight years in prison after being convicted of murdering his 22-year-old girlfriend, University of Toronto student Elizabeth Bain, who vanished in June 1990.

"Williams was the first," Klatt said, describing him as a "rare and different type of killer" – and someone who has shown us the future. With the development of new technology, such as small Iphones and other high-quality image recording equipment, Klatt suggests some murderers will take the opportunity to videotape or photograph their killings so they can relive the experience or even share their images with others, in the same way child pornography is distributed through underground computer networks. With more people having the ability to instantly record events, Klatt has no doubt others will follow in Williams' footsteps and take pictures of victims as they are struggling to survive murderous attacks. "It's common for criminals to take something from a crime scene, he said. "This is often known as a "trophy" and in some cases shared with others. Since they do take trophies, I fully expect in the future, killers will make use of modern technology to record their crimes. They get off...looking at what they have done."

There is an ironic twist that now links Williams to the homicide case involving Robert Baltovich, which MKD investigators had delved into. After a review of the evidence against him, Ontario's top court quashed his conviction and ordered a new trial. However, after prosecutors refused to proceed, Baltovich was released from custody. When Williams was charged with the murders of Lloyd and Comeau, Baltovich issued public statements suggesting the disgraced colonel could be responsible for the disappearance of Elizabeth Bain. Williams attended classes at the university several years earlier and was familiar with the areas on the campus where the avid runner often jogged. Bain, who was dating Baltovich at the time she disappeared, has never been found and any further investigation is stymied without a body.

One of the most recent movies featuring a killer making gruesome videos of his victims is the Poughkeepsie Tapes. Rumoured to have been based on a true case, it was in reality total fiction. In the horror film, police discover about 800 videos. They detail murders but, like Williams, the fictional slayer documented the crimes from the abduction of individuals to their deaths plus mutilation of their bodies in the town of 33,000 people midway between Albany and New York City. The film is portrayed as a documentary and because its release came only a few years after Kendall Francois pleaded guilty in August 2000 to murdering eight women in Poughkeepsie, some people surmised that it was a true account of his case. In fact, Francois was arrested after a prostitute escaped from his home, where he was attempting to strangle her. While being questioned by detectives about the attack, Francois, who was 27 at the time, confessed to the killings which took place between October 1996 and August 1998. Several bodies were located when police searched his home, but nothing was found to indicate that any of the victims had been photographed or video-taped as the motion picture portrayed.

Although Clifford Olson, who is considered to have been Canada's most callous serial killer, didn't photograph his victims, on one occasion he tape-recorded the screams of a 14-year-old girl as she was being murdered. He later called the family's home to play the daughter's anguished cries over the telephone. Between January 1980 and August 1981, Olson murdered 11 young people in the heavily-populated lower mainland area of British Columbia. The victims, ranging in age from nine to 18, were only linked together when Olson convinced justice officials to pay a reward of $10,000 for each killing that he helped them solve. At that time, the 11 murders were unsolved and some bodies had not been located. Olson freely confessed to one homicide, but wanted a total of $100,000 for details of the other slayings, plus information where six of his victims were buried. He sought the money to finance a trust fund for his wife and infant son, knowing that he would be spending the rest of his life in prison. In fact, he died in prison at the age of 71 on September 30, 2011. A career criminal with both juvenile and adult convictions, Olson began his killing spree on November 17, 1980, when 12-year-old Christine Weller was abducted while riding her bicycle in Surrey, British Columbia and driven to an isolated area where she was repeatedly stabbed. Police found her body on Christmas Day. Thirteen-year-old Colleen Daignault of Surrey was raped and murdered on April 16, 1981 after being offered a part-time job by Olson. Her skeletal remains were found in a wooded area five months later. Days after arriving from Saskatchewan to visit his mother and two younger siblings in Vancouver, 16-year-old Daryn Johnsrude was lured from a mall on April 22, and later bludgeoned to death with a hammer. His body was found on May 1, but police discovered nothing to link these three cases and had no idea a serial killer was in their midst.

On May 19, Olson clubbed 16-year-old Sandra Wolfsteiner to death after convincing the Langley, British Columbia teenager that she would be paid to help him clean windows at a cottage in the Fraser Valley, which straddles the border with Washington state. Police initially believed that Wolfsteiner had run away from home. A month later, on June 21, Ada Court vanished while waiting for a bus in Coquitlam, British Columbia to return to her home in Burnaby. It was two months before her remains were discovered at the side of a logging road. Nine-year-old Simon Partington vanished while riding his bicycle in Surrey. The July 2 disappearance in the same vicinity where, eight months earlier, the Weller girl had gone missing, prompted investigators to consider the possibility of a serial predator. They found no evidence at that time to link the cases, but pressure mounted when 14-year-old Judy Kozma disappeared July 9, after accepting a ride from Olson in New Westminster. She was killed after being plied with alcohol and knock-out pills, and when her body was found two weeks later in a wooded area, it was very evident that young people were being targeted.

Olson picked up Raymond King at a Canada Manpower employment centre on July 23, in New Westminster after the 15-year-old was offered a job washing windows – a ploy the killer routinely used to lure other teenagers. Raymond was taken to an isolated camping area new Alpine Lake, where he was clubbed with a rock and his body dumped beside a trail. On July 25, Sigrun Charlotte Arnd, an 18-year-old visitor from Germany, was killed after meeting Olson in a Coquitlam bar. Her body was discovered after his $100,000 fee was put into a trust fund for Olson's wife and child.

His job offer ploy was used to convince Terri Lyn Carson to accompany Olson on July 27, after she was picked up at a bus stop in Surrey. The 15-year-old was plied with alcohol and drugged before being raped and strangled. Her body was dumped in a rural area along the Fraser River. Olson's final victim, 17-year-old Louise Marie Chartrand, was murdered on July 30, 1981 after being picked up while hitch-hiking in Maple Ridge, just east of Vancouver. After drugging his Quebec-born victim, Olson drove to Whistler, British Columbia, where he beat her with a hammer and buried the young woman's body in a shallow grave.

Canadian Paul Bernardo did take videotape of his wife, Karla Homolka, involved in sexual activity with one of their victims. But there was no pictorial evidence of the killings. In the United States, Rodney Alcala, a rapist and serial killer who was sentenced to death in 2010 for five murders between 1977 and 1979, had more than 1,000 photographs of young women and boys hidden in a storage locker. The majority of the photographs were of individuals in sexually-explicit poses, but none depicted people after their deaths. Investigators believe Alcala, who in 1978 appeared as a bachelor on the Dating Game television show, may be responsible for slaughtering 50 to 130 women across the country and suggest that some of the photographs are of his victims before they were murdered. Another killer, who had young women posing for photographs he took before they were slain, is Christopher Bernard Wilder, but there is no evidence he snapped pictures during or after his murders. Wilder, born in Australia in March 1945, was known as the Beauty Queen Killer and murdered at least eight women across the United States. He was implicated in numerous other rapes and sex slayings, but investigators did not get any collaborating evidence – since he died when his gun discharged during a struggle with a police officer in New Hampshire in April 1984. At the time of his death, he was making his way to Canada because federal politicians had abolished capital punishment and he was facing the electric chair if captured in the United States.

Like Williams, Wilder was bent on committing the perfect crime. He was also wealthy, intelligent and had an interest in photography. Very much aware of the ability by authorities to identify serial offenders when crimes occur in the same area, Wilder moved from Florida to another state and then crisscrossed the United States, using both Interstate and secondary highways, before heading towards Canada. The Sydney native was later implicated in the January 1965 deaths of two 15-year-old girls, Marianne Schmidt and Christine Sharrock. But that came after Wilder fled to the U.S. following his indictment on sexual assault charges involving two other 15-year-old Australian victims. Since Wilder's rapes and torturous homicides had similarities to the attacks that Williams committed, it is possible that the colonel could have escalated to this type of behavior if not caught shortly after killing his second victim.

Wilder, who was on the FBI's Most Wanted list, would approach his victims and offer money for them to pose for him on the pretext of submitting their photographs to a modeling agency. His first murder victim in the U.S. is believed to have been 20-year-old Rosario Gonzalez, an aspiring model who had competed in the Miss Florida beauty pageant with his girlfriend, Elizabeth Kenyon. Wilder ran into Gonzalez in February 1984 at the Miami Grand Prix, where he was racing his car. He asked her to model for him and she hasn't been seen since. His 23-year-old girlfriend vanished two weeks after Gonzalez disappeared and also remains missing. Investigators later learned that Wilder had built a device that would use power from a car battery to stun victims and knock them out with a high-voltage charge.

Murders linked to him include 21-year-old Teresa "Terry" Ferguson, who was lured into a car on March 18, 1984 at a shopping mall in Indian Harbor Beach, Florida and found fatally stabbed two days later in a swamp 100 miles away; 24-year-old Terry Diane Walden vanished March 23 after dropping her four-year-old daughter at a daycare center in Beaumont, Texas and her beaten, stabbed and bound body was discovered three days later in a canal; after being raped, beaten and stabbed to death, 20-year-old Suzanne Logan's body was dumped in a reservoir. She had been abducted March 25 from a shopping mall in Oklahoma City; 18-year-old Sheryl Bonaventura was found dead in Utah on May 13 – stabbed and shot – after being picked up March 29 at a mall in Grand Junction, Colorado by a man who had asked her to be a model. The daugther of a casino executive, 17-year-old Michelle Korfman, willingly left to get her photograph taken after meeting a man on April 1 during a fashion show at the Meadow Mall in Las Vegas. Her remains were found six weeks later in the Angeles National Forest in the San Gabriel Mountain region of Los Angeles County in California.

While in California, Wilder abducted 16-year-old Tina Marie Risico near Torrance, a beach-front community south of Los Angeles. After being threatened with a gun, the victim was held captive for several days at a motel located just minutes from the Mexican border, where she was repeatedly jolted with electrical charges and raped. The torture turned the teenager into a slave-like zombie and she willingly went with Wilder to help lure other victims to his vehicle. He drove first to Taos, New Mexico, about 850 miles away, and then another 1,300 miles to Merrillville, an Indiana town with less than 30,000 residents. There were no killings along this route, but it appears that Wilder, who was an avid reader of once-banned sex novels, was making a pilgrimage to the remote U.S. town where D. H. Lawrence, the author of Lady Chatterley's Lover, had a ranch. The author's cremated ashes are in a chapel near Toas and there is some memorabilia on display in local buildings, including several of his paintings. Wilder's attacks resumed in Merrillville when his teenage companion brought Dawnette Sue Wilt to the car on the pretense that her photographer-friend was looking for fresh-faced girls to do some modeling. She was stunned with an electrical charge and raped repeatedly before being taken on April 12 to a wooded area some 600 miles away between Penn Yan and Barrington, New York, where she was tied up and stabbed. Dawnette survived, however, and gave investigators descriptions of the couple who had told her they were making their way to Canada.

Only a few hours after stabbing her, Wilder drove to Victor, New York where his still-traumatized young passenger called 33-year-old Beth Dodge over to their car in a mall parking lot. Dodge, a wife and mother, was taken to the outskirts of the community where she was shot and her body dumped into a gravel pit. Wilder then used her car to drive Risico to Boston, where she boarded a plane to Los Angeles while he headed north towards Canada. He tried to overpower a 19-year-old woman in a parking lot between Beverly and Wenham in Massachusetts before driving north into New Hampshire. That would-be victim fought him off and called police with a description of the distinctive gold Pontiac TransAm that was stolen when Dodge was killed. Wilder, who was taking back roads, was less than 10 miles from the Canadian border crossing at Hereford, Quebec when spotted by two New Hampshire state troopers, Leo "Chuck" Jellison and Wayne Fortier. Jellison had Wilder in a bear hug when the fugitive's gun discharged and the trooper was hit in the chest with the .357 magnum slug after it passed through the suspect's body. Wilder died instantly, but doctors were able to save the police officer's life. Apart from the serial killer's interest in the writings of D. H. Lawrence, investigators found a copy of The Collector, a 1963 novel by John Fowles about a young woman who dies while being held captive in a wine cellar. Wilder had basically memorized the 250-page book, which was later turned into a motion picture.

Among others taking photographs of victims was a British couple that also made a 16-minute audio-recording of a 10-year-old girl as she was being killed the day after Christmas in 1964. Like Williams' victims, the girl was forced to pose naked before being raped and strangled. It is one of the earliest-known cases in which anyone took pictures prior to a slaying, and became evidence of a horrific killing spree in Manchester, England known as the Moor Murders. In that case, 26-year-old Ian Brady and 22-year-old Myra Hindley became lovers after meeting at work. Both had difficulties as children. Brady, who was raised by adoptive parents when his mother couldn't afford to look after him, enjoyed abusing animals and hurting younger children. Hindley, from an early age, was encouraged by her alcoholic father to use her fists to settle arguments. This diabolical pair became obsessed with sadism and pornography, and within a short time hatched a plan to rape and murder unsuspecting victims.

Their first target, 16-year-old Pauline Reade, was lured into a van by Hindley on July 12, 1963 to help find an expensive glove she claimed to have lost on the nearby Saddleworth Moor. Brady arrived on his motorcycle moments later, on the pretext of helping to search for the glove and Pauline innocently walked with him to a desolate spot where she was raped and her throat slashed. On November 23, the couple stopped their vehicle beside 12-year-old John Kilbride and offered him a ride home. They then used the same story about losing a glove and took the boy to the sprawling grassy area where he was sexually abused, stabbed and strangled with a shoelace. Their next victim was 12-year-old Keith Bennett, who they convinced to get into their van on June 16, 1964. Brady walked Keith onto the moor with the same story of needing help to find a missing glove. He was also sexually attacked before being killed. Ten-year-old Lesley Ann Downey was driven to the couple's home on December 26, 1964, after agreeing to help with some packages that Hindley and

Brady had loaded into their vehicle. Once inside the house, the young girl was stripped naked, photographed and raped prior to her death. The couple had a tape recorder running, which captured the girl begging to go home and then screaming before a ligature was pulled tight around her neck. She was later buried on the moor.

Hindley's brother-in-law saw Brady killing the fifth victim, 17-year-old Edward Evans, and notified police. Officers found the young man's body in a bedroom in the couple's home. David Smith, who had married Hindley's younger sister, arrived unannounced there on October 6, 1965 and saw Brady beating Evans with the blunt end of an axe. He helped the killer wrap the body in plastic and agreed to come back the next day and join Brady on his drive to the moor for burial. Instead, Smith made his way home and walked with his wife to a pay phone to report the killing to police. While investigating the slaying, detectives found the photographs of the Downey girl and other pictures taken on the moor – where the remains of three victims were found. Police have been unable to find Bennett's body, but the couple insisted that he is buried in the same area. After giving them life sentences, the presiding judge described the murders as "truly horrible" and the couple "two sadistic killers of the utmost depravity."

Serial killer Tsutomu Miyazak was hanged at the age of 45 on June 17, 2008 in Tokyo, Japan after being sentenced for killing four young girls. Evidence revealed that he photographed the victims – four-year-old Mari Konno, seven-year-old Masami Yoshizawa, four-year-old Erika Nanba and five-year-old Ayako Nomoto – before and after death. The gruesome images also showed that he ate some of the remains and drank their blood. Letters containing graphic details were also mailed to families telling how the children were murdered. The charred remains of Mari were sent to her parents along with photographs of the clothing their daughter had been wearing, plus some the child's teeth. It is obvious that Miyazaki, known as the Otaku Murderer, the Little Girl Killer and Dracula, was much more extreme and depraved than Williams. His case, however, demonstrates the bizarre depths that someone can sink to once their life takes on another dimension in a dark world. Police in Japan found more than 5,000 horror and explicit adult videos in Miyazaki's apartment, plus photographs and videotaped recordings of the little victims he murdered between 1988 and 1989.

Dean Corll, known as the Candy Man, took photographs of some victims he tortured, raped and eventually murdered in Texas. The slayings occurred during a four-year period that began in 1970 and involved at least 28 boys, most in their mid-teens. The victims were rendered unconscious with drugs and alcohol, stripped naked and then strapped to a wooden board on which they were tortured before being slain. Police found photographs of at least 16 of them taken before they were killed, most likely so that Corll could use them to relive the euphoria he achieved while committing rape and murder. There were no pictures taken during the tortures or after death. The mass murder spree was uncovered when the 33-year-old was shot to death on August 8, 1973 in the Houston suburb of Pasadena. Corll's killer was one of his teenaged cohorts – who had come to fear for his life after being drugged and strapped to a torture board. His captor had only agreed to release 17-year-old Elmer Wayne Henley if he promised to kill Rhonda Williams, a 15-year-old girl he had brought to the house along with another potential victim, 19-year-old Tim Kerley. All three had been bound and gagged by Corll after being plied with drugs and alcohol. Instead of killing the two victims, however, the teenaged boy turned the gun on his tormentor and fired several times.

Corll became involved in a gay lifestyle after serving a 10-month stint in the United States Army. He was honourably discharged after being drafted in August 1964 and there is nothing on his record to indicate homosexual tendencies or any concern regarding his behaviour during basic training or later, when stationed at Fort Hood in Killeen, Texas, 140 miles south of the Dallas Forth Worth metroplex area.

Henley called police and began recalling the names of victims, between 13 and 20, who had been sexually abused, tortured and killed in specially-built rooms at homes and apartments which Corll occupied throughout Houston. The killer, who got the moniker the Candy Man because his family owned a local candy company, paid two teenaged friends $200 for each victim they brought to his lair. Henley and 18-year-old David Brooks showed police where various victims were buried. Most had been strangled or shot. The accomplices are both serving life in prison for participating in the murders. Police later revealed that 11 of the 16 photographs found at Corll's home identified victims of the murder spree, including several who had been friends of Henley and Brooks.

Prison buddies Lawrence Bittaker and Roy Lewis Norris made plans to go on a killing spree in 1979 and, like Williams, they wanted photographs as trophies of their crimes. Bittaker, 38 at the time, and Norris, who was 30, bought a silver-colored windowless van and prowled beach areas along a 20-mile section of the California coast between Santa Monica and Torrance. Before abducting their first victim, 16-year-old Lucinda Cindy Schaeffer, on June 24, 1979, the pair searched out isolated spots where victims could be killed. They also took photographs of girls who flocked to the surf and sandy playgrounds near Los Angeles. Around 500 photographs of teenagers, including pictures of three victims, were found by police when Bittaker and Norris were arrested. Schaeffer had just left a meeting at her church when the two men offered her a ride. She refused, but was dragged into the van and driven to the San Gabriel Mountains where she was raped and throttled with a coat hanger before being thrown from a nearby canyon cliff. Caught up in the frenzy of the killing, the pair had forgotten to photograph her. Two weeks later, on July 8, Polaroid photographs were taken of 18-year-old Andrea Joy Hall, showing her gripped with fear just prior to being stabbed twice in the side of the head with an ice pick. The young woman had been bound and gagged after being picked up while hitchhiking. She was driven to a desolate area where she was beaten and raped before her death.

Fifteen-year-old Jackie Gilliam and 13-year-old Leah Lamp became victims when they accepted a ride while sitting on a bench at a bus stop. The driver told them he was heading to Hermosa Beach, but they immediately realized he was going in the opposite direction. They tried to escape when the van pulled into a park, but were overpowered and bundled into the back of the vehicle. Lamp was struck in the head with a baseball bat before both were bound, gagged and then driven to the mountain region. The teenagers were sexually molested and tortured for two days. In addition to taking photographs, Bittaker and Norris tape-recorded the sounds as the two captives screamed and begged for their lives. On September 5, 1979, the 15-year-old girl was recorded crying out for mercy as an ice pick was plunged into her head. Leaving the spike imbedded in her skull, both men then took turns strangling her before clubbing the 13-year-old girl with a sledgehammer and then manually strangling her. Both bodies were also dropped from the nearby cliff. Police later found 24 photographs showing Bittaker engaged in various sex acts with Gilliam, but evidence showed the younger girl, who was a virgin, was not raped. When investigators eventually found the site were the bodies were dumped, they located only partial remains of Gilliam and Lamp. Animals had dragged off and devoured the other victims.

On September 30, the killer pair pulled a 17-year-old victim into their van and began sexually assaulting her near Manhattan Beach. The young woman was able to escape and reported the attack to police. A few weeks later, she picked out photographs of Bittaker and Norris from a stack of mug shots that police asked her to look over. Meanwhile, on Halloween night, 16-year-old Shirley Lynette Ledford was spotted by the pair while she hitchhiked around 10:45 p.m. in the vicinity of Sunland Boulevard and Tuxford Street, north of Burbank. She was sexually attacked after climbing into the van. The two men kept a tape recorder running while torturing the teenager. They pinched Ledford's nipples and vaginal area with pliers and vice grips which had been used in the earlier attacks – not only mistreat the victims, but to tighten coat hanger wire around their necks until they could no longer breathe. After killing the girl, the pair dumped her body on the lawn of a home near the spot where she had been hitchhiking.

Bittaker is awaiting execution after being sentenced to death for his part in the slayings, but Norris received a life sentence after offering to testify for the prosecution. Like Williams, he waived his right to speak to a lawyer before being interviewed and initially denied everything during police questioning. He later confessed and told how the five teenaged girls had been stalked, tortured and strangled. Norris also detailed how the final victim was repeatedly beaten with a three-pound sledgehammer and forced to endure other torture so that screams could be recorded as a trophy of their killing spree. In addition to finding an audio tape which recorded the last 20 minutes of Ledford's life, investigators also discovered photographs of another victim who they could never identify – and the pair refused to provide any information about that girl's killing. Although Bittaker and Norris were convicted of five murders, some law enforcement officers in Los Angeles believe the pair could be responsible for up to 40 slayings.

A 29-year-old woman who survived a murder attempt in Los Angeles by the Grim Sleeper on November 20, 1988 startled detectives when she revealed that Polaroid photographs were taken after she was shot. It wasn't until the suspected killer, Lonnie David Franklin, was arrested in the summer of 2010 that investigators realized the extent of his killing spree, which began in 1985 and continued to 2007. Franklin was charged with murdering 10 women, aged between 14 and 36, but police have linked at least six other cases to him and believe there could be other victims. Investigators began looking into numerous cold cases after finding more than 1,000 photographs of women, varying from teenagers to middle-aged victims, in Franklin's home following his arrest. Some of the photographs were 30 years old and police had difficulty identifying many of the individuals, some who appeared to be unconscious. Enietra Margette Washington, the individual who survived the 1988 sexual assault and shooting, told investigators that her attacker snapped several pictures with his Polaroid camera before pushing her from the vehicle. At that time, detectives had become aware of killers taking photographs of murder victims as trophies, but could not imagine an individual grabbing their camera and taking pictures of a just-shot victim being dumped from a car. It was as though Franklin was using the technology then available to document the killing as it occurred, like Williams later did with his video equipment. Franklin, who was 57 when arrested, had killed seven women before shooting Washington. He then waited 14 years before renewing his craze, and murdered three other women. Police linked the deaths through DNA and a $500,000 reward was offered by the Los Angeles Police Department when investigators realized the Grim Sleeper had reawakened and was again murdering women on the city's south side.

Another bizarre case in which video and still images were taken of victims prior to their murders involves two

California men who, like Williams, had served in the military. Leonard Lake and Charles Ng met in 1983 and in less than two years may have killed as many as 25 people, including two babies. Although law enforcement authorities have not formally indicated the purpose of the videos, the men may have experimented with the idea of producing so called "snuff films" in which the star of an explicit sex film is seemingly murdered. As mentioned earlier, there is no evidence that these type of x-rated movies having ever been commercially available or that these serial killers took video of any of their victims as they were being murdered. Police did find videotape of individuals being sexually assaulted and tortured, plus photographs of juvenile girls posing provocatively, but there were no images of anyone being slain or depicting dead bodies.

The men formed a bond because they had both served in the military. Lake had a troubled childhood and was raised by his grandparents in San Francisco, Just 19 when he joined the U.S. Marine Corps in 1965, he was left mentally scarred after serving a couple of tours in the Vietnam War. When discharged in 1971, Lake earned money acting in porn films, but later became paranoid and was sent to prison a couple of times on weapon charges. He married and tried living in a hippie commune, but eventually moved to a ranch that his wife owned near Wilseyville, in California's sparsely-populated Sierra foothills. It was there that Lake built a fortified bunker as protection from what he feared was a pending nuclear conflagration. After meeting Ng in 1982, the pair started living on the property. Born in Hong Kong in 1960 to wealthy parents, Ng was kicked out of several schools after stealing from fellow students. He was also expelled from private schools in England and Canada for petty crimes. Returning home, Ng finally finished high school and got a student visa to attend college in California, but quit before completing one semester. Several months later, even though he was not a United States citizen, Ng enlisted in the Marine Corps. While stationed in Hawaii, he was jailed for 14 years after being convicted of stealing a cache of automatic weapons. He escaped from a military prison and made his way back to California, where he linked up with Lake.

It was a fluke that caused police to stumble on the pair's macabre murder spree. Ng was caught shoplifting in San Francisco, but ran off before police arrived. He left behind the car he was driving and a gun equipped with a silencer was located during a search of that vehicle. Lake later tried to claim the automobile while identifying himself as 26-year-old Robin Stapley, an individual who had vanished several weeks earlier. Investigators also learned that the previous car owner, 39-year-old Paul Cosner, was missing. Lake was taken to an interview room at a police precinct, but before detectives could intensify their interrogation, he committed suicide by swallowing two cyanide pills that were hidden under the collar of his shirt. Earlier in the interview, he gave police Ng's name and mentioned the names of several victims who were slaughtered at the bunker. Investigators found written logs and videotapes which outlined some of the horror that had taken place on the property and a scheme Lake had to re-populate the world with sex slaves after a nuclear holocaust. His plan, Operation Miranda, was named after the young woman who in the book, The Collector, was kidnapped and held captive.

Ng fled and made his way to Canada, where he was arrested on June 6, 1985 after shooting a department store security guard when caught shoplifting in Calgary, Alberta. The guard recovered and Ng was incarcerated for almost five years. The United States Justice Department applied to extradite Ng to face multiple murder charges, but Canadian authorities initially refused the request because the serial killer might be executed if convicted.

After a great deal of pressure from average Canadians who feared Ng would be released and given sanctuary, the government relented, and in 1998 he was returned to California where he was sentenced to death when convicted on 12 counts of murder. The remains of Stapley and Cosner were found on the property, along with other bodies believed to be 29-year-old Harvey Dubs, his 33-year-old wife, Deborah, and their 16-month-old son, Sean; 27-year-old Lonnie Bond, his 19-year-old wife, Brenda O'Connor, and their two-year-old son, Lonnie Jr.; 18-year-old Kathleen E. Allen and her 23-year-old boyfriend, Michael S. Carroll; 36-year-old Charles Gunnar, an army buddy who was the best man at Lake's wedding; and Lake's 32-year-old brother, Donald, who had vanished in July 1983.

The gruesome evidence found during a search of the 75-acre site confirmed that people had been slaughtered at the Calaveras County survivalist compound. Police acknowledged that most of the victims were known to either Lake or Ng, but others had vanished while camping in the area or were lured to the bunker from as far away as San Francisco. Investigators found five bags of charred bone fragments, identification belonging to individuals who had been reported missing, several hundred pornographic photographs and videotapes showing the two men involved with different women. Although there were images of victims being sexually abused and tortured, there were no video recordings of anyone being murdered. On one tape, Kathleen Allen is seen being forced to undress and submit to a rape assault after being threatened with death. The video also shows a bayonet being used to cut clothing from Brenda O'Connor, who is begging for her tormenters to tell her that her baby is safe. The young woman is finally broken and agrees to their demands for sex after being convinced her little son is alive. At the point where O'Connor is raped, both her child and husband had already been killed. Another video found by police shows a dishevelled and bearded Lake delivering a rambling and sometimes incoherent speech describing how life will continue if the region is destroyed by nuclear war or an earthquake. He also made numerous notations in a collection of diaries and journals. One comment reads: "God meant women for cooking, cleaning house and sex, and when they are not in use, they should be locked up."

The bunker contained tiny soundproof, self-contained isolation chambers where victims could be held in isolation; various restraints, numerous weapons, ammunition, a quantity of female lingerie, a torture chamber and a main bedroom. Outside there was a pyre on which bodies could be cremated, several shallow graves, a partial skull, jewellery, metal tubing, wallets, credit cards and a large quantity of silver dollars.

Although not all bodies were recovered, police are confident that Lake and Ng killed at least 11 other people. They include 25-year-old Jeff Gerald, a part-time musician who worked as a mover in San Francisco; 24-year-old Cliff Peranteau, also a mover; three transients, known only by street names, who vanished in San Francisco; 30-year-old Jeffrey D. Askren, a resident of Sunnyvale, California, whose car was found near Lake's property a few days after he was reported missing in April 1984; and an individual identified by the name Randy Johnson. The bodies of two black men found on the property have never been identified. They were also unable to confirm the existence of 25-year-old Thomas D. Myers of Saratoga, California, after locating several items belonging to a man by that name on the property. A separate investigation linked Ng to the slaying of 36-year-old Donald Giulietti. The San Francisco disc jockey was shot in the head by a Chinese man who came to his home in response to an ad offering sexual services in an underground gay newspaper. Ballistic tests showed the murder weapon was a .22-

caliber semi-automatic pistol equipped with a silencer, which police found at the bunker. Giuliette's roommate, who recovered from wounds after being shot in the chest in the July 11, 1984 incident, also identified Ng as the assailant.

Muslim extremists have been video-taping their brutal torture and murder of kidnap victims, in addition to making visual recordings of attacks on military convoys. These images are key tools in a propaganda campaign designed to demoralize countries which declared a war on terrorism following the September 11, 2001 slaughter of people in New York, Washington and Shanksville, Pennsylvania. Extremist groups, including al-Qaeda and other militant Islamic organizations, began posting video and still images of barbaric executions shortly after troops from numerous countries joined a coalition organized by the United Nation's Security Council to destroy terrorist training camps and wipe out terrorism worldwide. The leaders of the terror groups ordered these graphic pictures to demoralize soldiers. They also seek to reduce the general public's appetite for war throughout the free world and make it easier for anti-war activists to pressure elected representatives to withdraw support for military action in the Middle East. One of the most chilling videos, which was widely available on the Internet and shown on television stations across the war-torn region, was the beheading of 38-year-old Daniel Pearl, a writer with the Wall Street Journal. He was kidnapped in January 2002 by a group of militants in Karachi, Pakistan.

It is now obvious that the video camera has become a popular tool for any killer who is seeking to have more than 15 minutes of fame. When 32-year-old Anders Behring Breivik unleashed a reign of terror which left 77 dead and more than 300 injured in Norway on July 22, 2011, he left a lengthy manifesto urging other mass murderers to videotape their carnage. It is widely rumoured that Breivik, a right-wing extremist, was carrying some type of video camera as young people at a youth camp on Utoya Island, 23 miles northwest of Oslo, were verbally taunted before he shot them. About 90 minutes before the massacre at the event sponsored by the ruling Labor Party, a fertilizer bomb was detonated outside the government's offices in Oslo, killing eight people. It was the same type of explosive that was used in the April 19, 1995 bombing at the Alfred P. Murrah Federal Building in Oklahoma City. That blast, which killed 168 people and injured almost 700 others, including 19 children, was carried out by Timothy McVeigh, an anti-government extremist who was branded as a domestic terrorist. McVeigh was executed by lethal injection and an accomplice, Terry Nichols, is serving a life sentence for his role in the Oklahoma devastation.

While investigating the background of Breivik following the bombing in Norway's capital, plus the shooting rampage, police discovered a 1,518-page manifesto which was written over a nine-year period. It calls for civil warfare to stem the immigration flow of Muslims into European countries. The manifesto includes instructions for anyone taking direct action to carry a specific type of video camera so that their violence can be videotaped and widely promoted via the Internet, in a bid to encourage others to wage similar campaigns. "This extremely small and lightweight field camera is used to document your operation," the manifesto notes. "Some governments may seize the movie (after you are neutralized) and publish it … while others may bury it or even destroy it to protect the multiculturalist ideology."

Officials have never officially announced that Breivik took video, but speculation is rampant that investigators have viewed images taken by the killer during the slaughter.

In southern France, it appears the motorbike-riding gunman who murdered people at a Jewish school after earlier attacks in which three soldiers were killed, was wearing the same type of camera Breivik recommended. French authorities began searching the Internet for video images of the March 19, 2012 shooting rampage outside the school in Toulouse, where 30-year-old teacher Jonathan Sandler and his two children, aged four and five, were mowed down with automatic gunfire. A security camera captured images of the gunman with a GoPro video camera strapped to his body. After killing the trio, he ran into the school's yard and executed a seven-year-old girl with a gunshot to the head after pushing her to the ground. Branded by French President Nicolas Sarkosy as a "monster," the heartless killer gunned down an off-duty French paratrooper on March 11 after making arrangements to sell him his motorcycle, and four days later on March 15, he fatally shot two soldiers as they were withdrawing money from an automatic teller machine in Montauban, a community 30 miles north of Toulouse. The killer, who yelled out the Arabic phrase "Allahu akbar" – God is Great – before opening fire while driving past the soldiers on his scooter, was 23-year-old Mohammed Merah. The al-Qaeda sympathizer was identified by a 200-member police task force that was assigned the task of tracking him down. Merah was killed when heavily-armed "special forces" police officers raided his apartment. No images of the attacks were posted on the Internet. Merah did, however, send his video recordings to the Al Jazeera Arab television network. But they were never broadcast.

It is easy to compare Russell Williams with the serial killers listed in this chapter. He shares similarities with the majority of them and there's a strong likelihood that many other women would have been raped and murdered had the police not intervened. Williams escalated rapidly from panty-stealing raids at neighbouring homes to sex-related homicides. Officially he wasn't a serial killer, since he'd only taken two lives. However, considering the pattern and frequency of his burglaries, although not an absolute certainty, it seems logical to conclude Williams would have continued to kill.

Because he was so calculating and methodically recorded the killings of Jessica Lloyd and Marie-France Comeau, police had "a gut feeling" that he may have already murdered other victims. Investigators with Canada's Military Police compiled records of his travels, including extended visits to several places across North America and the United Arab Emirates. Law enforcement agencies in the various locations were asked if there were any unsolved homicides coinciding with the time Williams was in their jurisdictions. Authorities in the United States commenced an investigation into at least one unsolved slaying, but so far no evidence – including analysis of DNA samples – links Williams to the victim.

Questions were also raised about his possible involvement in several unsolved rapes and murders in Toronto, which occurred while Williams was attending university in the city. He admitted developing a fetish for female underwear while in his 20s but insists he has confessed to all the crimes he ever committed. Despite his denial, Ontario Provincial Police investigators were assigned to review several cold cases, including the rape and stabbing death of 19-year-old Kathleen MacVicar at the Trenton base on June 13, 2001. The victim was discovered two days later in a heavily-treed area. She had recently moved from her hometown of Glace Bay, Nova Scotia and was staying with an aunt and uncle who lived on the base. Another case that gave police concern was the August 27, 1987 sexual assault and slaying of 21-year-old Margaret McWilliam along a jogging path in a Scarborough park near the school campus Williams was taking classes. The victim was from Deep River, a community where he lived as a child, but so far police have found nothing to link the colonel turned killer with her homicide.

Apart from investigations to determine if Russell Williams is implicated in other crimes, there will also be ongoing debate about why he became a killer and how far he would have escalated if not caught by police. It's impossible to predict what Williams would have done, and as the case with all individuals who transform themselves into serial killers, society is left with many unanswered questions.

Chapter Sixteen

Russell Williams is virtually impossible to profile, pigeonhole or categorize. There is no doubt that he is the killer of two women, a rapist and sexual deviant. But at the same time, Williams is someone who managed to conceal a dark side while maintaining what appeared to be a normal life during his rise towards the upper echelon of Canada's military. He has traits that could have him branded or classified as a sociopath, but his behavior has psychiatrists looking in other directions. No evidence was presented during court proceedings as to his psychological status and society may never learn the results of assessments that he will undergo during his incarceration.

When imposing sentence, Justice Robert Scott said Williams will be remembered as "a sado-sexual serial killer" and will "remain a very sick individual" even though he's not criminally insane. Showing the world-wide appeal this case received, Australia's Sydney Morning Herald carried an article which quoted the judge saying: Williams is a "sick and dangerous man."

He began his crimes as a sexual deviant, without confronting victims, but escalated into a serial predator. In addition to targeting the homes and sanctity of adult women, it became evident to spectators in the courtroom that Williams had an unnatural interest in young girls. Photos displayed by prosecutors during the court hearing clearly showed him becoming aroused in 13 bedrooms where pre-teens slept. Many pieces of underwear he masturbated onto obviously belonged to young girls, as did several of the pairs of panties he obviously could barely squeeze into while modeling for self-portraits.

Even before these sickening images stunned the courtroom filled with relatives, friends, local residents and newspaper writers, details of his atrocities had left people outraged. Fearing for his safety, authorities created a security cordon around the courthouse, including a tall temporary screen, some police officers were toting submachine guns and snipers positioned on nearby rooftops.

In the end, despite the anger and overwhelming sense of his betrayal, Russell Williams was sent to prison for life. He is automatically eligible for parole after serving 15 years, but it unlikely he will ever be released even though there are automatic reviews of his sentence after 25 years. Only Canada's worst criminals spend their remaining lives behind bars.

But even in the days leading up to his lifetime sentence, people around the world who saw him, or read accounts about the collapse of his rising military star, pondered how someone who was so outwardly successful could develop into such a twisted villain. People who knew him from his university, high school and band days were quoted in newspapers as describing him quite differently to how he was recalled in the military. On one hand Williams was a jokester and music lover, while others remember him as someone who was aloof, meticulous and a person who wanted to be in control.

Photography has been an interest from his teenage years and a video posted on a Heathrow Airport film company's website in London, England shows him handing his digital camera to a British military aide so that he could have a photo of himself standing beside Queen Elizabeth. He had just flown the Queen and members of the royal entourage from Canada to England.

The arrogance that Williams displayed and his confidence that he could beat the system was evident after he voluntarily agreed to a request for an interview by Detective Sergeant Smyth, a member of the Ontario Provincial Police Behavioral Science Unit. William wore the same boots that he had on the night he kidnapped and killed Jessica Lloyd and willingly gave police his BlackBerry plus samples of his DNA. He obviously wasn't naive about genetic fingerprint technology, but seemed to blindly ignore the reality that samples of his saliva could directly connect him to some of the crime scenes. He may have assumed that by allowing swabs to be taken from inside his mouth, police might not proceed with the extra step and actually test his DNA. But that conclusion would have been a definite risk and Williams is not the type of person to take such a gamble. He can be better described as someone who is calculated and carefully weighs situations as they arise.

But far from being the perfect criminal, Williams made several key mistakes that helped police gather the necessary evidence to identify him as the perpetrator they were seeking: He left DNA at some of the homes he broke into in Ottawa; minute amounts of his blood were found in Marie-France Comeau's bathroom; his saliva was on Jane Doe's neck; he kept the boots worn while abducting Lloyd; and – most importantly – ran out of time while raping Jessica and was forced to take her to his home in Tweed as the light of dawn approached. The presence of his vehicle in the field beside her house, where it was spotted by a patrolling Belleville Police officer, plus footprints matched to Williams' boots, helped seal his fate.

The prosecutor even stressed during his summation in court that the abduction and murder of Jessica Lloyd was the crime that finally "brought Mr. Williams down."

When confronted with irrefutable evidence by Detective Sergeant Smyth during his initial interview, Williams had the right to remain silent and retain a lawyer, but instead he permitted the interrogation to continue. He had already agreed to fully cooperate and after being read his rights and signing consent forms, he gave a sample of his DNA; handed over his boots, allowing police to compare the tread with impressions found near Lloyd's home; and surrendered his handheld communication device for analysis. The process took a little over half an hour and it was 5:04 p.m. when Williams returned to the interview room at Ottawa Police headquarters. After comparing the footwear impression with photographs of footprints taken at the crime scene, experts determined that the tread pattern was a perfect match and the colonel was likely responsible for the disappearance of Jessica Lloyd.

At 6:21 p.m., Smyth shows Williams the footprint evidence and also mentions that police were about to commence searches at the homes he owned in Ottawa and Tweed. It was another hour and ten minutes before Williams finally broke down and admitted responsibility for murdering Jessica and gave the location where he'd dumped her body.

The killer was no longer a mystery figure, but investigators now needed to locate a great deal more evidence to collaborate what Williams had told them. At this point Smyth didn't realize he was face to face with the first man in the world to document in written words and pictorial images the various crimes he'd committed. Even the casual way Williams had mentioned that investigators would find what he described as "almost four hours" of video didn't give a hint as to the true volume of recorded and digital images that were "deeply hidden" in a complex system of files on his home computer. He told Smyth the video-taking during the attack on Jessica "pretty much covers everything" and also mentioned taking still pictures before adding that he also took images at the home of Marie-France.

Investigators were actual "astounded" when they later discovered that details of his crimes had been documented and the murders of Marie-France Comeau and Jessica Lloyd had been videotaped almost in their entirety. Additionally there were graphic photographs and video of the incidents involving Jane Doe and Laurie Massicotte plus other evidence found during various searches which helped develop an air-tight case against Russell Williams.

Even after being formally charged with the two murders and sexual assaults, Williams still insisted he didn't need a lawyer and was questioned until 1:33 a.m. The interrogation would have gone on longer, but Detective Sergeant Smyth needed Williams to take police to the location where he'd dumped Jessica Lloyd's body.

The testing of material collected through vaginal swabs and from under her fingernails didn't confirm an exact DNA match with Williams, but the results didn't rule him out as a suspect.

But police amassed a great deal of other evidence. Two Hi-8 video tapes showing the attack on Lloyd and a SanDisk memory card containing 325 digital photographs were found by police inside a piano at Williams' house in Tweed. Two 500 Gigabyte Laci hard drives, containing similar evidence, were discovered hidden above ceiling tiles in the basement of his Ottawa home. Almost a hundred photographs of underwear and other garments stolen during burglaries in Ottawa and Tweed were hidden in folders on his computer. Police also seized camera and video recording equipment, several items Williams had in the "rape kit" when he entered the homes of the two murder victims, plus the assortment of women's clothing stolen during the various break-ins.

Searchers also discovered the black cap and scarf that Williams had used to leave only his eyes uncovered and a book – the LSI Guide to Lock Picking.

During the interrogation Williams was asked if he hadn't been caught, would his crime spree have continued. He told Detective Sergeant Smyth that was a difficult question to answer, admitting he would have likely kept breaking into homes, but hoped that he would not have attacked anybody else. Williams also indicated he made the decision to confess because he didn't want to amass large legal bills and to minimize the impact of his crimes on his wife.

Williams couldn't explain what triggered his behavior, but in 2007 developed a strong desire to steal undergarments. That was just before his first break-in, but he did acknowledge having a fascination with lingerie since his 20s or 30s.

Members of the team assigned to the Russell Williams investigation, known as the Hatfield Project, worked closely with Canada's military police to trace the colonel's movements when the various crimes were committed. He wasn't at the base when Marie-France Comeau was killed nor at the time of Jessica Lloyd's abduction.

Williams, by all accounts, never met Lloyd before breaking into her isolated rural home. And he appears to have had only brief conversations while on duty with Comeau while shuttling VIPs on military flights. In the end, neither Comeau or Lloyd knew who unmercifully ended their lives. After Comeau begged her attacker to "have a heart, please" Williams appeared to be more concerned with how his video was recording her last gasps. Then, continuing his meticulously-organized public life, he drove to Ottawa for an important military meeting, later downloading his treasured images onto his computer's external hard drive.

Similarly, after killing Lloyd and dragging her body into his garage, Williams drove to Trenton and ferried a contingent of Canadian troops to California on a large military aircraft. He appeared "quite normal" to several people who saw him before the flight took off and no one at the Canada Forces base had any idea that he had just callously murdered a young woman.

It's remarkable that Williams managed to leave so few clues and vary his various crime scenes. This made it extremely difficult for police to initially connect the dots and establish a linkage. In the narrative assembled for the courts in the Williams' case, investigators make the assertion that crimes which remain a mystery to police are ones in which there are no clues and no evidence that point them toward a particular suspect. "These crimes were the subject of intensive investigation by the police, but without having anyone to identify as a suspect, the police have little to work with," the court brief stated. "In Ottawa there was no evidence and no clues that led to any one suspect. Despite surveillance and undercover operations, the police still could not identify any suspects."

The narrative indicated that only one of the Tweed break-ins was reported to police, and in that case it was 10 days before the authorities were notified. No evidence was found at that home, and investigators also didn't turn up any significant clues to immediately identify who might have been responsible for the degrading assaults on Jane Doe and Laurie Massicotte.

"When Ms. Comeau was murdered, there was nothing beyond suspicion to link the crimes, and again, no clues left behind that caused them to identify Mr. Williams or anyone else," says the police brief, which was read aloud in the courtroom. "The first break came when Ms. Lloyd disappeared. There wasn't much left behind then either.

But the police observed those footwear and tire track impressions, and using those meager clues, they managed to identify the perpetrator and build an overwhelming case against him ... They did an outstanding job."

Belleville Police Chief Cory McMullan expressed the same sentiment about the efforts police made to track down the sex fiend. "The cooperation and seamless operation between the investigating partners was key to the apprehension of Russell Williams," she told members of the Belleville Police Services Board shortly after he was sent to prison for life. "Everyone worked side by side, sharing quarters and commitment to the investigation." The police chief also announced that a community gathering was scheduled for October 22, 2010 in the Belleville Market Square behind the city hall. "The rally has been organized to show support to the Williams' victims and their families," she said. "It will provide an opportunity for people to come together to continue with the healing process."

Days after Williams received the maximum sentence allowed under Canadian law, Belleville and the other communities were still reeling from the nightmarish wounds that had been inflicted on so many people. There was the sense of personal security being violated, the thoughts that a respected leader could commit vile acts in the bedrooms of teenage and even prepubescent youngsters, the outrage stemming from women being photographed in depraved poses in the sanctity of their own homes and the feeling of utter helplessness and despair, knowing that two vibrant young women in the prime of their lives had been slaughtered in savage sexual assaults. Russell Williams had confessed his guilt to each and every charge as they were read out in court, but average, normal-thinking people, could not come to grips with the enormity of his crime spree and the devastation that he had wreaked on so many families.

Long-time Toronto Sun feature columnist Michele Mandel described Williams as a person who spent hours as the meticulous director of his own snuff films. In one article during the trial, she said Williams starred as a rapist and torturer of two women for personal gratification.

In this sense, it is impossible to find a description that properly fits Russell Williams.

In the midst of his interrogation, just after admitting that he'd killed Jessica Lloyd, Williams scribbled apology letters on lined paper. Was this a genuine outpouring after being consumed with guilt, or further gestures to torment his victims and the families of those who were murdered?

To the 20-year-old woman he confronted at her Tweed home as her newborn baby slept nearby, Williams wrote:

"I apologize for having traumatized you the way I did. No doubt you'll rest a bit easier now that I've been caught."

His letter to Laurie Massicotte reads: "I am sorry for having hurt you the way I did. I really hope that the discussion we had has helped you turn your life around a bit. You seem like a bright woman who could do much better for herself. I do hope that you find a way to succeed."

The letter penned to Ernest Comeau, the father of Marie-France Comeau stated:

"Mr. Comeau,

I am sorry for having taken your daughter, Marie-France, from you. I know you won't be able to believe me, but it is true. Marie-France has been deeply missed by all that knew her."

And his message to Roxanne Lloyd, mother of Jessica Lloyd, seemed a bit more personal but didn't include her specific request to – "tell my mom I love her."

"Mrs. Lloyd,

You won't believe me. I know. But I am sorry for having taken your daughter from you. Jessica was a beautiful, gentle young woman, as you know.

I know she loved you very much – she told me so again and again. I can tell you that she did not suspect that the end was coming – Jessica was happy because she believed she was going home.

I know you have already had a lot of pain in your life. I am sorry to have caused you so much more."

Since the letters seem to lack sincerity, people in the courtroom didn't think Williams was being honest when he stood and apologized for his crimes. Even Burgess couldn't tell if he was remorseful. "I don't think we'll ever know that for sure."

Williams continues to be a cold, emotionless person and an individual who seems to lack feelings. He showed no real compassion or true concern for those he attacked, even though, at times, he displayed some kindness. More likely he was toying with his victims, much like he did with Lloyd when he promised she would be going home, moments before she was bludgeoned.

When you equate his crimes with Robert Pickton, who killed 49 women and fed their remains to his pigs, it's hard to call Williams a monster. It's possible he may have gone on to take the lives of other victims, but police ended his spree. You also can't brand him as a new kind of killer because the homicides he committed cannot be compared in any fashion to the way Michael Briere ended the life of 10-year-old Holly Jones on May 12, 2003 in Toronto. During a 90 minute period the sadistic killer abducted the young girl in broad daylight, dragged her into his home, raped and murdered her and then dismembered her body. As police scoured the neighborhood looking for the missing girl, Briere put several of her severed pieces into garbage cans and then discarded green plastic bags containing her head and torso along Toronto's waterfront. The 35-year-old software developer was arrested six weeks later and police discovered this was the first crime he had ever committed. Briere, who pleaded guilty to first degree murder and was sentenced to life in prison, told the court Holly was abducted when he was obsessed with a craving to kill after viewing images of child pornography. There were reports that police discovered some child porn on one of the computers that Williams used, but there was no mention of the images during court proceedings and he was never charged with possession of such material.

It is natural and common for a person to wonder about criminals. How does someone like Williams evolve? While criminologists and analysts will study Williams the remainder of his life, scant time was spent in the courtroom – where he sat near a standard portrait photograph of the Queen – trying to find out why Williams turned into a killer. Instead the prosecutor focused on the victims and the impact the perpetrator had while preying upon them.

Emphasizing that Williams will likely spend the rest of his life behind bars, prosecutor Lee Burgess said he didn't think it was necessary to have him declared a dangerous offender. He suggested no parole board in the future would allow Williams to be released from prison once they see and hear the evidence that led to his life sentence. Burgess said Williams had left a legacy of fear in the communities where his crimes were committed and betrayed the men and women of the military. He also said it was important to provide the facts and make public graphic details to show the progression and nature of his crimes. "It was important for the public to know ... what a danger this man really is," he later told a reporter from the Belleville Intelligencer.

The prosecutor said the only other good to come from the case of a man he called "one of the worst offenders in Canadian history" was "the job the police did." Well aware of the naysayers and critics, Burgess reminded the court that with only one break-in at a home in Tweed reported – even then by someone who just saw a man running away from a home – a pattern only emerged later. After reading the brief prepared for the court, he said "it was the best police work I'd seen in 20 years on the job and it was two police services that worked in concert to bring it together. They had a little luck that helped them."

Chief McMullan, who several months earlier had joined other officers at Jessica Lloyd's funeral service, lauded the two forces for doing "a fantastic job," telling The Intelligencer staff that the investigation and court case were "a very smooth process. We're extremely pleased with the way the justice system has worked through this case." More importantly, she said in the interview, "the community can start healing," taking comfort with the knowledge that Williams – who McMullan deliberately referred to as "Mr." instead of "colonel" – would remain behind bars. She described the crimes as "horrific" and said investigators had to deal with some "very disturbing" evidence. Officials actually blocked the video display screens in the courtroom so people in the public gallery would be shielded from the more graphic evidence showing the victims being raped and murdered.

Detective Inspector Chris Nicholas of the Ontario Provincial Police, the lead investigator on the case, said no one should have to look at the grisly and bizarre images that Williams recorded during his attacks. "I think it's one thing to look at a photograph of a male wearing female underwear and then it's another thing to watch a male person raping and murdering people."

Although Williams was portrayed in court as one of Canada's worst offenders, he will forever be known as the first person in the world to fully document his crimes with written notes and photographs, as well as with sound and video recordings.

Once standing tall in his uniform, saluting his Queen, greeting the prime minister, cabinet ministers and other dignitaries, inspecting and commanding troops, he wore an ill-fitting black suit while in the courtroom prisoner's box. He looked dejected, but in an act of defiance would sometimes sit reading a newspaper as several crown attorneys described his crimes in detail. Williams only seemed to take an interest when particularly dramatic photos he took during his murderous exploits were being displayed. He sobbed while apologizing for the pain and suffering he'd caused not only to the victims but to his family, friends and military colleagues. The military was particularly hard hit by his betrayal and want nothing more to do with Russell Williams. Basically all connections he had with the Canadian Armed Forces have been obliterated. In addition to his uniforms being burned, his SUV and all evidence seized from his homes were ordered destroyed. His name has also been removed from the plaque which honors all commanders who served at the Trenton base.

Until a new high-security prison is built, Williams will be housed in the segregation wing of Kingston Penitentiary. The facility constructed in the early 1800s on the shore of Lake Ontario by British Royal Navy prisoners, is about an hour's drive from the base he once commanded. For his own protection, Williams is allowed to spend an hour a day by himself in the prison's exercise yard and the remainder of the time, he's relegated to a 9-feet, 10-inch by 8-feet, 2-inch cell. He has no direct contact with other inmates on the range which holds inmates – mostly child killers – who would be immediately murdered if they were put in with the general prison population. Bernardo is in the same segregation area and some of Canada's most notorious criminals have languished there while prison authorities worked to find them a facility where they could be safely housed. Some of those accommodated in the high-security isolation unit are "out of control" and Plexiglas shielding has been erected to protect guards and others walking past cells from being hit with urine or feces which is routinely thrown by these inmates.

Recently one of these "severely demented" inmates was transferred to a prison in British Columbia after both Bernardo and Williams complained about his terrorizing behavior. They voiced concern for their well-being and safety after Richard Wills, a former Toronto police constable who has been in the unit since 2007 for strangling his girlfriend, howled and ranted incessantly, and often hurled body waste from his cell. Even behind bars, prisoners have rights. They include protection from harassment, and detrimental treatment by prison guards or other inmates.

Sadly, Williams and many of those on Kingston's segregation range, gave no consideration to the rights of their victims and stole the most precious gift from them – their lives.

Epilogue

No doubt there will be stories of other deranged people and those they prey upon. That is, sadly, the story of humankind throughout history.

It is only by recording such stories, however, that we learn grim lessons – hoping that in knowing such details, history may not repeat itself. From childhood we grow into adulthood, inheriting a world around us that is filled with wonder and beauty, of good people and bad, sadness and sometimes grim reality.

Being able to continue can be a challenge, especially for those who fall victim to predators of all descriptions. Survival is a basic human instinct. And knowledge helps us survive.

Today there is nothing in Belleville, Brighton or Tweed to remind residents of the horror that occurred in those communities. The homes of the murdered women have changed hands and others who were victimized are moving forward with their lives. Motorists travelling the stretch of road between Belleville and Tweed drive through the traffic light at Honeywood Corners and don't slow down when passing the home where Jessica Lloyd lived. Although a number of residents living near Marie-France Comeau sold their homes after the murder, other people have moved into the area and it continues to be a thriving community. There's a notice warning would-be bandits that homes are protected by Neighborhood Watch and a large sign on the tract of land where Williams parked his van before killing Comeau tells potential new homes buyers the locality offers a comfortable, secure and leisure lifestyle.

Russell Williams' military biography

Colonel Russ Williams enrolled in the Canadian Forces in 1987 after having obtained a degree in Economics and Political Science from the University of Toronto. He received his Wings in 1990 and was posted to 3 Canadian Forces Flying Training School where he served for two years as an instructor on the CT134 Beech Musketeer, during which time he earned an A2 instructional category and had the opportunity to fly with the last iteration of the Musket Gold.

In 1992 Colonel Williams was posted to 434 (Combat Support) Squadron in Shearwater where he flew the CC144 Challenger in the electronic warfare / coastal patrol role. He was subsequently posted to 412 (Transport) Squadron in Ottawa where he continued to fly the Challenger, this time in the VIP transport role. Promoted Major in November 199 he was  posted to Director General Military Careers where he served as the multi-engine pilot career manager.

Colonel Williams attended the Canadian Forces Command and Staff Course from August 2003 to June 2004, where he obtained a Master of Defence Studies from the Royal Military College. Following promotion to Lieutenant-Colonel in June 2004 he was appointed Commanding Officer 437 (Transport) Squadron, a post he held for two years, during which time he served for six months as the Commanding Officer Theatre Support Element – Camp Mirage (December 2005 – June 2006).

Colonel Williams was posted to the Directorate of Air Requirements in July 2006 where he served as Project Director for the Airlift Capability Projects Strategic (CC177 Globemaster III) and Tactical CC130 Hercules J), and Fixed-Wing Search and Rescue. In January 2009 he was posted to the Canadian Forces Language School in Catineau for a 6-month period of French language training, during which he was promoted to his current rank.

A keen photographer, fisherman and runner, Colonel Williams and his wife Mary Elizabeth are also avid golfers.

Military statement when Williams was convicted

On October 21, Russell Williams, former commander of 8Wing Trenton, was sentenced to two concurrent terms of life in prison, with no chance of parole for 25 years, for the first-degree murders of Corporal Marie-France Comeau and Jessica Lloyd.

The crimes committed by Mr. Williams are deeply upsetting to us all. Over the last few months, I have spoken with many of you in town halls across the country and on missions overseas. Like all Canadians, you and I have been shocked and repulsed by the crimes he committed. During these conversations, you expressed your sympathy and compassion for the victims and the families affected by this terrible tragedy.

I also listened to CF personnel of all ranks as they expressed their bewilderment and anger at the betrayal of our institutional ethos of truth, duty, and valour. Because of his heinous crimes and his subsequent criminal conviction, Mr. Williams has lost the privilege of calling himself a member of the CF community.

With the conviction and sentencing completed, and following my recommendation, the Governor General has revoked Mr. Williams' commission, an extraordinary and severe decision that may constitute a first of its kind in Canadian history.

Further, the following actions will now be taken: Stripping Mr. Williams of his medals; termination and recovery of his pay from the date of arrest; denial of severance pay; and promptly releasing Mr. Williams from the CF under "service misconduct", which is the most serious release item possible.

As a consequence of his release from the CF for service misconduct, and of the revocation of his commission, Mr. Williams no longer has a rank as a member of the CF.

I wish to point out that under the *CF Superannuation Act*, there are no grounds to revoke his pension, and a court martial would not have any impact on these accrued benefits.

Some have questioned why Mr. Williams has not also been charged under the military justice system. I believe we need to understand why this is so. It is because there is no jurisdiction under the code of service discipline to try persons charged with murder where those murders took place in Canada. Mr. Williams was therefore tried and convicted of all of these 88 charges under the Criminal Code of Canada by a civilian court.

Additionally, there will be no further court martial on these matters because the *National Defence Act* specifically prevents an individual from being tried by court martial where the offence or any other substantially similar offence arising out of the same underlying facts have been previously dealt with by a civilian court. This basic principle, sometimes called "double jeopardy", is fundamental within our civilian and military justice system. With his current convictions and sentence to life imprisonment, justice has already been served.

Now more than ever, this is a time for us to come together and heal as a community. We are doing everything we can to assist those in need of counselling or other support. I urge anyone who is feeling upset or concerned to seek assistance and to talk about it. While doing so, we will not forget Cpl Comeau, Ms. Lloyd and the many other victims – and their families. They will remain in our thoughts and prayers forever.

It is time to move forward, to be strong and proud, because Mr. Williams' actions are not reflective of the values of the men and women who serve in the CF, whose integrity and self-sacrifice come through loud and clear in words and deeds each day. Whether helping Canadians at home or abroad, or providing the hope of a better future to the people of Haïti, Africa or Afghanistan, I have seen our ethos of truth, duty, and valour at work and making a difference in the world.

You have reason to hold your head high. Be strong and proud! I am proud to be your Chief of the Defence Staff.

—General Walt Natynczyk

Russell Williams' Commission Revoked

News Release - October 22, 2010

OTTAWA – Upon the recommendation of General Walt Natynczyk, Chief of the Defence Staff, His Excellency the Right Honourable David Johnston, Governor General and Commander-in-Chief of Canada, has signed the documents revoking the commission of Russell Williams and approved his release from the Canadian Forces (CF).

"Mr. Williams committed horrific crimes and he is not worthy of the oath he took to serve as an officer of the Canadian Forces," said MacKay. "The Canadian Forces have undertaken all available actions to ensure that all possible sanctions are imposed against Mr. Williams and all possible benefits will be withdrawn from Mr. Williams, starting with the Governor General's revocation of his commission this morning."

"All Canadians have been stunned by the tragic events that led to the sentencing of Mr. Williams," said General Natynczyk. "His actions have constituted a fundamental breach of trust, duty and valour, upon which the commission is based. The removal of his commission and release from the CF is an important step towards closure for the CF community and Canadians alike. We will not forget Corporal Marie-France Comeau, Jessica Lloyd and the other victims and their families."

As a consequence of the revocation of Mr. Williams' commission, he no longer possesses a rank as a member of the CF. The administrative process to release Mr. Williams from the CF is now being finalized, including the following actions that are now being taken:

- stripping Mr. Williams of his medals;
- termination and recovery of his pay from the date of arrest;
- denial of severance pay; and
- his prompt release from the CF under "service misconduct" – which is the most serious release item possible.

The governor general is commander-in-chief of Canada. As such, the governor general plays a major role in recognizing the importance of Canada's military at home and abroad. Among these duties, the governor general signs Commissioning Scrolls. Every officer, for the discharge of his or her duties, holds a commission granted by the governor general on behalf of Her Majesty Queen Elizabeth II and countersigned by the Minister of National Defence. Along with the authority to grant such commissions is the authority of the governor general to revoke them.

Additional photographs

Williams salutes Queen Elizabeth as she exits Canadian military aircraft after trans-Atlantic flight during 2005 official visit to Canada

Williams attending the University of Toronto; below a high school yearbook photo and his graduation picture.

View of Jessica Lloyd's home showing front basement window where Williams saw the young woman working out and the rear deck leading to her kitchen

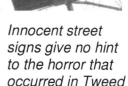

Innocent street signs give no hint to the horror that occurred in Tweed

The unpaved road in front of the Cosy Cove Lane home where Jessica Lloyd was brutally murdered

Tranquil view from the rear of the cottage home (left) where Jessica Lloyd was held captive before being killed by Russell Williams

About the authors

Cal Millar retired after a lengthy, award-winning career as a general assignment reporter at the Toronto Star, Canada's largest newspaper. Through the years he has concentrated his writing on crime and policing issues and has also had a lengthy involvement with Crime Stoppers. The author of two other books, Find my Killer and I'm Missing – Please Find me, Millar is married with two adult children, and a grandson. He resides in Burlington, Ontario, Canada.

Ian Robertson was born in Ottawa and has been a journalist for more than 40 years. He is a writer for the Toronto Sun and has co-authored another book, Prince Edward County: An Illustrated History. His father was an officer with the Royal Canadian Air Force and he is familiar with Canadian Forces Base at Trenton and the local communities where he worked as a reporter at both the Belleville Intelligencer and the Kingston Whig-Standard before moving to Toronto. Robertson has won writing and photography awards

for crime, agriculture and business news. He also writes a regular column in the Canadian Stamp News and has won awards for features on Canadian history.